TAX PROCEDURE AND TAX FRAUD
IN A NUTSHELL

Third Edition

By

Camilla E. Watson
Professor of Law
University of Georgia

Mat #40149479

© West, a Thomson business, 1998
© 2006 Thomson/West
     610 Opperman Drive
     P.O. Box 64526
     St. Paul, MN 55164–0526
     1–800–328–9352

Printed in the United States of America

ISBN–13: 978–0–314–14646–5
ISBN–10: 0–314–14646–6

TEXT IS PRINTED ON 10% POST
CONSUMER RECYCLED PAPER

For Patricia T. Morgan,
whom I am honored to have known

*

†

PREFACE

Federal tax practice and procedure is a burgeoning and ever more important area of the tax law. Many tax cases are won or lost on procedural grounds alone, and more and more law schools are incorporating tax procedure courses into their curricula. This book is intended as a supplement to the various casebooks and treatises on federal tax practice and procedure, especially *Federal Tax Practice and Procedure* by Watson and Billman. It summarizes the legal rules and provides a broad overview to the area, occasionally inquiring into the policy behind the law, and pointing out conflicts among the circuits and gaps in the law. This is not intended to be an exhaustive analysis of the law, however, nor of its historical development.

The tax practice area is divided into two general categories: civil tax practice and criminal tax practice. The last four chapters of this book are devoted to the criminal aspect of tax practice and covers the investigation of tax crimes, the substantive crimes (both Title 26 and Title 18 offenses), the important procedural aspects of criminal tax practice, and likely defenses. The most important recent development in this area has been the Supreme Court's decision in the consolidated *Booker* and *Fanfan* case, pertaining to the Federal Sentencing Guidelines, discussed in Chapter 18. Because this is a very recent decision, the numerous questions that this decision raises have yet to be addressed.

PREFACE

This book replaces Patricia Morgan's Tax Procedure And Tax Fraud (in a nutshell), although Pat's work will never be forgotten. Those familiar with that work will note that the organization of this book differs somewhat. For one, the standards governing tax practice and the ethical issues that commonly arise in such a practice are addressed in Chapter 3 instead of at the end of the book. As Pat had initially stated, this chapter should be of particular interest to students and practitioners alike. Some chapters have been expanded to incorporate recent developments and areas of interest, such as tax shelters. A new chapter on bankruptcy has been added.

Finally, I would like to express my thanks and deep appreciation to my friends and colleagues with whom I discussed various aspects of this book and who provided moral support and encouragement. These include Julian Cook, Caroline Harris John, Margaret V. Sachs, Charles R.T. O'Kelley, and Alan Watson. I also thank my assistant, Sylvia Stogden.

Athens, Georgia

October, 2005

OUTLINE

Chapter 1. Overview of the Federal Tax System

Chapter 2. IRS and Treasury Department Rulemaking

Chapter 4. Disclosure of IRS Materials and Confidentiality of Return Information

Chapter 5. Federal Tax Returns and Compliance

Chapter 6. Further Compliance: Audits and Administrative Appeals

Chapter 7. The Assessment Procedure and Statutes of Limitations

Chapter 8. Overpayments: Administrative Refunds

Chapter 9. Remedies to Absolve the Harshness of the Statute of Limitations on Assessments and Claims for Refund

Chapter 10. Civil Penalties and Interest

Chapter 15. Additional Civil Litigation Considerations

Chapter 16. Criminal Investigations

Chapter 17. IRS Investigatory Powers and Techniques

Chapter 18. Federal Tax Crimes

Chapter 19.   Defenses to Criminal Charges

*

TABLE OF CASES

References are to Pages

TABLE OF CASES

TABLE OF CASES

XXIX

TABLE OF STATUTES

UNITED STATES

UNITED STATES CODE ANNOTATED
5 U.S.C.A.—Government Organization and Employees

11 U.S.C.A.—Bankruptcy

UNITED STATES CODE ANNOTATED
18 U.S.C.A.—Crimes and Criminal Procedure

26 U.S.C.A.—Internal Revenue Code

TABLE OF STATUTES

UNITED STATES CODE ANNOTATED
26 U.S.C.A.—Internal Revenue Code

TABLE OF STATUTES

UNITED STATES CODE ANNOTATED
26 U.S.C.A.—Internal Revenue Code

UNITED STATES CODE ANNOTATED
26 U.S.C.A.—Internal Revenue Code

UNITED STATES CODE ANNOTATED
26 U.S.C.A.—Internal Revenue Code

TABLE OF STATUTES

UNITED STATES CODE ANNOTATED
26 U.S.C.A.—Internal Revenue Code

UNITED STATES CODE ANNOTATED
26 U.S.C.A.—Internal Revenue Code

UNITED STATES CODE ANNOTATED
26 U.S.C.A.—Internal Revenue Code

UNITED STATES CODE ANNOTATED
26 U.S.C.A.—Internal Revenue Code

UNITED STATES CODE ANNOTATED
26 U.S.C.A.—Internal Revenue Code

UNITED STATES CODE ANNOTATED
26 U.S.C.A.—Internal Revenue Code

UNITED STATES CODE ANNOTATED
26 U.S.C.A.—Internal Revenue Code

UNITED STATES CODE ANNOTATED
26 U.S.C.A.—Internal Revenue Code

28 U.S.C.A.—Judiciary and Judicial Procedure

31 U.S.C.A.—Money and Finance

TABLE OF STATUTES

UNITED STATES CODE ANNOTATED
31 U.S.C.A.—Money and Finance

*

TABLE OF TREASURY REGULATIONS

TREASURY REGULATIONS

*

TABLE OF REVENUE RULINGS

REVENUE RULINGS

REVENUE PROCEDURES

IRS NOTICES

*

TAX
PROCEDURE
AND TAX FRAUD
IN A NUTSHELL

Third Edition

*

CHAPTER 1

OVERVIEW OF THE FEDERAL TAX SYSTEM

§ 1.1 The Role of Federal Taxes

Taxes are the principal source of revenue for the federal Government, accounting for about two-thirds of all budget receipts. In taxable year 2003, federal tax receipts totaled more than $1.97 trillion, about half of which represented income taxes paid by individuals. In contrast, corporate income taxes for the same year amounted to only $194 billion, representing about 10% of the total federal tax revenues. This represents a declining trend in the importance of corporate taxes, measured both by the percentage of total tax revenues and by the percentage of Gross Domestic Product (GDP). Prior to World War II, only a small percentage of our population (about 5%) was required to file federal income tax returns. Currently, however, a large majority of Americans must file returns or be listed as dependents on another's return. For example, during the 2003 filing season, over 130 million individuals filed federal income tax returns.

Given the huge numbers of returns and the importance of the federal income tax to our society, fair and efficient administration of the federal tax

1

laws is essential. Our federal tax system is built upon the idea of "voluntary compliance": that is, each person is expected to account annually for his income and deductions and to pay the proper amount of tax. To foster voluntary compliance, the Government must impose taxes that are viewed as fair and must penalize those who fail to comply. During the late 1970s, our voluntary compliance system eroded due to widespread perceptions that wealthy individuals could avoid paying taxes by use of "tax shelters," that most people "cheated" on their federal income taxes, and that the IRS was so overburdened that those who cheated most likely would never be caught. Ironically, these perceptions persist today. But back in the 1970s and 1980s, both the IRS and Congress placed part of the blame for these perceptions on the civil penalty system, which they perceived as unfair and ineffective in ensuring compliance with the tax laws. In late 1989, Congress reacted by enacting the Improved Penalty Administration and Compliance Tax Act ("IM-PACT"), which completely overhauled the civil penalties under the Code to make the tax laws fairer and to provide additional penalties for noncompliance. The changes made by IMPACT are discussed further in Chapter 10. Recently, Congress has enacted tougher legislation designed to curtail the use of abusive tax shelters. These are discussed in Chapter 3.

During the period from 1988 to 1998, Congress enacted further legislation designed to minimize the perceived unfairness of the civil penalties and to provide greater fairness to taxpayers in the administration of the federal tax laws, particularly in the audit and collection process. The first Taxpayer Bill of Rights Act (TBRA 1) was enacted in 1988, with a second (TBRA 2) in 1996, and a third (TBRA 3) in July 1998 as part of the IRS Restructuring and Reform Act of 1998. These Acts ensure that taxpayers involved in disputes with the Internal Revenue Service (the "IRS" or the "Service") are apprised of their rights and are provided remedies for wrongful conduct by the IRS. Provisions of the TBRAs are discussed throughout this book, but particularly in Chapters 11, 14, and 17.

§ 1.2   The Treasury Department and the IRS

The IRS is a branch of the Treasury Department, and it is headed by the Commissioner of Internal Revenue. The Secretary of the Treasury Department has the authority and responsibility to administer the internal revenue laws (*see* I.R.C. § 7801), but the Treasury Secretary has delegated much of this authority to the IRS Commissioner. Both the Treasury Secretary and the IRS Commissioner are appointed by the President, with the advice and consent of the Senate.

A. *Organization Prior to 1999*

Prior to 1953, the IRS was known as the Bureau of Internal Revenue. Today, the IRS employs more than 114,000 employees nationwide. Its principal office (known as the "National Office") is in Washington, D.C. and its mission is to develop nationwide policies and programs for the administration of the tax laws. The National Office issues rulings (both private "letter" rulings and so-called Revenue Rulings with general applicability) and provides central executive control of the organization. Until the early 2000's, the IRS was organized according to a three-tiered pyramid structure with the National Office at the top, four Regional Offices (each headed by a Regional Commissioner), and thirty-three District Offices (each headed by a District Director). Regional Commissioners were charged with executing the policies and programs of the IRS and with supervising the District Directors in their region. Audits, collection activities, and investigations were conducted by divisions of the District Offices. Tax returns were (and continue to be) processed by the 10 Service Centers located throughout the country.

The Office of the Chief Counsel furnishes legal advice to the IRS in all matters pertaining to the administration and enforcement of the internal revenue laws. Lawyers from the Office of the Chief Counsel represent the Commissioner in Tax Court litigation. Prior to 1999, the Office of the Chief Counsel of the IRS was part of the Treasury Department's legal division. Thus, the Treasury Secretary (not the IRS Commissioner) had direct authority over the Chief Counsel. The Appeals Office, whose functions are described in Chapter 6, was part of the Chief Counsel's Office, and thus was not subject to supervision by the IRS.

B. *IRS Restructuring and Reform Act of 1998*

In 1997 and 1998, several proposals to reorganize the IRS received careful attention from Congress. On July 22, 1998 President Clinton signed into law the IRS Restructuring and Reform Act of 1998 (RRA), which significantly altered the organization and operation of the IRS. This Act required the IRS to review and restate its mission to place a greater emphasis on serving the public and meeting taxpayers' needs. As such, the Commissioner was required to implement a plan to reorganize the IRS by eliminating or modifying the three-tiered organizational structure (national, regional and district offices), and replacing it with organizational units serving taxpayer groups with similar needs. When the restructuring was completed, the National Office retained much of its former organization, but the Regional and District officers were replaced with four operating divisions. These are (1) the Wage and Investment Income Division (W & I), which serves approximately 88 million taxpayers whose income taxes are paid primarily through third-party withholding, (2) the Small Business and Self–Employed Division (SB/SE), which serves approximately 33 million fully or partially self-employed taxpayers and small businesses with assets of $10 million or less, (3) the Large and Mid–Size Business Division (LMSB), which serves approximately 210,000 of the largest filers, with assets over $10 million, and (4) the Tax Exempt Organizations and Governmental Entities Division (TE/GE), which serves approximately 24 million filers who generally pay no income tax, although they may pay employment taxes, and withhold and remit income taxes on the wages of their employees.

The operating divisions are supported by four functional units and two service organizations. The functional units focus on specific areas and issues. These are Criminal Investigation (CI), Appeals, Communications and Liaison, and the National Taxpayer Advocate. The CI Division coordinates with the Chief Counsel's office to investigate potential criminal violations of the tax laws and related financial crimes. The Chief Counsel reports directly to the Commissioner instead of to the Treasury Secretary. The Appeals Office has authority to resolve tax controversies without litigation. The RRA requires that the Appeals Function be assured its independence, so the Act includes a specific prohibition of *ex parte* communications between Appeal officers and other IRS employees to the extent that such communications appear to compromise the independence of the Appeals officers. The Communications and Liaison Division coordinates communications between the IRS and taxpayers and Congress. It also assures proper collection, use, and protection of information to accomplish the objectives of the IRS. The National Taxpayer Advocate assists taxpayers in resolving problems with the IRS quickly and fairly, coordinates with the operating divisions to identify potential administrative problems, and represents taxpayers' interests in the formulation of policies and procedures.

Note that as the reorganization progresses, the IRS continues to use the terms "district director" and "district offices" in some of its publications. In addition, there are IRS employees in the former District Offices, most of whom coordinate taxpayer filing and customer service in the W & I operating division. Each operating division has a Division Commissioner and a senior level management team, and each operating division has its own compliance team that is divided into areas. The compliance teams are discussed further in Chapter 6.

The service organizations, the Agency Wide Information Systems Services and the Agency Wide Shared Services, provide internal support to the IRS. Information Systems is responsible for meeting the IRS's information technology needs, while Shared Services provides common services such as facilities management and procurement. A chart reflecting the reorganization of the IRS appears at the end of this Chapter.

The RRA also ordered the creation of an IRS Oversight Board to "oversee the Internal Revenue Service in its management, conduct, direction, and supervision of the execution and application of the internal revenue laws." (RRA, § 1101; IRC § 7802.) The establishment of the nine-member Board was delayed until 2000, however, because of partisan wrangling over the appointment of the members. The nine members of the Board consist of the Commissioner, the Treasury Secretary (or, if the Secretary so designates, the Deputy Secretary of the Treasury), a federal employee appointed by the

President with the advice and consent of the Senate, and six members from private industry who are appointed by the President with the advice and consent of the Senate. Appointments are for 5–year staggered terms. While the Board has broad powers with respect to funding, organizational structure, modernization, and internal management, there are some restrictions on its power. For instance, it may not receive confidential tax return information, interfere in the case of any specific taxpayer, or implement tax policy.

The Act requires appointment of the Commissioner (as under current law, by the President with the advice and consent of the Senate) for a five-year term, as opposed to an unspecified term. It further requires that the appointee "have a demonstrated ability in management." (RRA, § 1102; IRC § 7803.) The Act allows for the reappointment of the Commissioner for additional five-year terms, and permits the President to remove the Commissioner at will. The Act authorizes the appointment of other IRS officials, such as the Chief Counsel, the Taxpayer Advocate, and the Treasury Inspector General for Tax Administration. It further authorizes the Commissioner to employ such number of persons as he or she deems proper for the administration and enforcement of the internal revenue laws.

In reaction to reports of potential improper influence by Executive Branch officers, the Act makes it a felony for the President, Vice President or other specified Executive Branch employees to request (directly or indirectly) that any officer or employee of the IRS conduct or terminate an audit of any person, or otherwise investigate (or terminate the investigation of) any person. (RRA, § 1105; IRC § 7217.)

Other major aspects of the Act are discussed elsewhere in this book: electronic filing is discussed in section 5.2.A and the Taxpayer Bill of Rights Act 3 (Title III of the IRS Restructuring and Reform Act of 1998) is discussed in numerous sections.

C.   *Office of Professional Responsibility*

Those who represent taxpayers before the IRS are subject to regulation by the Director of Practice, who is the head of the Office of Professional Responsibility (OPR), formerly the Office of the Director of Practice. The OPR is supervised by the Senior Counselor to the Commissioner, who has the authority to render the agency decision in disciplinary proceedings when decisions by the Administrative Law Judges are appealed. See further discussion, Chapter 3.

§ 1.3   Justice Department

The Tax Division of the Justice Department plays a significant role in the administration of the federal tax laws. Lawyers from the Tax Division represent the Government in refund suits (civil actions in United States district courts and the Court of Federal Claims, discussed in Chapter 14) and in civil suits challenging the validity of Treasury regulations and IRS rulings. In addition, Tax Division lawyers in the Criminal Section supervise the prosecution of criminal tax cases. Typically, the role of the Criminal Section is limited to reviewing criminal cases developed by the IRS and forwarding them for prosecution to United States Attorneys. In particularly complex or otherwise significant cases, lawyers from the Criminal Section will try the cases or offer substantial assistance to the United States Attorneys trying the cases.

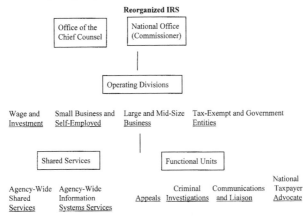

CHAPTER 2

IRS AND TREASURY DEPARTMENT RULEMAKING

The Treasury Department and the IRS issue many different types of rules, regulations, and statements of position. The precedential value of these different types of statements varies, as does the formality with which they are adopted. The Secretary of the Treasury is authorized by the Internal Revenue Code to prescribe rules and regulations to enforce the Code. *See* I.R.C. § 7805(a). Although the Treasury Secretary officially issues most of the regulations under the Internal Revenue Code, the regulations are drafted by the Office of the Chief Counsel.

"Rules" or "regulations" are promulgated by the Treasury Department following formal rulemaking procedures prescribed by the Administrative Procedure Act ("APA"), 5 U.S.C. §§ 551 *et seq*. The APA was enacted in 1946, some 25 years after the enactment of § 7805(a). The fact that the tax authorities are subject to the APA often has been overlooked or forgotten, perhaps because of the substantial body of precedent developed by the courts prior to the enactment of the APA.

11

Both the Code and the APA use the terms "rules" and "regulations" interchangeably. Although there are different types of regulations, all except purely procedural regulations (discussed in § 2.2, *infra*) bear the characteristic of being adopted pursuant to procedures prescribed by the APA. On the other hand, revenue rulings, private letter rulings, determination letters and other IRS statements of position have less precedential value and are not subject to formal APA rulemaking procedures. A chart outlining the hierarchy of tax authorities and statements of position appears at the end of this Chapter.

§ 2.1 Treasury Regulations

There are three types or classes of regulations governing federal tax matters: legislative, interpretive and procedural. The first two types are promulgated by the Treasury Department, and are binding on the Treasury and the IRS, while procedural regulations are issued by the IRS and are not always binding on the agency.

Section 553 of the APA requires that all "substantive" or legislative regulations be published in final form in the *Federal Register* at least 30 days prior to their effective date. The purpose of this requirement is to give the public notice of the proposed rule and an opportunity to comment on it. Although neither interpretive regulations nor procedural regulations are subject to these notice provisions, the Treasury Department follows the section 553 requirements when it promulgates interpretive regulations. Regulations that have been proposed by the Treasury Department but not yet adopted as final are known as "proposed regulations." If there is substantial adverse public comment or internal disagreement within the Treasury Department about the wisdom of a particular proposed regulation, it can languish for years in the status of a merely proposed regulation and not be released as a final rule.

An exception to the notice and comment procedures of section 553 exists for cases in which the agency believes the procedures are "impracticable, unnecessary, or contrary to the public interest." Particularly in the recent past, the Treasury Department has frequently invoked this exception in promulgating *temporary regulations* for prompt guidance following significant tax legislation. Temporary regulations are often issued in "question-and-answer" form, reflecting the Treasury Department's positions on the most obvious and frequently noted issues generated by the legislation. Temporary regulations must also be issued as proposed regulations, but they expire if not finally adopted within three years of the date they are issued. I.R.C. § 7805(e).

A. *"Legislative" and "Interpretive" Regulations*

Section 7805(a) directs the Treasury Secretary "or his delegate" to "prescribe all needful rules and regulations for the enforcement" of the Code. Regulations promulgated under this grant of authority are known as "interpretive" (or "interpretative") or "general authority" regulations. In addition to the blanket authority of section 7805(a), specific authority to issue regulations is often contained in discrete sections of the Code. When regulations are issued pursuant to such specific authorization or direction, they are "legislative" or "specific authority" regulations that have the force and effect of law unless they exceed the scope of the legislation, are unreasonable, or are not issued according to prescribed procedures.

Under the APA, a legislative regulation is one that is based on a congressional delegation of authority to resolve ambiguities in an incomplete statute. It creates new duties or obligations that are binding on all parties. Legislative regulations are promulgated under the notice and comment procedure and have the force and effect of law. An interpretive regulation, on the other hand, merely interprets existing law. It does not create new duties and it does not bind either the agency or any of the other parties.

In the recent past, Congress has expanded its reliance on the grant of legislative rulemaking authority, with the result that the Treasury Department's role in the drafting of substantive tax law has dramatically increased. Unfortunately, the burgeoning workload imposed on the Treasury Department also has resulted in significant periods of delay between the passage of new legislation and the issuance of authoritative guidance from the Treasury. An infamous example is section 385, enacted in 1969, which directed the Treasury "to prescribe such regulations as may be necessary or appropriate to determine whether an interest in a corporation is to be treated * * * as stock or indebtedness." Section 385(b) lists certain factors that "may" (but need not be) included in the regulations. More than thirty-five years later, regulations still have not been adopted, although regulations were proposed and withdrawn. The Treasury Department indicated in 1983 that it was "continuing to study" the issue.

B. *Judicial Review of Regulations*

Legislative regulations enjoy a great deal of deference from the judiciary. They are regarded as having the force and effect of law, because Congress has explicitly delegated to the agency its authority to draft substantive law. Therefore, a court is not free to strike down a legislative regulation that is properly issued procedurally and that is within the scope of the legislative grant. According to the Supreme Court, "[w]here the Commissioner acts under specific authority, our primary inquiry is whether the interpretation or method is within the delegation of authority." Rowan Companies v. United States (S.Ct.1981). Courts can strike down legislative regulations that conflict with the statute, that are beyond the scope of the statute, or that are otherwise unreasonable, although this happens only rarely. *See, e.g.,* Rite Aid Corp. v. United States (Fed. Cir.2001).

Interpretive regulations generally have been given less deference by the courts than legislative regulations. In 1944, the Supreme Court held that the degree of judicial deference afforded a general authority regulation depends upon "the thoroughness evident in its consideration, the validity of its reasoning, its consistency with earlier and later pronouncements and all those factors which give [the regulation] power to persuade, if lacking power to control." Skidmore v. Swift & Co. (S.Ct.1944). This is known as "traditional deference," under which a court owes such a regulation "respectful consideration," although the court is the final arbiter of whether the regulation is reasonable. Later, the Court held that interpretive regulations are entitled to deference if they "implement the congressional mandate in some reasonable manner." National Muffler Dealers Assoc., Inc. v. United States (S.Ct.1979). The Court provided several factors to be considered in making this determination: "whether the regulation harmonizes with the plain meaning of the statute, its origin and purpose," whether it was issued contemporaneously with the statute, "the length of time the regulation has been in effect, the reliance placed on it, the consistency of the Commissioner's interpretation, and the degree of scrutiny Congress has devoted to the regulation during subsequent re-enactments of the statute." *Id.* The Court also clarified that the "choice among reasonable interpretations is for the Commissioner, not the courts." *Id.*

In the wake of these cases, critics complained that it was illogical to distinguish between legislative and interpretive regulations because there was little difference between them, except for the congressional grant of authority (specific versus general) to the Treasury Department to promulgate regulations. They argued that this was a minor exception because both types of regulations are promulgated under the notice and comment procedures of the APA, and both create duties and have binding effect.

In 1984, the Supreme Court again addressed the issue of judicial deference to regulations. In *Chevron U.S.A., Inc. v. Natural Resources Defense Council, Inc.* (S.Ct.1984), the United States Supreme Court stated:

> When a court reviews an agency's construction of the statute which it administers, it is confronted with two questions. First, always, is the question whether Congress has directly spoken to the precise question at issue. If the intent of Congress is clear, that is the end of the matter; for the court, as well as the agency, must give effect to the unambiguously expressed intent of Congress. If, however, the court determines Congress has not directly addressed the precise question at issue, the court does not simply impose its own construction on the statute, as would be necessary in the absence of an administrative interpretation. Rather, if the statute is silent or ambiguous with respect to the specific issue, the question for the court is whether the agency's answer is based on a permissible construction of the statute.

In footnote 11, the Court noted:

> The court need not conclude that the agency construction was the only one it permissibly could have adopted to uphold the construction, or even the reading the court would have reached if the question initially had arisen in a judicial proceeding.

Thus, *Chevron* deference does not differentiate between the different types of regulations and under *Chevron* the court is no longer the primary interpreter of the statute. Instead, it must accept the interpretation of the promulgating agency unless the regulation is contrary to the "unambiguously express intent of Congress" or "the statute is silent or ambiguous with respect to the specific issue" and the agency's interpretation is not "based on a permissible construction of the statute."

The regulation at issue in *Chevron* was not a tax regulation, however, and the Supreme Court has sent mixed messages about whether *Chevron* deference applies to interpretive regulations. This has caused considerable debate over whether *Chevron* deference applies to Treasury regulations issued under § 7805(a). The courts currently are split on the issue, with the Sixth Circuit holding that interpretive regulations are entitled to *Chevron* deference, while the Fifth Circuit has determined that *Chevron* deference does not apply to interpretive regulations. The Tax Court and the Seventh Circuit take the position that there is no distinction between the *National Muffler* standard and the *Chevron* standard. In fact, the Tax Court has held that "deference only establishes the framework for judicial analysis; it does not displace it." Georgia Federal Bank, F.S.B. v. Commissioner (Tax Ct.1992). There appears to be general agreement, though, that *Skidmore* deference no longer applies to tax regulations.

In *United States v. Mead Corporation* (S.Ct.2001), the Supreme Court considered whether a tariff classification ruling of the United States Customs Service was entitled to judicial deference. Although the Court did not address the issue of judicial deference to regulations, it stated that the test for *Chevron* deference is whether "Congress would expect the agency to be able to speak with the force of law when it addresses ambiguity in the statute or fills a space in the enacted law." In determining whether this test has been met, the Court stated:

> We have recognized a very good indicator of delegation meriting *Chevron* treatment in express congressional authorizations to engage in the process of rulemaking or adjudication that produces regulations or rulings for which deference is claimed. It is fair to assume generally that Congress contemplates administrative action with the effect of law when it provides for a relatively formal administrative procedure tending to foster the fairness and deliberation that should underlie a pronouncement of such force. Thus, the overwhelming number of our cases applying *Chevron* deference have reviewed the fruits of notice-and-comment rulemaking or formal adjudication. That said, and as significant as notice-and-comment is in pointing to *Chevron* authority, the

want of that procedure here does not decide the case, for we have sometimes found reasons for *Chevron* deference even when no such administrative formality was required and none was afforded.

C. *Retroactivity of Treasury Regulations*

Under the APA, rules or regulations generally have future (or prospective) effect only. See the definition of "rule" under the APA at section 551(4). Until recently, Code section 7805(b) (which was enacted long before the APA), had the opposite effect: it established a presumption that regulations would have retroactive effect. Under the Taxpayer Bill of Rights Act of 1996 (the second TBOR) section 7805(b) was amended to establish a new rule that most regulations will now have prospective (or future) effect only. Under amended section 7805(b), any temporary, proposed or final regulation issued after July 30, 1996 must have an effective date that is no earlier than the date on which the regulation is filed with the Federal Register, unless one of the exceptions listed in section 7805(b) applies. Those exceptions include regulations issued within eighteen months of the enactment of the statute to which the regulation relates. Other exceptions permit retroactivity to prevent abuse and to correct procedural defects.

§ 2.2 IRS Procedural Regulations

Regulations describing the organization of the IRS and its "housekeeping" rules are set forth in the IRS Statement of Procedural Rules, which is contained in 26 CFR Part 601. These regulations are preceded by "601" and are cited, for example, as "26 C.F.R. § 601.509," to distinguish them from regulations issued by the Treasury Department. Legislative and interpretive regulations, issued by the Treasury Department, are cited differently, and the number immediately following the § symbol identifies the type of tax provision they implement. Income tax regulations, for example, are preceded by a "1," and are cited as follows: "Reg. § 1.61" (which indicates a regulation under section 61 of the Code). Procedural regulations are promulgated by the IRS, not the Treasury Department, and are not subject to the notice-and-comment requirements of the APA. Unlike legislative and interpretive regulations, procedural regulations may have retroactive effect. I.R.C. § 7805(b)(6).

Some regulations address matters of procedure, but are not "procedural regulations," as that term is defined above. For example, rules establishing taxpayer obligations to file certain forms or furnish certain information are often included in interpretive regulations. When such procedural matters are included in an interpretive or legislative regulation, the Treasury Department follows the APA notice-and-comment rules and the regulations are not "procedural," although they cover matters of procedure. Similarly, regulations interpreting the administrative and procedural sections of the Code, which are cited as "Reg. §§ 301.6001" et seq., are treated as interpretive regulations.

While legislative and interpretive regulations are binding authority on both the Service and taxpayers, the Service will not always be bound by its procedural rules. The Internal Revenue Manual is a lengthy volume of procedures prescribed by the IRS as procedural regulations to be followed by IRS personnel. Generally, procedural rules that affect individuals' rights will be binding on an agency, even if the rules are stricter than the law otherwise requires. *See* Morton v. Ruiz (S.Ct.1974). However, where the procedural regulation was not relied upon by the taxpayer, and it had no effect on her conduct, failure by the IRS to comply with the procedural rule does not require that the evidence obtained in violation of the rule be suppressed. United States v. Caceres (S.Ct.1979) (failure to follow procedures in Internal Revenue Manual). Generally, it appears that if the right granted under the procedure is relatively minor, and if the relief necessary to correct the failure by the IRS to comply is relatively harsh, there is little likelihood that the taxpayer's challenge to the IRS action will be sustained.

§ 2.3 IRS Rulings

Rulings issued by the IRS have less precedential value than the "rules" or "regulations" discussed in the preceding sections. The IRS issues two basic types of "rulings": revenue rulings and letter rulings (usually called "private letter rulings" or "PLRs"). In the hierarchy of tax statements of position, revenue rulings are lower than regulations but higher than letter rulings. The IRS also issues other types of statements of position, such as revenue procedures and determination letters, which are discussed at § C, *infra*. The IRS rulings program has become increasingly important as the tax laws have become more complex and more frequently amended. Particularly in business transactions involving large sums of money, the parties may condition the transaction on receipt of a favorable ruling if the law is uncertain.

A. *Revenue Rulings*

Revenue rulings are official agency interpretations of tax laws or treaties, as applied to specific facts. Revenue rulings are issued by the IRS National Office, rather than the Treasury (which issues regulations), and the notice and comment procedures of the APA are not followed. Revenue rulings are published in the Internal Revenue Bulletin (abbreviated as "I.R.B.") and collected in bound form in the Cumulative Bulletin (abbreviated "C.B."). A revenue ruling can be easily located by its official citation. For example, the revenue ruling that is cited as "Rev. Rul. 84–108, 1984–2 C.B. 32" is located in the second Cumulative Bulletin for 1984 at page 32.

Although revenue rulings are binding on the Service and on taxpayers, their applicability is limited by the specific fact situations to which they are addressed. Thus, the IRS cautions taxpayers as follows:

Taxpayers generally may rely upon revenue rulings published in the Bulletin in determining the tax treatment of their own transactions and need not request specific rulings applying the principles of a published revenue ruling to the facts of their particular cases. However, since each revenue ruling represents the conclusion of the Service as to the application of the law to the entire state of facts involved, taxpayers, Service personnel and others concerned are cautioned against reaching the same conclusion in other cases unless the facts and circumstances are substantially the same.

Thus, reliance on a revenue ruling is warranted only if the facts and circumstances are "substantially the same" as those described in the ruling.

B. *Letter Rulings*

If there is no clear authority for determining the tax consequences of a transaction, the taxpayer may request a ruling on the issue. Advance planning is crucial: the IRS will rule only on prospective transactions or transactions that are completed, but for which the return has not been filed. The IRS will not issue a ruling on a hypothetical situation or on alternative plans for a proposed transaction. In addition, there are numerous issues on which the Service will not rule. These issues or areas are referred to as the "no-rulings list" and are identified in revenue procedures that are updated annually. See, e.g., Rev. Proc. 2005–1. According to the Service, the no-rulings list is comprised of areas involving "inherently factual" questions. Rev. Proc. 2005–3. These revenue procedures also list areas in which the Service will "not ordinarily" rule, plus areas in which the Service has temporarily suspended ruling.

Letter rulings are issued to specific taxpayers and may not be relied upon by other taxpayers. Letter rulings are not officially published and were not available to the public until 1976. In that year, two circuit courts of appeals held that letter rulings were subject to disclosure under the Freedom of Information Act (discussed in Chapter 4), and Congress responded by enacting section 6110 of the tax Code, which removed applicability of the Freedom of Information Act and established rules for public inspection of letter rulings, determination letters and technical advice memoranda. Although section 6110(i)(3) states that "a written determination may not be used or cited as precedent," the previously private rulings are a valuable research source that afford insight into the IRS's position on many issues and are in fact relied on by tax planners.

Although section 6110 requires public access to "written determinations," which it defines as including rulings, determination letters and technical advice memoranda, taxpayers need not fear that their identities will be revealed if they request a ruling. Under section 6110(c), identifying information (such as names, addresses and "other identifying details") are to be deleted before the document is made available to the public.

Not surprisingly, there was (and continues to be) an enormous demand for rulings. In its 1988 fiscal year, for example, the IRS issued 24,827 letter rulings. In response to the increased demand on the Service, Congress enacted legislation in 1987 requiring the Treasury Department to establish a program of "user fees" for rulings, determination letters and other types of agency determinations. The schedule of fees is published in the first Revenue Procedure each year. See, e.g. Rev. Proc. 2005–1, App. A. The amount of the fee depends on the type of request and varies from $50 to $6,000 (if postmarked before March 1, 2005) or $7,000 (if postmarked after). The fee must be paid in advance, and the Service will return any request that is not accompanied by the proper fee.

It is not always advisable to request a ruling when the tax consequences of a transaction or course of action are uncertain. One must balance the possible positive effect of a favorable ruling that will prevent subsequent problems on the issue against the possible negative effect of receiving an adverse ruling. Particularly if the available information (such as revenue rulings and letter rulings) indicates a probability that the ruling will be adverse, and if the taxpayer is determined to pursue the transaction, requesting a ruling could be a serious mistake. Although ruling requests may be withdrawn, and usually are withdrawn when an adverse ruling appears imminent, the National Office can notify the applicable Area Examination

Team of the withdrawal, which could increase the taxpayer's chance of audit.

Another factor that may influence the decision whether to request a ruling is timing. If the transaction must be completed by a certain date, obtaining a timely ruling may not be possible. The Service must contact the requester within 21 calendar days of its receipt of the ruling request, to discuss the request informally and possibly request additional information, but processing of the requests is done only "in regular order and as expeditiously as possible." Rev.Proc. 2005–1. Expedited treatment may be requested, but it will be granted only if the Service believes there is a "compelling need" for it. Examples of what the IRS does not consider sufficient grounds for expedited treatment include the scheduling of a closing date for a transaction or the possible effect of fluctuation in the market price of stock. *Id.*

To minimize delay, the ruling request should contain all the information and documents required under the revenue procedure, which is issued annually as the first revenue procedure. For example, Revenue Procedure 97–1 contains applicable rules for rulings requested during 1997. This same revenue procedure contains guidelines for requesting determination letters and information letters, as well as for entering into closing agreements (discussed in Chapter 6).

Some of the essential contents of a ruling request include:

1. An executed power of attorney (on Form 2848) if the request is being submitted by a taxpayer's authorized representative, rather than by the taxpayer himself.

2. A "perjury declaration," signed by the taxpayer, stating: "Under penalties of perjury, I declare that I have examined this request, including accompanying documents, and to the best of my knowledge and belief, the facts presented in support of the requested ruling or determination letter are true, correct, and complete." If the taxpayer is a corporation, the person signing the perjury declaration must be an officer who has personal knowledge of the facts. Similarly, if the taxpayer is a trust or partnership, the declaration must be signed by a trustee or partner with personal knowledge of the facts.

3. A "complete statement of all of the facts relating to the transaction," together with "true copies of all contracts, wills, deeds, agreements, instruments, and other documents." Further, all "material facts" in documents must be identified in the letter requesting the ruling, and not merely incorporated by reference, and there must be "an analysis of their bearing on the issue or issues, specifying the provisions that apply."

4. An "issue not pending statement," signed both by the taxpayer and by the authorized representative, declaring that the issue presented is not identical to an issue that is contained in a prior return of the taxpayer, or is being considered or

examined by the IRS with respect to the taxpayer, or is involved in pending litigation involving the taxpayer.

5. A statement that the issue is not clearly and adequately addressed by any existing authority.

It is advisable to include a request for a conference in the ruling request. Unless requested in writing with the initial filing or "soon" thereafter, the Service is not required to grant a conference. Conferences are normally scheduled only if an adverse decision is expected or the IRS thinks it would be helpful.

The legal effect of a letter ruling is limited to the requesting taxpayer and the precise facts described in the request. A favorable ruling will preclude the IRS from challenging the position approved in the ruling. However, rulings may be modified or revoked retroactively, as discussed in § 2.4, *infra*.

C. *Other IRS Statements of Position*

In addition to revenue rulings and letter rulings, other types of IRS statements of position include:

1. *Revenue Procedures.* The IRS issues revenue procedures, and publishes them in the Internal Revenue Bulletin, to inform the public of procedural rules that affect taxpayers' rights and duties. Revenue rulings, on the other hand, interpret the tax laws as applied to a specific set of facts. Like revenue rulings, revenue procedures are easily located in the I.R.B. or Cumulative Bulletin by their citation. For example, Rev.Proc. 88–1,1988–1 C.B. 557

is located in volume 1 of the 1988 Cumulative Bulletin at page 557.

2. *Determination Letters.* These are written statements issued by a Director of an Operating Division applying "clearly established rules" to a completed transaction. Determination letters have the same legal effect as a letter ruling, but differ from rulings in that they are issued by an Area Director (rather than the Associate Chief Counsel), apply only to completed (as opposed to prospective) transactions, and will be issued only if clearly established rules justify their issuance. Most determination letters involve the "qualification" of employee benefit plans and the tax-exempt status of organizations.

3. *Technical Advice.* Technical advice, also known as a TAM, is issued in memorandum form to a Director or Area Director (Appeals) by the Office of the Chief Counsel in response to technical or procedural questions that may arise during the examination of a taxpayer's return or during the consideration of a claim for refund or credit. TAMs provide guidance on the proper interpretation and application of the tax laws, regulations, treaties, revenue rulings and other precedents. Employees of the IRS may initiate the request for technical advice, or the taxpayer may initiate the request if he believes the IRS has dealt with an issue inconsistently or that the issue is so complex or novel that National Office consideration is warranted. Like letter rulings and determination letters, TAMs apply only to the specific case in which the advice was

requested and may not be used as precedent by any other taxpayer. Also like letter rulings and determination letters, TAMs are available to the public only after identifying information has been deleted.

4. *Acquiescence or Nonacquiescence*. When a tax case is decided adversely to the Government, the IRS will announce (in the Internal Revenue Bulletin) whether it will alter its position to accept the court ruling (acquiescence) or will continue to litigate the issue and maintain its position (nonacquiescence). Indications of acquiescence or nonacquiescence appear in the case citation as "acq." or "nonacq." An acquiescence "in result only" means that the IRS expressly disagrees with some or all of the reasoning underlying the decision. Prior to 1991, the IRS issued its acquiescence or nonacquiescence only in regular Tax Court decisions. After 1991, the acquiescence program was expanded to include Tax Court memorandum decisions and cases decided by other courts (i.e., the United States District Courts, the United States Court of Federal Claims, and the Circuit Courts of Appeal). Although the IRS publishes a statement in each volume of the Cumulative Bulletin that "acquiescences in adverse decisions shall be relied on by revenue officers and others concerned as conclusions of the Service," the Supreme Court has held that retroactive revocation of an acquiescence (resulting in assessment of a deficiency against a taxpayer) is not an abuse of discretion. Dixon v. United States (S.Ct.1965). According to the Court, "Since no reliance [on the published acquiescence] was warranted, no notice

[of the Service's intent to retroactively revoke it]
was required."

5. *Actions on Decisions.* Rulings adverse to the
Government on tax issues in any federal court,
including the Tax Court, trigger the preparation of
an "action on decision" ("AOD") memorandum explaining why the Government should or should not
appeal. AODs are prepared by lawyers in the Office
of the Associate Chief Counsel (Litigation) and are
intended for internal use by IRS personnel in cases
with similar issues. AODs are available to the public
under the Freedom of Information Act and, like
letter rulings, they are published by commercial
publishers, but they may not be relied upon by the
public as precedent.

6. *IRS Pamphlets and Booklets.* The IRS is not
bound by statements or positions in its unofficial
publications, such as handbooks and pamphlets.
Some courts, however, have found it an abuse of
discretion to apply retroactively a regulation that
contradicts an unofficial statement of position on
which the Service has invited reliance by promising
that any modification would have prospective effect
only.

7. *Other Written and Oral Advice.* Most taxpayers' requests for advice from the IRS are made
orally. Unfortunately, the IRS is not bound by answers or positions stated by its employees orally,
whether in person or by telephone. According to its
procedural regulations, "oral advice is advisory only
and the Service is not bound to recognize it in the

examination of the taxpayer's return.'' 26 C.F.R. § 601.201(k)(2). In rare cases, however, the IRS has been held to be equitably estopped to take a position different from that stated orally to, and justifiably relied on by, the taxpayer.

The Omnibus Taxpayer Bill of Rights Act (TBOR 1), enacted as part of the Technical and Miscellaneous Revenue Act of 1988, gives taxpayers some comfort, however. It amended section 6404 to require the Service to abate any penalty or addition to tax that is attributable to advice furnished in writing by any IRS agent or employee acting within the scope of his official capacity. Section 6404, as amended, protects the taxpayer only if the following conditions are satisfied: the written advice from the IRS was issued in response to a written request from the taxpayer; reliance on the advice was reasonable; and the erroneous advice did not result from inaccurate or incomplete information furnished by the taxpayer. Thus, it will still be difficult to bind the IRS even to written statements made by its employees, and as was true before, taxpayers may be penalized for following oral advice from the IRS.

§ 2.4　Retroactive Revocation of Rulings

Although section 7805(b) now generally prohibits the issuance of regulations with retroactive effect, it permits the Service to modify or revoke retroactively rulings, determination letters, acquiescences, and other statements of position. There are limits on the authority to make such revocations retroactively, however, and in some cases, courts have held it an abuse of discretion to revoke or modify a ruling retroactively.

A. *Basic Rules*

In 1957 the Supreme Court upheld a retroactive revocation of a determination letter that an organization was tax-exempt, ruling that the IRS may correct a mistake of law retroactively unless retroactive revocation amounts to an abuse of discretion. Automobile Club of Michigan v. Commissioner (S.Ct.1957). In that case the Supreme Court distinguished a case decided the previous year by the Third Circuit, *Lesavoy Foundation v. Commissioner* (3d Cir.1956), in which the Third Circuit had nullified a retroactive revocation of a tax-exempt status determination. The Third Circuit found the action to be an abuse of discretion because the organization had disclosed all material facts to the Service when it applied for tax-exempt status and the effect of the retroactive revocation would have made the organization "liable for a tax bill so large as to wipe it out of existence." As these cases illustrate, whether retroactive revocation amounts to an abuse of discretion depends upon the particular facts involved, including the harshness of the result to the taxpayer.

Courts have been very reluctant to hold that a retroactive revocation of a published IRS position amounts to an abuse of discretion. As discussed in § 2.3 C, *supra*, the Supreme Court refused to find an abuse of discretion when the IRS retroactively revoked its acquiescence in a Tax Court decision, even though the taxpayer had relied on the acquiescence. Dixon v. United States (S.Ct.1965). The *Dixon* Court found that the taxpayer was not justified in relying on the acquiescence, and thus was not entitled to notice prior to a change of position by the IRS.

B. Discriminatory Treatment as Abuse of Discretion

One circumstance that courts have found to amount to an abuse of discretion is an arbitrary distinction between similarly situated taxpayers. In *Baker v. United States* (11th Cir.1984), the Eleventh Circuit listed factors to be considered and concluded that the Service had abused its discretion when it denied retroactively a deduction of flight training benefits that were subsidized by the taxpayer's veterans benefits, while denying only prospectively the deductibility of other types of educational expenses subsidized by veterans benefits. The *Baker* court found that there was no rational basis for this "arbitrary distinction." Ruling on the identical issue, the Ninth Circuit upheld the Service's actions, finding that there was a "rational basis" for the distinction. Manocchio v. Commissioner (9th Cir. 1983). The dubious logic employed by the Service and accepted by the Ninth Circuit to justify the distinction was that general educational benefits are in the nature of a living stipend, while flight training payments are reimbursements for actual tuition and fees.

In extraordinary circumstances, a taxpayer may prevail on a discriminatory treatment claim involving private letter rulings (as opposed to revenue rulings, at issue in *Baker*). Although letter rulings may not be relied upon as precedent by anyone other than the taxpayers who request them, the IRS is not permitted to treat similarly situated taxpayers with identical issues in grossly disparate fashion. The facts of *International Business Machines Corp. v. United States* (Ct.Cl.1965) are remarkable and provide the only available guidance for when a discriminatory treatment argument in the context of letter rulings will succeed.

The *IBM* case involved two competitors, IBM and Remington Rand, both engaged in manufacturing and marketing large computer systems. On April 13, 1955, Remington requested a ruling that would permit it to avoid certain tax liabilities arising out of its computer sales and rentals. On April 15, just two days later, the IRS issued a favorable ruling to Remington. On July 13, 1955, having learned of Remington's ruling, IBM sought a similar ruling in a letter marked "Urgent! Please Expedite" that recited: "In view of the extreme urgency of this matter, your immediate ruling, wire collect, is respectfully requested." After spending more than two years processing IBM's request, the Service ruled against IBM.

That same year, both IBM and Remington filed for refunds of taxes already paid on past sales and rentals of computers. Remington's refund claim was allowed, but IBM's was rejected. In 1958, the IRS revoked Remington's favorable ruling, but did so prospectively only. The net effect of these actions was a comparative $13 million loss to IBM. The court found that the Commissioner had abused his discretion in favoring one competitor over another. Subsequent cases have essentially limited the *IBM* case to its facts, holding generally that "[t]axpayers without rulings are entitled only to be taxed the same as other taxpayers without rulings." Bookwalter v. Brecklein (8th Cir.1966).

HIERARCHY OF TAX AUTHORITIES

Authority	Issued by	APA notice and comment	Binding on	Cite
Internal Revenue Code	Congress	No	All taxpayers	I.R.C. §
Legislative regulations*	Treasury	Yes	All taxpayers	Reg. §
Interpretive regulations**	Treasury	Yes	All taxpayers	Reg. §
Temporary regulations	Treasury	No	All taxpayers	Reg. §
Proposed regulations	Treasury	Yes	All taxpayers	Prop. Reg. §
Procedural regulations	IRS	No	IRS (Sometimes)	26 C.F.R. §
Revenue rulings	IRS	No	All taxpayers	Rev.Rul.
Revenue procedures	IRS	No	All taxpayers	Rev. Proc.
Letter rulings	IRS	No	Taxpayers who request	P.L.R.
Technical advice memoranda	IRS	No	Taxpayers on whose behalf issued	T.A.M.
Acquiescence, or nonacquiescence	IRS	No	No one	Acq. or nonacq.

*   Authorized by specific Code section (other than section 7805)
** Issued under blanket authority of section 7805

CHAPTER 3

THE HAZARDS AND
STANDARDS OF
TAX PRACTICE

§ 3.1 "Practice" Before the IRS

Practice before the IRS consists of interaction with any of its officers or employees "relating to a taxpayer's rights, privileges, or liabilities" under the tax laws or regulations. This includes "preparing and filing documents, corresponding and communicating with the IRS, and representing a client at conferences, hearings, and meetings." Circular 230, § 10.2(d)(see discussion of Circular 230, § 3.3, and throughout this Chapter). On the other hand, the preparation of a tax return does not constitute practice before the IRS, nor does appearing as a witness or furnishing information requested by the IRS. Circular 230, §§ 10.2(a) and 10.7. The right to practice before the IRS is statutory. 5 U.S.C. § 500. Lawyers in good standing and certified public accountants have a statutory right to practice before the Service, as long as they file written declarations of their qualifications. Enrolled agents are individuals who lack the special training of lawyers and certified public accountants, but who qualify to practice before the IRS by passing certain examinations or by past employment with the IRS. 5 U.S.C. § 500. Enrolled actuaries also are authorized by the Treasury Department to practice before the Service to a more limited degree.

A. Powers of Attorney

An authorized representative enters her appearance as a taxpayer's representative by filing a declaration of qualification and a power of attorney executed by the client. 26 C.F.R. §§ 601.501–.509. Before a power of attorney is filed, the representative will not be allowed to act on behalf of the taxpayer or receive confidential tax information about the taxpayer.

The IRS has special forms for this purpose. Form 2848 is a general power of attorney form on which the client indicates the types of actions the representative may take for him. It contains a declaration to be executed by the attorney or other representative (under penalty of perjury) indicating qualification to practice before the IRS and awareness of Circular 230. The Regulations require a power of attorney in proper form before a representative may execute documents on the client's behalf or receive a check refunding tax, penalties or interest. 26 C.F.R. § 601.502. Once the power of attorney has been filed, the IRS contacts the representative, rather than the taxpayer, unless the representative hinders the IRS in its audit or investigation. 26 C.F.R. § 601.505(b). In such cases, the

Regulations provide procedures for bypassing the representative. *Id.*

Form 8821 is a limited power of attorney, known as a Tax Information Authorization, by which a taxpayer authorizes a representative to receive and inspect confidential tax information pertaining to the taxpayer. Unlike the Form 2848, the Form 8821 does not contain a section for the representative to declare her eligibility to practice before the IRS and awareness of Circular 230.

B. *Regulation of Return Preparers*

The majority of taxpayers use a return preparer to prepare and file their tax returns. An income tax return preparer is any person who, for compensation, prepares any tax return or claim for refund. IRC § 7701(a)(36). This includes any person who prepares a substantial portion of a return or who furnishes a taxpayer with sufficient information and advice so that the completion of a return is largely a mechanical or clerical matter. Reg. § 301.7701–15(a)(1). While some preparers, such as attorneys, CPAs, and enrolled agents are subject to strict federal and state licensing requirements, ethical obligations, and continuing professional education, preparers who do not fall into these categories are not required to meet minimum competency standards. In fact, the regulations provide that a "person may be an income tax return preparer without regard to educational qualifications and professional status requirements." Reg. § 301.7705–15(a)(3). Since the quality of these preparers may vary widely, and this disparity can adversely affect the federal tax system in general, the National Taxpayer Advocate has recommended that Congress require Federal Tax Return Preparers ("FTRPs") to register and certify that they can demonstrate skill and competency in federal tax return preparation.

C. *Regulation of Tax Practitioners*

Attorneys advising clients on tax matters owe a dual obligation: they must represent the client fairly and use available legal means to reduce the client's tax liability; to do less would deprive the client of tax benefits to which he is legally entitled. On the other hand, the attorney also owes an obligation to the Government and the public to support and implement our self-assessment system. Taking "aggressive" positions, in the hope that the client's return will not be audited, or attempting to conceal the transaction with confidentiality agreements and/or the use of complex transactions involving offshore companies, violates the duty owed to the public when the position underlying the transaction is legally unsupportable. By counseling such positions, or acquiescing in them, the lawyer is assisting in the evasion of taxes, with a resulting loss of both tax revenue and respect for our tax system.

Most lawyers are aware of the criminal penalties for aiding and abetting, and many are aware of the civil aiding and assisting penalty of the Code, section 6701. Certainly, most tax advisors would not consciously advise a tax return position that would or might expose them to such penalties. The problem, however, is not so simple. Because the tax laws are so complex, and have been so fundamentally and frequently overhauled in the past two decades, the "correct" reporting position is not always self-evident. Given a choice between a conservative position, which might cost the taxpayer more than he actually, ultimately owed, and an aggressive position, which might cost the public tax revenues, which position can or should the lawyer advise? And is the lawyer absolved of any culpability if she advises the client that the position is not supported by adequate authority, but the client decides to take the position and risk possible penalties?

The answers to these questions are continuing to evolve. Standards established by Congress now are based on those of the American Bar Association ("ABA"), the American Institute of Certified Public Accountants ("AICPA") and the Treasury Department. Regulations governing practice before the Treasury are known as "Circular 230," the official title of which is "Regulations Governing the Practice of Attorneys, Certified Public Accountants, Enrolled Agents, Enrolled Actuaries and Appraisers before the Internal Revenue Service."

§ 3.2 Professional Standards

A. The "Reasonable Basis" Standard

Although neither the ABA nor the AICPA directly regulates tax practice, each has a professional code (the ABA's Model Rules of Professional Conduct and the AICPA's Code of Professional Ethics), and each has committees that occasionally issue opinions dealing specifically with tax practice. In 1965 the ABA's Standing Committee on Ethics issued Formal Opinion 314, adopting the infamous "reasonable basis" standard. Under this standard, a lawyer could recommend a return position favorable to the client "as long as there [wa]s a reasonable basis" for the position, with no attendant duty to disclose or "red flag" the position on the return. In 1977 the AICPA adopted a similar "reasonable support" standard.

Opinion 314 characterized the giving of tax advice and the representation of clients under tax audit as adversarial, and concluded that the lawyer's role in each should be governed by the same ethical rules governing litigation. But the failure to distinguish between advising with respect to a return and representing the client under audit, prompted many to question the Opinion and to predict serious erosion of the voluntary compliance system. Nevertheless, the reasonable basis standard prevailed, perhaps because it mirrored the tax system's standard for taxpayer behavior: the no-fault penalty of section 6662(d) was not introduced until 1982, so that only the negligence penalty was available to curtail taxpayer manipulation of the system. A reasonable basis for the return position thus shielded both the client and the lawyer from sanctions.

Because reliance on the advice of a lawyer after full disclosure provides a defense to criminal sanctions, as well as the negligence and fraud penalties, and because some lawyers interpreted the reasonable basis standard as permitting favorable opinions on very dubious positions, the reasonable basis standard deteriorated in the 1970s. Taxpayers sought favorable opinions to insure against penalties, and lawyers stretched the standard to accommodate the clients' tax-minimizing goals, particularly in the area of tax shelter offerings. As one judge observed in acquitting a taxpayer of criminal charges:

> Surely it would be unfair to judge the client's criminal liability on a stricter standard than his lawyer's ethical obligation. * * *
>
> The scheme in the instant case is a very aggressive one. The Court is somewhat shocked that it was approved by competent counsel. * * * [T]he literature in the entire area of tax avoidance planning, particularly the A.B.A. opinion, tends to take a rather cavalier attitude toward obviously questionable schemes. [United States v. Yorke, unpublished opinion, D.Md. July 19, 1976.]

The ABA's Standing Committee reacted to the mounting criticism by issuing Formal Opinion 346 in 1981, setting forth stricter guidelines for the issuance of "tax opinions" in publicly offered tax shelters. For such offerings, the reasonable basis standard was replaced with requirements that the lawyer assess the likelihood that the claimed tax benefits more likely than not would be realized by the investors. The Treasury subsequently amended Circular 230 to incorporate the tax shelter standards of Opinion 346. (See further discussion, § C., *infra*).

Meanwhile, Congress decided in 1982 to enact the no-fault penalty of section 6662(d), under which a taxpayer (but not his advisor) could be penalized for understatements of income even in the absence of negligence. Enactment of section 6662(d) created a disturbing anomaly: lawyers and accountants apparently could freely advise clients to take a position on a return if there was any reasonable basis for it; taxpayers who reported such positions, without disclosing them, would be liable for the penalty unless there was substantial authority for the position or the position was "red-flagged" on the return. The legislative history of section 6662(d) reveals that Congress intended the "substantial authority" standard to be stricter than the "reasonable basis" standard. On the other hand, the "substantial authority" standard is less strict than, and requires less authority than, a "more likely than not" to succeed standard, which section 6662(d) applies to tax shelter items.

B. The "Realistic Possibility" Standard

In 1985 the ABA issued Opinion 85–352, in which it abandoned the "reasonable basis" standard, but opted for a completely new standard to replace it. Under this new standard, the return position must have "some realistic possibility of success" if litigated. The ABA clearly rejected the more stringent "substantial authority" and "more likely than not" standards, and opted instead for a litigation-oriented standard akin to Rule 11 of the Federal Rules of Civil Procedure. As Opinion 85–352 states:

> In summary, a lawyer may advise a reporting position on a return *even where the lawyer believes the position probably will not prevail, there is no "substantial authority" in support of the position, and there will be no disclosure of the position on the return.* However, the position to be asserted must be one which the lawyer in good faith believes is warranted in existing law or can be supported by a good faith argument for an extension, modification or reversal of existing law. This requires that there is *some realistic possibility of success* if the matter is litigated. In addition, in his role as advisor, the lawyer should refer to potential penalties and other legal consequences should the client take the position advised. [Emphasis added.]

The response to this Opinion was not uniformly enthusiastic. Many believed that the ABA had not sufficiently addressed the problems created by the reasonable basis standard. In response, the ABA appointed a Special Task Force to study the new standard. It concluded that the "some realistic possibility of success" standard was intended to be stricter than the "reasonable basis" standard as interpreted by many lawyers. To provide guidance, the Special Task Force stated that a position having only a 5% or 10% chance of success would not meet the new standard, but that one approaching a 30% chance of success should be sufficient. Report of the Special Task Force on Formal Opinion 85–352, 39

Tax Lawyer 635, 638 (1986). The "realistic possibility" standard is thus stricter than the "reasonable basis" standard, but more lenient than the "substantial authority" standard.

Obviously, Opinion 85–352 did not cure the anomaly created by the taxpayer standard of section 6662(d) (substantial authority) being stricter than the standard governing lawyers ("reasonable basis" and later, "some realistic possibility of success").

C. *Tax Shelter Opinions*

During the 1970s and early 1980s, the widespread proliferation of tax shelters, usually bearing the official stamp of approval of a lawyer's tax opinion, fostered the negative public perception of lawyers as "hired guns" whose help in evading taxes could be bought for the right price. One direct and unfortunate result was an erosion of our system of self-assessment. As the public increasingly believed that most people cheated on their taxes, and that most wealthy individuals and corporations were assisted in doing so by crafty tax professionals, the stigma attached to "cheating" or "fudging" began to disappear. The problem worsened in the 1990's with highly publicized corporate accounting scandals and abusive tax avoidance transactions. The Treasury Department, Congress, the organized bar, and the accounting profession all have attempted to address the problem, resulting in special provisions to counter the spread of these abusive tax avoidance schemes.

Tax shelter opinions present special problems because not all tax professionals who issue such opinions conform to the high standards that are expected of them, and because third parties may rely on the advice of the lawyer who renders a tax shelter opinion. Because of the latter factor, the principles of ABA Formal Opinion 314 have little application. In recognition of this short-coming, the ABA issued Formal Opinion 346 on June 1, 1981. This Opinion defines a tax shelter opinion as "advice by a lawyer concerning the federal tax law applicable to a tax shelter if the advice is referred to either in offering materials or in connection with sales promotion efforts directed to persons other than the client who engages the lawyer to give the advice."

Initially, Opinion 346 prohibited lawyers from issuing negative tax shelter opinions that concluded that the proposed benefits from the shelters were not likely to withstand challenge by the Service. In response to a number of concerns raised about this provision, however, the ABA reissued the Opinion on January 29, 1982. Under the revised Opinion, if the lawyer concludes that the significant tax benefits probably will not be realized, the lawyer may issue a negative opinion, but the negative conclusion must be "clearly stated and prominently noted in the offering materials." In addition, the risks and uncertainties of the investment must be clearly stated at the outset of the opinion or in a clearly marked separate section of the offering materials. If the lawyer and the client cannot reach an agreement on the extent of disclosure to be made in the offering materials, the lawyer must withdraw from representing the client on this matter and refrain from issuing an opinion.

Opinion 346 also provides that a lawyer may not issue a false opinion and must be diligent in determining the facts, at all times obeying the ABA rules of ethics. This means that the lawyer must make clear to the offeror/client that she expects "full disclosure of the structure and intended operations of the venture and complete access to all relevant information." In rendering the opinion, the lawyer must relate the law to the actual facts, to the extent those facts are ascertainable when the offering materials are circulated. If not ascertainable, the lawyer may speculate, provided the speculation is reasonable and complete, and as long as the factual assumptions are clearly identified as such in the offering materials.

The lawyer also should ensure that she, or another competent professional, has considered all "material" tax issues. A "material" tax issue is one that would have a significant effect on sheltering income from federal taxes by providing deductions in excess of the income from the shelter, or credits in excess of the tax attributable to the shelter investment. In addition, the tax risks of the venture should be clearly disclosed, including an evaluation of the extent to which the tax benefits of the venture are likely to be realized. If it is not possible to make such an evaluation (where, for instance, the benefits are predicated upon a newly enacted Code provision with no regulations and obscure legislative history), the lawyer must fully explain why the evaluation cannot be made and assure full disclosure of the assumptions and risks.

§ 3.3   Administrative Standards—Circular 230

The ABA standards apply only to lawyers and only to the extent they have been adopted by the jurisdictions in which the lawyers are practicing. Similarly, the AICPA standards apply only to certified public accountants. Because the organized bar does not enforce its standard of conduct, such enforcement is left to the states, which have shown little interest in tax-related issues. Circular 230, on the other hand, applies to all persons authorized to practice before the IRS: lawyers, accountants, enrolled actuaries, and enrolled agents. "Circular 230" is the shorthand description of regulations issued by the Treasury Department governing practice before the IRS. Congress granted the Treasury Department authority to "regulate the practice of representatives of persons" before the Department and to suspend or disbar representatives who are "incompetent" or "disreputable" or who "violate regulations." 31 U.S.C. § 330. Regulations issued under this statute are found in Part 10 of Title 31 of the Code of Federal Regulations (a/k/a Treasury Department Circular 230), as revised from time to time.

Between 1986 and 1994 there was controversy over proposed amendments to Circular 230 that would have permitted censuring those practitioners who advised return positions that could have subjected the taxpayer to the substantial understatement penalty of section 6662(d). In 1994 the Treasury withdrew these controversial proposals and amended Circular 230 to conform to the "realistic possibility of success" standard adopted by Congress for return preparers under section 6694. In the "Explanation of Changes" contained in the final adoption of the amendments, the Treasury Department explained its reasoning for adopting the "realistic possibility of success" standard:

> To promote consistency in disclosure standards, the Circular 230 rules are patterned after the section 6694 rules and, therefore, a signing preparer must actually disclose (rather than merely advise disclosure of) nonfrivolous return positions that do not satisfy the realistic possibility of success standard. Because Treasury believes the realistic possibility standard is distinct from the not frivolous standard, these amendments to Circular 230 also distinguish between these two standards.

A. *"Best Practices"*

In an effort to "restore and promote public confidence in the tax system and in those who provide tax advice and other services," Circular 230 was amended in late 2004 to set aspirational (as opposed to mandatory) "best practices" for tax advisors. These practices were derived from the ABA Model Rules of Professional Conduct. Failure to follow the practices will not result in a sanction unless the failure violates other provisions of Circular 230. The practices are found at section 10.33 of Circular 230, which provides that all tax advisors must (1) communicate clearly with their clients regarding the terms of the engagement and the form and scope of the advice or assistance to be rendered, (2) establish the relevant facts, including evaluating the reasonableness of any assumptions or representations, (3) relate the applicable law, including potentially applicable judicial opinions, to the relevant facts, (4) arrive at a conclusion supported by the law and the facts, (5) advise the client regarding the importance of the conclusions reached, and (6) act fairly and with integrity in dealing with the IRS. Section 10.36 requires those who are responsible for overseeing a firm's practice of providing advice with respect to federal tax issues, or in assisting or preparing the submissions to the IRS, to take reasonable steps to ensure that the firm's procedures for all members, associates, and employees are consistent with the best practices described in section 10.33.

B. *Sanctions for Violations of Circular 230*

The American Jobs Creation Act of 2004 added new sanctions for violations of the provisions of Circular 230. In addition to disbarment or suspension, the Director of Practice may censure and impose monetary penalties against practitioners and may enjoin such practitioners to prevent further recurrences of Circular 230 violations.

The statutory grounds for disbarment or suspension include incompetence, disreputable conduct and violation of regulations prescribed by the enabling statute. 31 U.S.C. § 330(b). Circular 230 expands the statutory grounds for disciplinary actions. Violation of regulations, one of the statutory grounds for suspension or disbarment, includes violation of Circular 230. Circular 230 § 10.52.

"Disreputable conduct," which also justifies suspension or disbarment, includes conviction of any criminal offense under the Internal Revenue Code or of any offense involving dishonesty or breach of trust; giving false or misleading information to the IRS; attempting to influence an IRS employee; and "contemptuous conduct in connection with practice before the Internal Revenue Service," which includes "the use of abusive language." Circular 230 § 10.51.

C. *Disciplinary Actions*

Disciplinary action may take one of four forms: (1) private reprimand of the representative by letter from the Director of Practice, (2) public censure (published in the Internal Revenue Bulletin), (3) monetary penalties, or, for more serious violations, (4) prohibition from practice before the IRS.

The initiation of formal disciplinary proceedings begins with the filing of a complaint against a tax practitioner for violation of Circular 230. Generally, the complaint will be lodged with the Office of Professional Responsibility (OPR) by a revenue agent, since a client who has a complaint against a practitioner for bad tax advice or inadequate representation usually will be inclined to file a malpractice suit. The Director of Practice then usually sends the practitioner an allegation letter, informing the practitioner of the potential violations of Circular 230 the OPR is investigating and providing an opportunity for a response. Most cases end with no action taken, either because the Director concludes that there is no violation or because there is an agreement reached with the practitioner. In the future, monetary penalties also may be imposed against a practitioner who reaches an agreement with the Director.

In more serious cases, or where there is no agreement reached with the practitioner, the Director of Practice may initiate formal disciplinary proceedings by filing a complaint against the practitioner. Circular 230, § 10.60. The practitioner may file an answer within a relatively short period, usually 30 days. Failure to file an answer may result in a default decision against the practitioner, and the complaint must so inform the respondent. Circular 230, § 10.64.

The case will be heard by an administrative law judge (ALJ). The respondent may appear in person or be represented at the hearing. Following the hearing, the ALJ will make an initial decision, which will include findings and conclusions, the reasons for them, and an order of disbarment, suspension, reprimand, and/or monetary penalties, or an order dismissing the complaint. Circular 230 § 10.70. Within 30 days of the ALJ's decision, either party may appeal the decision to the Secretary of the Treasury, who then will make the final agency decision. If the representative wishes to appeal the final agency decision, she must petition the United States district court for review. If there is a final order of disbarment, the practitioner may petition the Director of Practice for reinstatement after five years have passed from the date of the final order. The Director of Practice may not grant reinstatement unless he is satisfied that the representative is not likely to violate the Regulations and that reinstatement would not be contrary to the public interest. Circular 230 § 10.81.

D. *Tax Shelter Opinions*

The late 1990's and early 2000's witnessed widely publicized accounting scandals involving bogus tax shelters marketed to large investors. These scandals led the Treasury Department to propose amendments to Circular 230 that address the standards of practice for professionals issuing tax shelter opinions. These recently finalized amendments provide standards for practitioners rendering written tax advice, including electronic communications, that might be considered part of an abusive tax avoidance transaction. Section 10.35 provides stringent requirements that must be met if the advice constitutes a "covered opinion." Several types of written advice fall within the category of "covered opinion." These include advice that concerns one or more federal tax issues arising from (1) a transaction required to be listed under sections 6011 and 6111 as a tax shelter transaction, (2) any plan or arrangement, the principal purpose of which is the avoidance or evasion of any tax, and (3) any plan or arrangement, a significant purpose of which is the avoidance or evasion of tax if the written advice is (a) a reliance opinion (i.e., an opinion that concludes at a confidence level of at least more likely than not that one or more significant federal tax issues will be resolved in the taxpayer's favor), (b) a marketed opinion (i.e., an opinion, including a "more likely than not opinion," that concerns a listed transaction in which the practitioner knows or has reason to know the opinion will be used or referred to by a person other than the practitioner or a member of the practitioner's firm in promoting, marketing, or recommending a tax shelter to one or more third parties), (c) subject to conditions of confidentiality, or (d) subject to contractual protection.

A "more likely than not opinion" is an opinion that concludes that there is a greater than 50 percent likelihood that one or more significant federal tax issues would be resolved in the taxpayer's favor if challenged. The written advice will not be considered a covered opinion, even though subject to conditions of confidentiality or contractual protection, if it prominently discloses that it is not intended to be used and cannot be used for the purpose of avoiding penalties. In the case of a marketed opinion, the written advice will not be considered a covered opinion if the advice prominently discloses that it was not intended to be used for the purpose of avoiding penalties and cannot be used for such purpose, and the advice further discloses prominently that it was written to support the promotion or marketing of the matters addressed, and that the taxpayer should seek advice, based on the taxpayer's particular circumstances, from an independent tax adviser. In addition, written advice regarding a plan or arrangement having a significant purpose of tax avoidance or evasion is not considered a covered opinion if the written advice concerns the qualification of a deferred compensation plan or is included in documents required to be filed with the Securities and Exchange Commission. There also is an exclusion for preliminary advice if the practitioner is reasonably expected to provide subsequent advice that satisfies the requirements of the regulations. Under certain circumstances, a practitioner may provide a limited scope opinion that considers less than all of the significant federal tax issues, provided the advice does not relate to a listed transaction or an arrangement that has as its principal purpose the avoidance of federal tax.

Section 10.35 further provides that a practitioner providing a covered opinion, including a marketed opinion, must (1) identify and consider all relevant facts and must not rely on unreasonable factual assumptions or representations, (2) relate the applicable law to the relevant facts and must not rely on unreasonable legal assumptions, representations or conclusions, (3) consider all material federal tax issues and reach a conclusion, supported by the facts and the law, with respect to each material federal tax issue, and (4) provide an overall conclusion as to the federal tax treatment of the tax shelter items and the reasons for that conclusion. In addition, the practitioner must meet the disclosure requirements of section 10.35(d), such as disclosing any compensation arrangement (other than with the client for whom the opinion is prepared) or referral agreement with any person in connection with the promoting, marketing or recommending of the tax shelter discussed in the opinion. In order to ensure compliance with these provisions, section 10.36 requires a firm to take reasonable steps to ensure that adequate procedures are in place to ensure that members, associates, and employees comply with the requirements of section 10.35. Any person responsible for ensuring compliance with section 10.35 who fails because of willfulness, recklessness, or gross incompetence to take reasonable steps to ensure that the firm has adequate procedures in place will be subject to discipline.

Written advice that does not constitute a covered opinion falls into the category of "other written advice" that is subject to the provisions of section 10.37. Under section 10.37, a practitioner must not (1) base written advice on unreasonable factual or legal assumptions, (2) unreasonably rely upon representations, statements, findings or agreements, (3) fail to consider all relevant facts, or (4) take into account the possibility that a tax return will not be audited, an issue will not be raised on audit, or that an issue is likely to be settled. Unlike section 10.35, section 10.37 does not require that the practitioner describe the relevant facts (including assumptions and representations), the application of the law to those facts, or the practitioner's conclusion with respect to the law and the facts. In the case of an opinion that the practitioner knows or has reason to know will be used or referred to by a third person (other than a member of the practitioner's firm) in promoting, marketing, or recommending to one or more taxpayers an entity, plan or arrangement that has as a significant purpose the avoidance or evasion of federal tax, a heightened standard of care will be used to determine whether the practitioner has failed to comply with the provisions of section 10.37. The rationale for such a heightened standard is that a practitioner's lack of knowledge of the client's peculiar circumstances poses a greater risk of violating the provisions of Circular 230.

Section 10.38 authorizes the establishment of advisory committees to review and make general recommendations regarding professional standards or best practices for tax advisors, including whether hypothetical conduct would give rise to a violation of sections 10.35 or 10.36. Each such committee is to be composed of at least five individuals authorized to practice before the Service. The membership of each committee is to be balanced among attorneys, accountants, and enrolled agents.

§ 3.4   Statutory Standards

A.   *Preparer Penalties*

In addition to the ethical and regulatory standards, tax advisors are subject to several civil penalties. The Tax Reform Act of 1976 added penalty provisions applicable to "income tax return preparers," defined in section 7701(a)(36) as any person or entity that prepares for compensation any return or claim for refund, or a substantial portion of a return or claim for refund. Under the Regulations, it is clear that furnishing legal advice that is directly relevant to determining the proper treatment of any item on a return can make a lawyer a "preparer," if the legal advice relates to a completed (rather than contemplated) action. Reg. § 301.7701–15.

Under section 6694(a), a return preparer will be subject to a $250 penalty if all of the following occur: "(1) any part of any understatement of liability with respect to any return or claim for refund is due to a position for which there was not a realistic possibility of being sustained on its merits, (2) any person who is an income tax return preparer with respect to such return or claim knew (or reasonably should have known) of such position, and (3) such position was not disclosed as provided in section 6662(d)(2)(B)(ii) or was frivolous." The return preparer penalty is not to be imposed if there was reasonable cause for the tax understatement and the preparer acted in good faith. I.R.C. § 6694(a).

Regulations issued under section 6694 explain that the "realistic possibility of success" standard is met "if a reasonable and well-informed analysis by a person knowledgeable in the tax law would lead such a person to conclude that the position has approximately a one-in-three, or greater, likelihood of being sustained on its merits." Regs. § 1.6694–2(b)(1).

If a return position does not satisfy the "one-in-three" chance of success test and the position is not frivolous, a preparer may avoid the penalty by disclosing the position. A preparer who is uncertain whether a position is correct, but confident that the position is not frivolous, should err on the side of caution and disclose the position to avoid the penalty. Curiously, taxpayers themselves are held to a higher standard under section 6662(d): they may avoid the 20% penalty only if there is substantial authority (a standard that is higher than the realistic possibility of success standard) or if they disclose the position and the disclosed position has a reasonable basis (again, a higher standard than the not-frivolous standard applicable to preparers). See further discussion of taxpayer penalties, Chapter 10. Both taxpayers and tax return preparers should disclose questionable positions on Form 8275 to avoid possible penalties.

Reasonable cause is generally a facts and circumstances determination in which the Service considers such factors as the extent and complexity of the error, good faith reliance on the advice of another preparer, and the preparer's normal office practices and whether those practices may have contributed to the error. Reg. § 1.6694–2(d).

To illustrate these various standards:

Standard	**% chance of success**
Substantial Authority (§ 6662(d))	34–50
Realistic Possibility of Success	33
Reasonable Basis	15–32
Frivolous	0–14

Position not disclosed: taxpayers' positions must have substantial authority; preparers' positions must have realistic possibility of success.

Position disclosed: taxpayers' positions must have reasonable basis; preparers' positions must not be frivolous.

Under section 6694(b) a preparer may be subject to a penalty of $1,000 per return for willful understatements of tax liability or for any reckless or intentional disregard of rules or regulations. A preparer may be liable under both sections 6694(a) and 6694(b), but if both penalties apply, the section 6694(b) penalty is reduced by the section 6694(a) penalty.

Return preparers are subject to a penalty of $50 for each failure to furnish a completed copy of a return to the taxpayer, for each failure to sign a return, and for each failure to furnish the preparer's identification number on a return. An annual maximum penalty for each of these three omissions is now $25,000. The penalty is not to be imposed for any omission due to reasonable cause and not to willful neglect. I.R.C. § 6695.

(1) Who Is A Return Preparer?

Might you be liable for the section 6694 penalty for helping a friend or relative with his return? The answer is no. Those who are subject to the penalty are limited to the following: persons who prepare for compensation all or a substantial portion of an income tax return or claim for refund. I.R.C.

§ 7701(a)(36). Note that this requires that the preparer receive compensation, and it excludes those who prepare estate or gift tax returns.

If you are an income tax return preparer within the definition of section 7701(a)(36), then you must sign the return as a preparer, and failure to sign as a preparer subjects you to a separate penalty under section 6695. But you cannot avoid the section 6694 penalty by failing to sign the return as a preparer; if you meet the requirements, you are subject to the section 6694 penalty regardless of whether you actually signed the return in question as a preparer.

Can you avoid the penalty provisions by providing substantial advice, but not physically filling out the return? The answer is no. Anyone who furnishes "sufficient information and advice so that completion of the return or claim for refund is largely a mechanical matter" meets the definition of a return preparer. Regs. § 301.7701–15(a)(1).

(2) Aiding and Assisting—§ 6701

As part of the Tax Equity and Fiscal Responsibility Act of 1982, Congress added section 6701, which authorizes the IRS to impose penalties on anyone who "aids or assists in, procures, or advises with respect to, the preparation or presentation of any material portion of a return, affidavit, claim, or other document in connection with any matter arising under" the tax laws. This language is obviously much broader than the definition of "income tax return preparer" for purposes of the section 6694 penalty. The aiding and abetting penalty can be imposed only if the person knows or has reason to believe that the document will be used in connection with any material matter arising under the tax laws and knows that if it is used, an understatement of tax liability will result. The penalty is $1,000, unless the actions pertain to a corporation's return, in which case the penalty is $10,000.

The aiding and abetting penalty can be imposed for "ordering (or otherwise causing) a subordinate to do an act." Providing purely mechanical or clerical assistance, such as typing or photocopying, is not sufficient to trigger the penalty. Unlike the section 6694 penalty, in which the taxpayer bears the burden of proof, the IRS has the burden of proving the propriety of imposing the aiding and abetting penalty. I.R.C. § 6703. The section 6701 penalty is mutually exclusive with the section 6694 penalty, so if the section 6701 penalty is imposed, the section 6694 penalty may not also be imposed.

B. Promoting Abusive Tax Shelters

Section 6700 imposes a penalty on any person who organizes, assists in the organization of, or participates in the sale of any interest in a tax shelter (defined as a partnership or other entity, investment plan or arrangement, or any other plan or arrangement, a significant purpose of which is the avoidance or evasion of federal income tax) if in connection with such activity the person makes or furnishes a qualifying false or fraudulent statement or a gross valuation overstatement. The amount of the penalty is equal to the lesser of $1,000 or 100 percent of the gross income derived (or to be derived) from the activity.

A gross valuation overstatement is defined as any statement made with respect to the value of property or services if the stated value exceeds 200 percent of amount determined to be correct and the value of the property or services is directly related to the amount of any deduction or credit allowable to any participant.

In an effort to crack down on the proliferation of abusive tax shelters, the American Jobs Creation Act of 2004 imposes a penalty of 50 percent of the gross income derived from the shelter activity if the activity involves a statement regarding the tax benefits of participating in a plan or arrangement where the person knows or has reason to know that such statement is false or fraudulent as to any material matter. The enhanced penalty does not apply to a gross valuation overstatement.

The section 6700 penalty applies to each sale and the penalty can be imposed along with any other penalties. Since the total amount of the penalty can be substantial, it can be waived upon establishing that there was reasonable cause for the valuation and that it was made in good faith, but only if the penalty is attributable to a gross valuation misstatement. (See Chapter 10 for a discussion of reasonable cause).

Another weapon against the proliferation of abusive tax shelters is found at section 6011, which requires promoters to disclose investment transactions designed to avoid or evade federal income taxes, and to maintain and furnish the government with a list of investors in these transactions. In this way, the Service hopes to identify abusive tax avoidance transactions at an early stage. Failure to timely disclose the required information with respect to a reportable transaction will result in a penalty of $50,000, applicable to returns with due dates after October 22, 2004. I.R.C. § 6707(a). The penalty is greater if the transaction constitutes a "listed transaction." See I.R.C. § 6707(b).

C.   Sanctions for Delaying or Frivolous Court Proceedings

Section 6673 authorizes the Tax Court to impose a penalty of up to $25,000 if it determines that a proceeding was instituted or maintained merely for delay or that the taxpayer's position was frivolous or groundless. Although this provision has existed since 1926, it was seldom used prior to the barrage of "tax protestor" cases beginning in the late 1970s. The maximum penalty was increased from $500 to $5,000 in 1982, and again to $25,000 in 1989. In 1986, Congress amended section 6673 to provide that an unreasonable failure by the taxpayer to pursue an administrative remedy can justify the Tax Court's imposition of the penalty.

The section 6673 penalty has been applied in various contexts, and is not restricted to the typical "tax protestor" cases. The Tax Court has imposed the penalty in cases involving highly leveraged tax shelters, particularly in situations in which the underlying issues have already been litigated and resulted in Government victories.

Section 6673(a)(2) authorizes the Tax Court to impose sanctions against attorneys and others representing parties before the Tax Court. If the court finds that such person "has multiplied the proceedings in any case unreasonably and vexatiously," the court may require the person to "pay personally the excess costs, expenses, and attorneys' fees reasonably incurred because of such conduct." If an attorney representing the Government is found to have engaged in such conduct, then the Tax Court is to order the United States to pay such amounts in the same manner as an award of such costs by a U.S. district court under 28 U.S.C. § 1927. This provision should cause attorneys for both sides to be more circumspect in advising litigation.

Section 6673(b)(1) authorizes courts other than the Tax Court to impose penalties of up to $10,000 against taxpayers who bring frivolous or groundless tax suits. Under section 6673(b)(2), any penalties, costs or damages assessed by any court under section 6673(b)(1) may be assessed by the IRS and collected in the same manner as a tax. The purpose of this provision is to permit sanctions imposed by all courts in connection with federal tax proceedings to be assessed and collected in the same manner as penalties imposed by the Tax Court. In addition, section 6673(b)(3) provides that federal appellate courts (the U.S. Courts of Appeal and the U.S. Supreme Court) may impose monetary sanctions, penalties or court costs in favor of the Government for frivolous appeals of Tax Court decisions and tax decisions of other federal tribunals, and that such awards may be assessed and collected in the same manner as a tax. Moreover, such orders may be registered with a U.S. district court and enforced as other district court judgments.

§ 3.5   Privileges and Protections

A.   *Federally Authorized Tax Practitioners' Privilege*

As part of the 1998 Taxpayer Bill of Rights Act 3, Congress extended the common-law privilege of confidentiality of communication historically enjoyed by attorneys and clients to tax advice furnished to a taxpayer-client by any individual who is authorized to practice before the Treasury. This new uniform privilege, contained in Code section 7525, applies to tax advice given after July 22, 1998. The new privilege applies only in non-criminal tax matters before the IRS and non-criminal tax proceedings in federal court brought by or against the United States. The privilege does not apply to communications concerning tax shelters (as defined in section 6662(d)(2)(C)(iii)) between a federally-authorized tax practitioner and a corporation or any of its shareholders or agents. The legislative history cautions that the new privilege applies only in circumstances in which the attorney-client privilege would apply, and notes that information disclosed to an attorney for the purpose of preparing the client's tax return is not privileged.

B. Attorney–Client Privilege

The attorney-client privilege is the oldest common law privilege for confidential communications. Its purpose is to "encourage full and frank communication between attorneys and their clients and thereby promote broader public interests in the observance of law and administration of justice." Upjohn Co. v. United States (S.Ct.1981). The privilege applies to communications made in confidence to obtain legal advice and the claim of privilege must be item-specific, rather than a general, blanket assertion of the privilege. The privilege belongs to the client and may be waived by the client, although a breach of confidentiality forfeits the client's right to claim the privilege. Also, if a taxpayer attempts to use a third-party reliance defense as reasonable cause to avoid an accuracy-related penalty (see § 10.2), such a defense may impliedly waive the attorney-client privilege.

C. Work–Product Doctrine

Materials prepared or collected by an attorney in preparation for litigation are protected from compelled disclosure under the attorney work-product doctrine. There are two classes of materials protected under this doctrine: (1) opinion work product—an attorney's research, analysis, legal theories and mental impressions assembled or created in anticipation of litigation, and (2) fact work product—documents and written statements of witnesses prepared for trial. The purpose of this doctrine is to preserve the quality of representation by preventing an opposing counsel from gaining access to an attorney's work product. The fear is that if an attorney's work product is not her own, she would be loath to reduce her thoughts and analyses to writing in preparation for trial. Unlike the attorney-client privilege, which can be waived by the client, the work-product privilege belongs to the attorney, and may be asserted by the attorney with or without consent of the client, although it too can be waived if the information is not kept confidential.

The work-product doctrine applies when it is reasonably anticipated that litigation could result, although the litigation does not have to be pending at the time the work product is created. The fact that such information may serve other purposes as well does not affect its status as work product. In the case of a tax controversy, work-product protection generally arises when an administrative dispute with the IRS is reasonably anticipated. United States v. Adlman (2d Cir.1998). If the possibility of such a dispute is remote or the information was prepared in the ordinary course of business or during the preparation of a client's tax returns, the information is not entitled to work-product protection. United States v. El Paso Co. (5th Cir.1982). By the same token, the work-product doctrine does not protect an accountant's tax accrual workpapers. United States v. Arthur Young & Co. (S.Ct.1984). Moreover, even if the information in question is work-product material, the information may be discoverable if the IRS demonstrates that the information is relevant or material to the determination of the correctness of the taxpayer's return. I.R.C. § 7602. In *Upjohn Co. v. United States,* however, the Supreme Court held that the government must make a stronger case for discovery when the information constitutes opinion work-product.

§ 3.6 Cash Transaction Reporting Requirements

Some people find it surprising to learn that attorneys and accountants are subject to cash transaction reporting requirements that were designed originally to combat money laundering. Section 6050I of the Code, enacted in 1984, requires anyone who receives more than $10,000 in "cash" in one transaction or a series of related transactions in connection with his trade or business to report the transaction and certain information about the payor of the money to federal authorities.

A. *Historical Development*

Congress decided in its enactment of the Bank Secrecy Act in 1970 to identify and tax the "underground economy" as well as the illegal economy involved in money laundering, drug trafficking and other illegal activities. Under this Act, financial institutions are required to file Currency Transaction Reports disclosing the receipt of more than $10,000 in a single transaction. Later, in 1986, Congress amended the Bank Secrecy Act to prohibit any individual from "structuring" transactions with the intent of avoiding the reporting requirements. That same year Congress enacted the Money Laundering Control Act of 1986 which criminalized money laundering, which is the conversion of proceeds of crimes into untainted "clean" currency while hiding the identity of the owner or the source of the tainted currency.

During the mid–1980s, the federal budget deficit was growing rapidly and Congress decided to take measures to combat the underground economy through which many individuals were avoiding tax on income by engaging in barter or cash transactions that were not reported as income by the recipient. Section 6050I was designed to achieve this result by creating a "paper trail" by extending the reporting requirement for receipt of large amounts of cash beyond financial institutions to include any person who receives more than $10,000 in "cash" in connection with a trade or business.

B.   *Definition of "Cash"*

Cash is defined generally as the coin and currency of the United States or any other country, as well as certain "near-cash" instruments in certain situations. "Near-cash" instruments (cashier's checks, bank drafts, traveler's checks and money orders) are treated as cash in two situations: designated reporting transactions (a retail sale of a consumer durable or collectible, or a travel or entertainment activity) and "any transaction in which the recipient knows that such instrument is being used in an attempt to avoid the reporting of the transaction under section 6050I." Regs. § 1.6050I–1(c)(1). Under these rules, an attorney who receives a cashier's check for services rendered is not required to report it under the "designated reporting transaction" rule, but may be required to report it under the knowledge test.

C. Related Transactions

The reporting requirement is triggered both by the receipt of more than $10,000 in cash in a single transaction and by the receipt of more than $10,000 in cash in related transactions. A related transaction is any transaction between a payor (or his agent) and the recipient within a 24–hour period. In addition, transactions are related if made outside the 24–hour period and the recipient knows or has reason to know that each transaction is part of a series of related transactions. Regs. § 1.6050I–1(c)(7). An example from the Regulations is helpful: Assume an attorney agrees to represent a client in a criminal case, with the fee determined on an hourly basis. In January the attorney bills the client $8,000 and the client pays in cash. No reporting is required (unless the attorney believes the transaction is suspicious—*see* discussion, § D., *infra*). In February the attorney bills, and the client pays in cash, $4,000. The attorney now must report the transaction because he has received more than $10,000 in related transactions.

D. Form 8300

Reporting under section 6050I is done by filing a Form 8300 with both the IRS and the payor of the cash. The Form 8300 must disclose the name, address and taxpayer identification number of the payor, the amount of cash received, and the date and nature of the transaction. Form 8300 also contains a box to be checked by the cash recipient if he believes the transaction is "suspicious," in which case he may voluntarily file the Form 8300 even if filing is not required because the cash involved does not exceed the $10,000 threshold. What is a suspicious transaction? Examples include an indication of possible illegal activity, an effort by the payor to persuade the recipient not to file the Form 8300, and other facts or circumstances that arouse the recipient's suspicion.

E. Penalties for Noncompliance

Failure to comply with the reporting requirement of section 6050I can trigger both civil and criminal penalties. The civil penalty for an unintentional failure to file a Form 8300 or an incorrect or incomplete filing is $50 per return, up to $250,000 per year. The civil penalty for intentionally disregarding the filing requirement or intentionally filing an inaccurate or false report is quite stiff: it is the greater of $25,000 per return or the amount of cash received in the transaction, up to $100,000. I.R.C. § 6721.

A willful failure to file the Form 8300 is a felony under section 6703, although other failures to file required returns under that section are misdemeanors. Willfully filing a materially false Form 8300 is a felony under section 7206. "Structuring" a transaction (or assisting in structuring) to avoid the reporting requirements is a felony under section 6050I(f), punishable under the felony provision of section 7203, which increases the failure to file penalty from one year to five years in the case of a willful violation of section 6050I. Attorneys who receive cash in connection with representing clients also may be subject to criminal prosecution under the Money Laundering Control Act, 18 U.S.C §§ 1956 and 1957. *See* § 18.3, *infra.*

F. *Assertion of Attorney–Client Privilege*

Many attorneys have refused to comply with section 6050I on the basis that compliance would violate the attorney-client privilege. Courts generally have rejected this argument. Absent special circumstances, client identity and fee information are not subject to the attorney-client privilege. Courts generally have found that no special circumstances exist to justify a lawyer's failure to comply fully with section 6050I. *See, e.g.,* United States v. Leventhal (11th Cir.1992) (disclosure not protected by special circumstance).

Courts also have been unreceptive to claims that compliance with section 6050I by attorneys would violate their clients' Fourth, Fifth and Sixth amendment rights. As one court stated, "[a]ppellants' allegations of unconstitutionality merit only brief discussion." United States v. Goldberger & Dubin (2d Cir.1991).

CHAPTER 4

DISCLOSURE OF IRS MATERI- ALS AND CONFIDENTIALITY OF RETURN INFORMATION

The tension between the citizens' desire for priva- cy and their simultaneous demand for access to Government information is more acute in the tax area than perhaps any other. Because our federal tax system is based on voluntary compliance, the Government must foster compliance by assuring citizens that information reported by them will remain private. Tax returns contain a wealth of information that many individuals and businesses might not furnish if not assured of confidentiality. On the other hand, the principle that secrecy breeds misconduct is reflected in numerous state and fed- eral laws ensuring public access to Government records. This chapter discusses the principal laws governing confidentiality of tax return information and mandatory disclosure of IRS documents and records.

§ 4.1   Freedom of Information Act and Priva- cy Act

The Freedom of Information Act ("FOIA") was enacted in 1966 as an amendment to the APA. Its legislative history reveals that Congress believed that individuals have a right of access to most information possessed by the Government and that public disclosure would help prevent Government abuse. Despite the FOIA's general policy of disclosure, numerous exemptions exist, including an exemption for information specifically protected from disclosure by other statutes.

FOIA litigation in the early 1970s forced the IRS to make public much information it previously had refused to disclose. For example, courts required the IRS to disclose private letter rulings, technical advice memoranda, and most of the Internal Revenue Manual. In 1976 Congress enacted section 6110 (discussed in § 4.3, *infra*) which now provides the exclusive rules for public disclosure of IRS rulings and similar statements of position.

The Privacy Act of 1974, another amendment to the APA, regulates agencies' use of information they have accumulated about individuals and prohibits the federal government from disclosing the information without the prior consent of the person to whom the information pertains. At the same time, the Privacy Act ensures that individuals and organizations will have access to many types of Government records concerning them, so that errors or inaccuracies in those records can be detected and corrected. As is true of the FOIA, the Privacy Act contains numerous exceptions, such as permitting disclosure to other Government agencies for "investigative purposes" or "routine use" or other listed purposes.

When it enacted the Privacy Act, Congress created a special commission to determine the types of safeguards that should be enacted for federal tax return information. The commission recommended that tax return information be more carefully protected than the Privacy Act guidelines required, and Congress adopted many of the recommendations in 1976.

Prior to 1976, federal tax returns and return information were treated as Government property and were routinely divulged by the IRS to other Government agencies. Spurred by the commission's recommendations and by testimony confirming numerous Watergate-era incidents involving the Nixon administration's use of tax return information in the ordering of audits for political purposes, Congress amended section 6103 and added new section 6110 to the Code as part of the Tax Reform Act of 1976. Section 6103 substantially supersedes the Privacy Act for taxpayer information and is the Code's own version of a privacy act, while section 6110 overrides the FOIA with respect to public access to certain types of IRS records. The legislative history of the 1976 enactments explained the need for the changes as follows:

> The IRS has more information about more people than any other agency in this country. Consequently, almost every other agency that has a need for information about U.S. citizens sought it from the IRS. However, in many cases the Congress has not specifically considered whether the agencies which had access to tax information

should have that access. * * * This, in turn, raised the question of whether the public's reaction to this possible abuse of privacy would seriously impair the effectiveness of our country's very successful voluntary assessment system. (Staff of Joint Comm. on Taxation, General Explanation of Tax Reform Act 314–15 (1976)).

Sections 6103 and 6110 did not resolve all the issues and problems, however. The following sections discuss the operation of these provisions and some of the continuing controversies in the clash between confidentiality and public access to tax information.

§ 4.2 Section 6103: The Code's Privacy Rules

A. *Confidentiality of Return Information*

Section 6103(a) provides the general rule that except as otherwise authorized by the Code, "[r]eturns and return information shall be confidential," and Government employees and others with access to such information are prohibited from disclosing it. "Returns" are defined to include any tax return, information return, declaration of estimated tax, and claim for refund, together with any amendment and any supporting documentation filed with any of such documents. "Return information" is defined to include the following:

—the taxpayer's identity;

—the nature, source or amount of any income, deductions, tax liability, etc.;

—any data received by the IRS in connection with any return;

—information concerning any possible or actual investigation of a return; and

—any part of any IRS written determination or background file document exempt from disclosure under section 6110.

All of the above types of information are confidential and may not be disclosed except in conformity with one or more of the exceptions contained in section 6103.

B. *Exceptions Permitting Disclosure of Return Information*

Although the "general rule" is that neither returns nor return information may be disclosed, numerous and lengthy exceptions are provided. The persons or agencies to which return information may be disclosed, and the purposes for which return information may be used, include the following:

1. Persons designated in writing by the taxpayer in a written request or consent to disclosure. Section 6103(c).

2. State tax officials and state audit agencies, pursuant to written request of the head of the state agency. Section 6103(d).

3. Persons or entities having a material interest in the information. For individual returns, this would include the taxpayer himself and certain others, in limited specific circumstances. Both spouses are entitled to jointly filed returns. Partners are

entitled to partnership returns, and record owners of 1% of a corporation's stock, together with other individuals, can be given access to corporate tax return information. Section 6103(e).

4.   Committees of Congress, the President, White House employees and other federal government employees not involved in the administration of tax laws are given access to return information under sections 6103(f), (g) and (i), although there are numerous restrictions and procedures to be followed.

5.   Employees of the Treasury Department, and Justice Department employees (including United States attorneys) who are "personally and directly" involved in a civil or criminal tax case, are given access to return information, without any need for written request. Section 6103(h). Section 6103(h)(4)(A) permits the disclosure of return information in judicial proceedings involving the taxpayer's civil or criminal tax liability.

6.   IRS employees may reveal return information to the extent such disclosure "is necessary in obtaining information, which is not otherwise reasonably available" in determining a taxpayer's tax liability. Section 6103(k)(6).

There are numerous additional exceptions. Disclosures that are not authorized by any of the exceptions give rise to a private cause of action for damages against the United States. I.R.C. § 7431(c). Section 7431 replaced former section 7217, in effect until 1982, which provided for an action for damages against a Government employee who made an improper disclosure of return information.

Two of the exceptions described above merit additional discussion. The first is the exception noted at number 6 above, which permits disclosure by IRS employees if disclosure "is necessary in obtaining information, which is not otherwise reasonably available" to determine a taxpayer's tax liability. I.R.C. § 6103(k)(6). Should this exception permit an IRS special agent who is conducting a criminal investigation of a physician to send letters to the doctor's patients stating that the doctor is under criminal investigation and asking for information from them? The Fifth Circuit reversed a district court's summary judgment in favor of the Government in a section 7431 damages action based on these facts, and remanded the case for a determination whether it was necessary to disclose that the doctor was under criminal investigation and whether the information sought was reasonably available from bank records and other sources. Barrett v. United States (5th Cir.1986). On remand, the court held that the disclosure was improper and that the IRS agent had not acted in good faith. Similarly, in a suit brought against an IRS special agent under former section 7217, the court found that disclosing to the taxpayer's clients that the taxpayer (a lawyer) was under criminal investigation and characterizing the taxpayer as "unscrupulous" were unnecessary and improper under section 6103. Heller v. Plave (S.D.Fla.1987). After concluding that such disclosures "depict a lack of integrity on the part of the government," the *Heller* court awarded the taxpayer $13,000 in damages from the IRS special agent.

The exception provided by section 6103(h)(4)(A), described in number 5 above, also deserves special mention. The courts are currently split on the following question: once return information is disclosed in a judicial proceeding, does it lose its confidentiality and thereby become publicly disclosable by Government employees? In a 1988 decision, the Ninth Circuit condoned the issuance of press releases by the IRS and U.S. Attorneys announcing the bringing of an injunction action against a taxpayer and the entry of guilty pleas by taxpayers charged with tax evasion. Lampert v. United States (9th Cir.1988). The *Lampert* court recognized that its decision was in conflict with that of some courts, but it agreed with the decisions of other courts that had permitted public disclosure of information that had already been disclosed in court proceedings. Factors that influenced the court's decision were that strict enforcement of section 6103 would hamper the Government's ability to publicize its tax law prosecutions and that court records are public and any member of the public is free to inspect them. *Lampert* could have a chilling effect on taxpayers considering litigation with the IRS because it specifically upheld the release of tax return information about taxpayers who were involved in civil injunction proceedings initiated by the Government. Presumably, this would permit the IRS to publicize any civil tax dispute that has reached the litigation phase.

On the other hand, the Fifth Circuit has concluded that since there is no exception in section 6103 for tax return information disclosed in a judicial proceeding, such information retains its protection under section 6103, "despite the fact that some of it is not entirely 'secret.'" Johnson v. Sawyer (5th Cir.1997). Under this view, the important question is not whether the information is "private" or "confidential," but whether the immediate source of the information in question is tax return information, and if so, whether it was wrongfully disclosed.

C. Standard of Review

If a person requests information from the IRS under the FOIA, and the IRS refuses to produce the information, claiming it is confidential "return information" under section 6103, the requester may sue to compel the disclosure. The outcome of the litigation will depend largely on the standard of review employed by the court, but the courts are split on the question of the appropriate standard of review.

An exception to mandatory disclosure under the FOIA is information "specifically exempted from disclosure by statute." 5 U.S.C. § 552(b)(3). The IRS claims that section 6103 displaces or preempts the FOIA, while numerous information requesters have argued otherwise, reasoning that the FOIA is the type of statute contemplated by the (b)(3) exception. If the view of the IRS is accepted, then a court reviewing the Service's refusal to disclose information must uphold the refusal unless it is arbitrary or an abuse of discretion. 5 U.S.C. §§ 701 et seq. Furthermore, the information requester bears the burden of proving the arbitrariness of the agency's refusal to disclose. On the other hand, if section 6103 does not supersede or displace the FOIA, then a court must review *de novo* the IRS's refusal to disclose, and the IRS bears the burden of sustaining its position. For a discussion of the issues and description of the split in the Circuits, see *Church of Scientology of California v. IRS* (D.C. Cir.1986), which held that section 6103 does not supersede the FOIA.

§ 4.3   Section 6110: Disclosure of IRS Written Determinations

When Congress amended section 6103 in 1976 to establish the Code's own privacy and confidentiality rules, it also enacted new section 6110, which requires the IRS to disclose all "written determinations," which is defined to include letter rulings, determination letters and technical advice memoranda. For definitions and discussion of these IRS statements of position, see Chapter 2. Section 6110 does not address or apply to information other than "written determinations," and confidentiality or disclosure of such information is governed by section 6103 and the FOIA.

In addition to the actual written determinations, section 6110 requires the disclosure of "background file documents," which include the request for the written determination and any documents or communications received by the IRS in connection with the request. The IRS need not disclose its own internal memoranda relating to the request.

As discussed in Chapter 2, the confidentiality of the identity of taxpayers who request rulings is protected by "sanitizing" mechanisms prescribed by section 6110(c). This section requires that all information that could identify a taxpayer, or that is otherwise privileged or confidential, must be deleted from the written determination before it is made public. Before the document is disclosed, the taxpayer's name, address and other "identifying details" must be deleted. As a result, publicly disclosed rulings tend to refer to "Taxpayer A" or to "Corporation X" that may be described as "incorporated under the laws of State B." Other required deletions, which track the "confidential" information exceptions to the FOIA, include "trade secrets and commercial or financial information obtained from a person and privileged or confidential."

The task of identifying the information which must be deleted is left to the taxpayer. The IRS is required to notify the taxpayer of its intent to make the information publicly available, and the taxpayer then has 60 days in which to furnish the IRS with a list of all information that should be deleted. If the taxpayer and the IRS cannot agree on any specific deletion, the taxpayer may petition the Tax Court for a determination of whether the disputed information must be disclosed. The Tax Court petition may be filed anonymously.

Section 6110 also contains rules designed to discourage the use of improper influence to affect the IRS rulings process. Under section 6110(d), if a third party (someone other than the taxpayer or his authorized representative) communicates with the IRS (in writing or otherwise) concerning any request for a written determination, the IRS must "red flag" the contact by describing it in its publicly disclosed ruling. The description of such third-party contact must include the date of the contact and a categorization of the type of person making the contact. For example, the contacting person might be identified as a "member of the same trade association" or the "taxpayer's Senator." Contacts or communications from other IRS employees need not be noted.

CHAPTER 5

FEDERAL TAX RETURNS AND COMPLIANCE

All taxpayers must prepare (or have prepared) and file federal income tax returns on which they must disclose and reconcile their annual financial transactions, determine their tax liability, and pay amounts due by certain dates. For the fiscal year 2004, there were more than 224 million federal returns filed, of which over 131 million were income tax returns. In order to properly administer the internal revenue laws, the IRS must ensure that these returns adhere to a uniform standard.

§ 5.1   What Constitutes A Return?

Forms or documents that are incomplete when filed by taxpayers with the IRS may not qualify as "returns" for purposes of the return filing requirement, penalties, and the statute of limitations. Generally, the law requires that the return be filed on the proper form, signed under penalties of perjury, and contain enough information to enable the Service to calculate the tax. *See* I.R.C. § 6011(a). In addition, the taxpayer must make an honest and reasonable attempt to comply with the requirements of the tax laws. Beard v. Commissioner (Tax Ct.1984). For a discussion of the types of errors that can cause a form not to qualify as a return, see § 7.2.C, *infra*.

Tax forms are available from IRS offices, libraries, and post offices throughout the country. Forms also can be obtained via the Internet at http://www.irs.ustreas.gov.

§ 5.2　Filing the Return

Under section 6091, returns are required to be filed by the due date with the IRS Service Center in the internal revenue district in which the taxpayer resides or is located. The due date of a return is determined by the type of return being filed. For example, individual taxpayers must file their income tax returns by the fifteenth day of the fourth month following the close of their taxable years. I.R.C. § 6072(a). Corporations must file their income tax returns by the fifteenth day of the third month following the close of their taxable years. I.R.C. § 6072(b). If the due date falls on a Saturday, Sunday, or legal holiday, the taxpayer has until the following business day to file the return. I.R.C. § 7503.

The general rule is that a return is considered filed when it is received by the IRS, but if a return is mailed before the expiration of the due date and is properly addressed, with proper postage affixed, the return is considered filed on the due date if the return is received by the IRS after the due date. I.R.C. § 7502. This is known as the "mailbox rule" and is discussed further in § 7.2.B, *infra*.

A. Electronic Filing

During the late 1990s and early 2000's, the growth in electronic filing of tax returns was explosive. Surely most Americans have noticed the proliferation of advertisements promising "instant tax refunds" that appear each tax filing season. As discussed below, such advertisements are misleading, but the growing popularity of electronic filing is creating novel problems and opportunities for fraud.

Electronic filing involves the transmission of tax returns or return information to the IRS via computer or phone. (Note, though, the IRS has discontinued the Telefile program after August 2005, so filing by phone is no longer an option). When the IRS receives the transmission, it processes and stores the information. Although electronic filing was first introduced on a nationwide basis only in 1990, in the 2003 filing season more than 53 million returns were filed electronically. In the IRS Restructuring and Reform Act of 1998, Congress directed the IRS to develop and implement a strategy to provide for the electronic filing of at least 80% of all tax returns by 2007.

(1) Mechanics of Electronic Filing

Until recently, taxpayers either had to hire a third party to file a return electronically or locate an IRS office that permitted free electronic filing. Now, however, taxpayers may file from their own homes using a computer. The IRS homepage on the internet (http://www.irs.ustreas.gov) explains the "e-file" options available and permits taxpayers to obtain forms and information such as IRS publications.

Businesses or individuals that prepare and file others' returns electronically are called "electronic return originators" (or "EROs"), and those who merely transmit (but do not prepare) returns are called "transmitters." The same party may be both an ERO and a transmitter. Taxpayers who utilize EROs pay preparation fees, filing fees and, if they opt for an expedited refund, a refund anticipation loan ("RAL") fee. Thus, the taxpayer is not really getting an instant refund, but instead is paying interest at a usurious rate on a loan from the ERO. Typically, the total fees for preparing, filing electronically, and making the RAL exceed $100. Nonetheless, nearly 12.7 million taxpayers opted to pay the fee in the 2002 tax season to obtain an RAL. As more taxpayers become aware of the different filing options, including the relatively easy filing from one's own computer, more taxpayers should opt for these alternative methods.

(2) Electronic Filing Fraud

In the early years of electronic filing, taxpayers devised numerous schemes to obtain refunds to which they were not entitled. Much, if not most, of this fraud involved improper claims of entitlement to the earned income tax credit (I.R.C. § 32), and much of it involved the use of fictitious or purchased social security numbers. In 1995, the Service took several steps to address the problem: it began delaying processing of returns claiming the earned income tax credit to allow sufficient time to verify the claim; it began checking social security numbers to verify that the numbers matched the names in IRS databases; and it sent paper (rather than electronic) refunds to all taxpayers who were filing returns for the first time, because about 30% of all detected fraud involved persons for whom the Service had no record of previous filing.

B.   *Extensions of Time To File*

An individual taxpayer may obtain an automatic four-month extension of time to file a federal income tax return by filing a Form 4868 (Request For Automatic Extension of Time to File U.S. Individual Income Tax Return). The request must be filed on or by the original due date of the return. Since an automatic extension of time to file does not extend the time to pay the tax, the taxpayer must estimate the amount of any remaining tax and must remit that amount with the Form 4868 in order to avoid penalties and interest. An extension beyond the four-month period may be obtained if the taxpayer submits a written request before the end of the extended period and provides a good reason for an additional extension. Such a request, however, must be approved by the IRS.

§ 5.3   Amended Returns

After the return has been filed, a taxpayer may find it necessary to file additional information, either because an item of income was omitted or because a refund or credit was not claimed on the original return. If an amended return is filed on or before the due date, the IRS considers the amended return to be the taxpayer's return. If, however, the amended return is filed after the due date has passed, the IRS has discretion to accept or reject the amended return because there is no Code provision that authorizes the filing of an amended return. Instead, amended returns are allowed administratively to promote the filing of true and correct returns. The Supreme Court noted in *Badaracco v. Commissioner* (S.Ct.1984) that an "amended return is a creature of administrative origin and grace." (*See* § 7.2.D, *infra*, for the effect of an amended return on the statute of limitations in the case of fraud).

§ 5.4 Payment

Payments of income tax are due quarterly and are paid either through employer withholding on wages of employees, or through estimated tax payments on amounts that are not subject to withholding. The obligation to pay the tax liability is separate and distinct from the obligation to file a return. Thus, an automatic extension of time to file the return does not convey an automatic extension of time to pay. Instead, the tax must be estimated and any remaining liability must be paid at the time the Form 4868 is filed, unless the taxpayer has obtained a separate extension of time to pay. Such an extension may be granted for up to six months in the case of an income tax return, but the taxpayer must make a showing of undue hardship. Such a showing is twofold: (1) the taxpayer must establish that the deficiency is not due to fault of the taxpayer (i.e., negligence, intentional disregard of rules and regulations, or fraud) (I.R.C. § 6161(b)(3)) and (2) the hardship must amount to more than "mere inconvenience" to the taxpayer. Reg. § 1.6161–1(b) and (c). If the taxpayer cannot pay the full amount of the tax, the taxpayer may submit an offer in compromise or attempt to negotiate an installment agreement. *See* discussion § 11.3.C and § 11.3.D, *infra*.

If a payment is not made by the due date, penalties and interest apply. If a taxpayer makes a showing of "reasonable cause" (see § 10.1, *infra*), the taxpayer will be able to avoid the delinquency penalties, but not the interest.

CHAPTER 6

FURTHER COMPLIANCE: AUDITS AND ADMINISTRATIVE APPEALS

The dreaded IRS audit performs a vital function in our tax laws: it is the method by which our system of voluntary compliance is enforced and measured. Of course, because taxes are withheld from wages, and returns are audited and penalties (both civil and criminal) are assessed, our system is perhaps more accurately referred to as one of enforced voluntary compliance or self-assessment. The possibility of returns being selected for audit coerces many taxpayers to file complete and truthful returns, while others simply do not file a return at all or are dishonest on their returns in hopes of beating the "audit lottery"—that is, never being audited.

When a return is filed, the taxpayer does not know whether the return will be examined carefully or not examined at all, except to check for computational mistakes. For the vast majority of returns, the simple checking of computation (and other minor matters) is the only examination ever performed, and the taxpayer's determination of his tax liability is accepted by the IRS and cannot be challenged after the statute of limitations has run. See Chapter 7, § 7.2 for a discussion of the statutes of limitations.

§ 6.1   Audits

Due to budgetary limitations, only a tiny minority of income tax returns are audited. For instance, during the 1990s, only about 1% of all individual income tax returns were audited. It is also obvious that the greater the amount of income involved, the greater the likelihood of audit. For individuals, the chance of being audited more than doubles if the person's income is over $100,000, but even so, only about 2% of all such returns are audited, although this number varies widely depending upon how the term "audit" is defined.

A.   *Selecting Returns for Audit*

Returns are selected for audit in several ways. The Internal Revenue Manual (Part IV) contains a wealth of information on the IRS's selection and examination procedures, and those seeking more detailed information than is warranted here should consult the IRM. Although some are selected after manual examination, most income tax returns are selected through a computer analysis called the "Discriminant Function" or "DIF" system, which is designed to identify returns with a high probability of error and a resulting significant tax change. For example, returns with enormous deductions that would appear beyond the taxpayer's financial ability (because claimed deductible expenses nearly equal reported income) will result in a high DIF score. After a total DIF score is assigned by the computer analysis, the returns with high DIF scores are examined manually to eliminate returns that do not warrant further examination and to determine the type of audit appropriate for the others. Some will be handled through the mail; those that are more complex will involve a meeting between the taxpayer and an IRS employee. Other methods of return selection are through the Information Reporting Program (IRP) in which return information is verified through the matching of information returns with tax returns and through manually examining returns requesting refunds.

B.   *Types of Audits*

Audits handled through the mail are conducted by IRS Service Centers and are known as "correspondence examinations." Typically they involve a written request from the IRS Service Center to substantiate items such as charitable contributions. If a taxpayer requests an interview or is unable to furnish the substantiation, the case will be dealt with by either an office audit or a field audit.

"Office audits "occur in an IRS office and are conducted by "tax auditors." Typically the scope of the office audit is restricted to specific "significant items" identified during the screening process. If a tax auditor uncovers significant items that were not previously detected, the scope of the audit can be expanded. More complex cases are handled as "field audits" by "revenue agents," who are not restricted in the scope of the audit to identified significant items. Revenue agents are generally more highly educated and experienced than tax auditors; thus they handle more complex cases. In a field audit, the revenue agent examines the taxpayer's books and records, usually at the taxpayer's home or business premises.

The revenue agent's first task is to identify items that may require adjustment. Next the agent verifies the accuracy of amounts reported by examining the taxpayer's books and records. Finally, the revenue agent analyzes the transactions underlying the return to determine whether the taxpayer has complied with the applicable law.

All field examinations must be conducted in accordance with what the Internal Revenue Manual refers to as "Audit Standards." One of these standards formerly required that "[i]ssues should be raised only when in the agent's considered opinion they have real merit; never frivolously, arbitrarily or for bargaining purposes." IRM 4233, § 210 (1976). As revised, however, the standards now require only that the agent "provide top quality service and apply the law with integrity and fairness to all." IRM 4.10.1.4 (1999). To provide guidance in implementing these standards, the IRM lists "examination techniques" applicable to all field audits, as well as detailed techniques for special circumstances. Detailed guidelines are also provided for specialized industries.

Another type of audit is the "calibration audit" or "compliance audit," designed to evaluate taxpayer compliance through random, specialized audits. The results of taxpayer compliance audits are used to develop the DIF formula used in selecting returns for audit. In the past, the IRS conducted compliance audits under the Taxpayer Compliance Measurement Program ("TCMP"). The TCMP involved compliance audits conducted as field audits where the revenue agent was required to examine the return and substantiate documents in detail. TCMP audits were suspended by Congress in 1995 on the basis that these so-called "audits from hell" were too intrusive. Recently, they have been replaced with National Research Program (NRP) audits, which accomplish the same objective in a less intrusive manner.

C. *Taxpayer Protections*

The Omnibus Taxpayer Bill of Rights Act (TBOR 1), enacted as part of the Technical and Miscellaneous Revenue Act of 1988, created important new safeguards for taxpayers under new section 7521 of the Code. First, it requires the IRS to deliver a comprehensive notice of taxpayer rights to every taxpayer it contacts concerning the determination or collection of tax. This notice must be in plain, nontechnical language and must explain, among other things: taxpayer rights; how to appeal an adverse decision (both administratively and through the courts); how to file complaints; and how the IRS can collect the tax it determines is due and owing through various collection procedures.

Other important audit rights and safeguards that were enacted as part of the Omnibus Taxpayer Bill of Rights Act include the following:

(a) Reasonable Time and Place. The IRS must issue regulations under I.R.C. § 7605 specifying standards for determining that audits be conducted at a reasonable time and place. Although section 7605 is not new, the IRS standards for determining a reasonable time and place were developed internally and no regulations existed. By requiring regulations, the Taxpayer Bill of Rights Act will subject the standards developed in the regulations to public notice and comment.

(b) Right to Representation and Consultation. During an interview with IRS personnel, a taxpayer is entitled to consult with and be represented by an attorney, a certified public accountant, an enrolled agent or other person authorized to practice before the IRS. If a taxpayer is unrepresented during an interview, but clearly indicates during the interview that she wishes to be represented or to consult with a representative, the interview must be suspended immediately. An eligible representative acting under a power of attorney can represent the taxpayer during an interview, and the IRS cannot compel the taxpayer to attend unless it issues an administrative summons. (*See* Chapter 17, § 17.1 for a discussion of IRS summonses.)

(c) Audio Recordings. Taxpayers may make sound (but apparently not video) recordings of interviews with IRS personnel. The taxpayer must request permission to record in advance and must do so on his own equipment (the IRS is not required to furnish recording equipment) and at his own expense. If the IRS intends to record the interview, it must so notify the taxpayer in advance and furnish the taxpayer (at his request and his expense) a copy of the transcript or tape.

(d) Notice of Rights During Audit and Collection. Before or during the first audit or collection interview, the IRS must explain the audit and collection process to the taxpayer. The legislative history indicates that this may be done by furnishing the written notice described above.

(e) Exceptions for Criminal Investigations. The safeguards listed in (b), (c) and (d) do not apply to criminal investigations. As under prior law, however, the taxpayer must be notified immediately if his case is being transferred to the Criminal Investigation Division ("CID").

Additional taxpayer protections were enacted in the 1998 Taxpayer Bill of Rights Act 3, as part of the IRS Restructuring and Reform Act of 1998. First, in response to numerous complaints, the 1998 legislation prohibits so-called "financial status" or "economic reality" audits, unless there is a reasonable indication that there is a likelihood of unreported income. (Act section 3412; IRC § 7602.). Section 7602 generally authorizes audits, and any reasonable method of determining tax deficiencies may be used. At present, however, the IRS may not base an audit solely on a taxpayer's lavish lifestyle without a reasonable indication that the taxpayer is concealing income from the federal tax authorities. I.R.C. § 7602(e).

§ 6.2   Resolution of the Audit

A. *Agreed Cases*

When the revenue agent or auditor has completed her examination of a return, she must explain any proposed adjustments to the taxpayer. If the taxpayer agrees with the proposed adjustments, he is asked to sign an appropriate form, which usually will have the effect of preventing the taxpayer from challenging any deficiency in Tax Court. Execution of the form (usually a Form 4159, "Income Tax Examination Changes," or a Form 870, "Waiver of Restrictions on Assessment and Collection of Deficiency in Tax and Acceptance of Overassessment") will not prohibit the taxpayer from paying the tax and filing a refund suit. Thus, consenting in writing to the proposed adjustments will not bar later refund litigation, but it will bar a Tax Court suit if the taxpayer signs a Form 4159 or Form 870. Adjustments agreed to by the taxpayer after an office audit are usually reflected in a Form 1902–E, "Report of Individual Income Tax Audit Changes," which does not prevent litigation of the deficiency in Tax Court. For a more detailed discussion of settlement and closing agreement forms, see § 6.4, *infra.*

B.   *"Unagreed" Cases*

If the taxpayer does not agree with the proposed adjustments, he can request a conference with the Appeals Office. The conference must be requested within 30 days after a "30–day letter" (proposed notice of deficiency) is sent to the taxpayer, notifying the taxpayer of the auditor's (or revenue agent's) findings, requesting that he agree to the findings, and advising him of his appeal rights. For conferences with the Appeals Office following an office audit, the taxpayer need not submit a written protest. (Protests are discussed in § 6.3.B, *infra*). To qualify for a conference with the Appeals Office following a field audit, however, the taxpayer must submit a written protest within 30 days of receipt of the "30–day letter," if the total proposed tax deficiency exceeds $25,000 for any taxable period.

If the taxpayer takes no action after receiving the "30–day letter," the IRS will issue a "notice of deficiency," also known as a "90–day letter" and discussed in detail in Chapter 7. The taxpayer then will have 90 days in which to pay the tax or file a Tax Court petition.

§ 6.3   Administrative Appeals

A.   *Appeals Office Conferences*

Failure to reach an agreement with the revenue agent or auditor does not mean that litigation is inevitable. The vast majority of all tax disputes are settled out of court, and the Appeals Office affords an excellent opportunity to avoid the expense and delay of litigation. As described in the Internal Revenue Manual, the role of the Appeals Office is to settle cases:

> The Appeals mission is to resolve tax controversies, without litigation, on a basis which is fair and impartial to both the Government and the taxpayer and in a manner that will enhance voluntary compliance and public confidence in the integrity and efficiency of the Service. (IRM § 8.1.1.1 (2003))

The Appeals Office has "exclusive and final authority" to settle tax cases. 26 C.F.R. § 601.106(a)(1). Thus, its decisions normally are not reviewable by or appealable to any other office or person within the IRS. Appeals Offices are located throughout the United States.

In deciding whether to seek a conference with the Appeals Office, it is important to remember that the Appeals Office can raise a new issue that was not detected by the examining agent. Thus, if there is a proposed deficiency of $5,000, but counsel is aware of another issue that could result in a much larger proposed deficiency, it may be advisable to pay the proposed deficiency, skip the Appeals Office conference and plan to file a refund claim. On the other hand, the Internal Revenue Manual (§ 8.6.1.4.2 (2001)) recognizes that raising new issues could justifiably irritate taxpayers, so in practice the Appeals Office raises new issues infrequently. Another factor to be considered in determining whether to seek an Appeals conference is that the failure to pursue an administrative remedy may result in the

Tax Court imposing a section 6673 penalty for frivolous cases or cases maintained merely for delay. See discussion of § 6673 in § 3.4.C.

Additional reasons to request an Appeals Office conference include the fact that the taxpayer will not qualify for an award of attorneys' fees against the Government if he bypasses the Appeals conference or other administrative remedies (see § 15.3 for a discussion of attorneys' fees). Moreover, the case will be referred to the Appeals Office for settlement after the Tax Court petition is docketed, so the Appeals Office will become involved whether the taxpayer requests a conference or not. See Rev. Proc. 87–24, 1987–1 C.B. 720. In summary, it is almost always advisable to seek an Appeals Office conference, because of the genuine possibility of settlement and to avoid penalties for failure to do so. Although the Appeals Office will become involved ultimately if the taxpayer chooses to skip the Appeals conference and file a Tax Court petition, it is better to meet with the Appeals Office before suit is filed in the hope of settling the matter, than to be forced to meet on an expedited schedule when litigation has begun.

If the taxpayer is able to settle the dispute with the Appeals Office, he typically will be asked to execute a Form 870–AD (Offer to Waive Restrictions on Assessment and Collection of Tax Deficiency and to Accept Overassessment), which is binding on the taxpayer and the Government. If some issues remain unresolved, the Form must be modified to reflect the open issues that are not covered by the agreement. Unless and until the appropriate form is executed by both the taxpayer and the Government, the case is not settled. Oral agreement between the Appeals officer and the taxpayer (or his representative) is not final and binding, and the agreement is subject to review within the Appeals Office. See § 6.4, *infra*, for a discussion of the various settlement and closing agreements.

B.   *The Protest*

If the proposed adjustments result from an office audit or involve $25,000 or less, no written protest is required to qualify for an Appeals Office conference. 26 C.F.R. §§ 601.105(d)(2); 601.106(c)(1)(i). For all other cases, a protest is required.

There is no specified form for a protest, but it is advisable to think of a protest as the taxpayer's opportunity to influence the case by thoroughly explaining and documenting his position. Skeletal protests that offer no new information and simply incorporate by reference other documents or information can be rejected as not constituting valid "protests." IRS Publication Number 5 describes the recommended contents of a protest, including the following:

1.   The taxpayer's name, address and identification number.

2.   The representative's name and a Power of Attorney on Form 2848 (if not already on file).

3.   Copy of or reference to the "30–day letter" and the audit report identifying the tax years involved and the proposed adjustments.

4. Statement that the protest is timely.

5. Description of the issues and a statement of the taxpayer's position on each issue.

6. Request for an Appeals Office conference.

7. Taxpayer's signature, under penalties of perjury, that the facts alleged are true (or representative's statement that she prepared the protest and knows the facts alleged to be true and correct).

8. Exhibits supporting or amplifying the taxpayer's position may be attached.

In preparing the protest, it is important to emphasize that there is legal or factual uncertainty involved, and that the Government would not be assured a victory in litigation. The Appeals Office is guided by a "hazards of litigation" standard, under which it must review the entire case (including the credibility of witnesses and the probative value of the taxpayer's evidence) to determine how a court would likely rule. See Rev. Proc. 2000–43. An Appeals Office conference following a carefully prepared protest affords an excellent opportunity for the taxpayer's representative to present the taxpayer's case, unhindered by any rules of evidence and without an advocate for the government's position arguing the other side.

§ 6.4   Settlements and Closing Agreements

The form that the taxpayer executes in settling his case determines the effect of the settlement on possible future litigation. The following forms are utilized: Form 870 (consent to assessment); Form 870–AD (agreement to assessment); Forms 866 and 906 (closing agreements); and collateral agreements. The purpose and effect of these types of agreements are described below.

A. *Form 870*

Form 870 is used to reflect an agreement between the taxpayer and the Government that is reached prior to an Appeals Office conference. Thus, if the taxpayer agrees with the revenue agent's report and the proposed adjustments it contains, the IRS will ask him to sign a Form 870. This form also is used to reflect an agreement reached with the Appeals Office in which the Government makes no concessions to the taxpayer.

The effect of executing a Form 870 (or Form 890 for estate or gift tax disputes) is to waive the statutory notice of deficiency (the "90–day letter") and consent to an immediate assessment and collection of the tax. I.R.C. § 6213(d). A taxpayer who signs a Form 870 may not litigate the tax deficiency in Tax Court, but may sue for a refund after paying the tax and filing a refund claim. Importantly, the IRS later may assess additional deficiencies for the same tax year covered by the Form 870.

B. *Form 870–AD*

Settlements reached with the Appeals Office are usually memorialized on a Form 870–AD (or Form 890–AD for estate taxes). Form 870–AD, when executed by the taxpayer, is an offer to waive the statutory notice of deficiency in exchange for the Government's concessions in the settlement. Unlike the Form 870, which expressly recognizes the taxpayer's right to seek a refund of taxes paid pursuant to it and which does not prevent the Government from assessing additional deficiencies, the Form 870–AD is intended to be final and binding on both the taxpayer and the Government. The taxpayer is prohibited from filing or prosecuting a claim for refund or credit, and the Government is prevented from reopening the case in the absence of fraud, misrepresentation or concealment of a material fact, or gross mathematical errors.

Taxpayers, however, have sought to avoid the effects of the Form 870–AD by suing for refunds and claiming that Form 870–AD is not binding because it does not conform to the requirements of I.R.C. § 7121. Section 7121, which prescribes the rules governing closing agreements, and section 7122, which contains rules for compromises, are the only types of agreements recognized in the Code itself as final and binding. The issue in such cases involving a taxpayer's suit for refund after executing a Form 870–AD is whether the taxpayer should be equitably estopped to litigate the claim, or whether the execution of the form should not be final and binding because it does not conform to section 7121. The Supreme Court in *Botany Worsted Mills v. United States* (S.Ct.1929), left open the question whether an agreement that is not binding under the statute may become binding through the doctrine of estoppel. In a 1985 decision, the Claims Court held that a taxpayer will be equitably estopped to litigate a refund claim that is covered by a Form 870–AD if three criteria are met: execution of the Form 870–AD resulted from mutual concessions or compromise; there was a meeting of the minds that the claims would be extinguished; and to permit the taxpayer to reopen the issues would be prejudicial to the Government in light of its reliance on the Form. Kretchmar v. United States, 9 Cl.Ct. 191 (Cl.Ct.1985); *accord*, Schneider v. United States, 89–2 U.S.T.C. ¶ 9522 (W.D.Mich.1989).

C.　*Closing Agreements: Forms 866 and 906*

As mentioned above, the only Code section that recognizes the finality of settlement agreements is I.R.C. § 7121. Formal compromises, authorized by section 7122, also are final and binding and are used in collection cases to bind the Government to accept less than the assessed amount. The only agreements that satisfy the formal requirements of I.R.C. § 7121 are Form 866 (which settles conclusively the taxpayer's total tax liability for the years in question) and Form 906 (which settles only one or more issues, but which can apply to future years for issues such as the proper basis of an asset that will affect future tax liability).

Because of the finality of Forms 866 and 906, the Service enters into such closing agreements "with great caution." IRM, Part VIII (Appeals), Closing Agreements Handbook 8.13.1.1.1 (2001). If a taxpayer wishes to obtain a closing agreement, he must present good reasons for it and convince the Service that the Government will not be disadvantaged by entering into the agreement. Regs. § 301.7121–1(a). Closing agreements may be entered into for a taxable period any time before a case involving that period is docketed in the Tax Court. Regs. § 301.7121–1(d)(1). Closing agreements may be set aside by either the taxpayer or the Government only for fraud, misrepresentation or malfeasance.

D. *Collateral Agreements*

When an issue has been settled that will affect other taxpayers' tax liability, the Service may condition any settlement on the execution of collateral agreements by the other taxpayers to abide by the settlement in filing their returns. For example, in an estate tax valuation controversy, the heirs may be asked to execute an agreement to use the valuation agreed to in the settlement as their basis (for the purpose of computing gain or loss on a later sale of the asset), rather than the valuation contained in the estate tax return. Collateral agreements also may be used to clarify a closing agreement or to collect funds in addition to those mentioned in the closing agreement.

CHAPTER 7

THE ASSESSMENT PROCEDURE AND STATUTES OF LIMITATIONS

§ 7.1   Assessment

Under the normal rules, a tax may not be collected until it has been assessed. Thus, assessment is the beginning of the collection process. Assessment is the recording of the taxpayer's name, address, TIN, the taxable period involved, and the nature and amount of the tax liability on an official list in the office of the Secretary. I.R.C. § 6203. Technically, the date of the assessment is the date that an assessment officer signs an Assessment Certificate (Form 23–C).

There are two general ways in which an assessment normally occurs. One is through the summary assessment process in which tax liability that is shown on a return is recorded in a summary record, even though the tax itself may not be paid. This amount is said to be "self-assessed." The other is through the recording of a deficiency, which normally occurs only at the end of the deficiency assessment procedure.

A. *Notice of Deficiency*

A deficiency is defined under section 6211 as "the amount by which the tax imposed exceeds the excess of (1) the sum of (A) the amount shown as tax on the return, plus (B) the amounts previously assessed (or collected without assessment) as a deficiency, over (2) the amount of any rebates (abatements, credits, refunds or other payments)." If no return is filed, the entire amount of the tax liability is a deficiency. If the return fails to show the full amount of the tax liability, the excess of the amount due over the amount shown on the return constitutes a deficiency. Thus, the deficiency is not determined by nonpayment of the tax, but by the amount of tax that is not shown on a return.

In order to collect a deficiency, the IRS first must mail a notice of deficiency (also called a "90–day letter") to the taxpayer's last known address in accordance with section 6213. The notice of deficiency gives the taxpayer 90 days (150 days if the notice is mailed to an address outside the U.S.) to file an appeal with the Service or to file a petition in the Tax Court. During the 90–day period, the IRS is prohibited from assessing the deficiency and the statute of limitations is tolled for the period that the Service is prohibited from assessing. This insures that the Service will have enough time to assess the deficiency when the 90–day period expires. See § 7.2.A, *infra*. Thus, the statutory prerequisites to the IRS's ability to assess a deficiency are (1) mailing a notice of deficiency and (2) waiting the

90 days (or longer if the taxpayer files a petition in the Tax Court).

B. *Waiver of Restrictions on Assessment*

A taxpayer may waive the right to a notice of deficiency and the 90–day period either by paying the tax liability or by signing a Form 870 or Form 870–AD, discussed in §§ 6.4.A and 6.4.B, *supra*. By doing so, however, the taxpayer also waives the right to contest the proposed deficiency in the Tax Court. See § 14.2, *infra*. Thus, a taxpayer who contemplates signing a waiver should be certain that he does not wish to contest the proposed deficiency.

C. *Jeopardy and Termination Assessments*

The IRS can bypass the normal rules governing assessment in situations in which it believes immediate collection action is necessary. Particularly in situations involving illegal income, the IRS must be able to seize a person's assets quickly when it is likely that a delay will permit the person to flee the country or conceal his assets. The Code permits the IRS to assess and collect a tax immediately without first sending a notice of deficiency if it appears that collection of the tax would be jeopardized by delay. There are two separate statutory authorizations: section 6851 permits the Service to terminate a taxpayer's taxable year and assess the tax due (known as a "termination assessment"); section 6861 permits immediate assessment of a tax already due (known as a "jeopardy assessment").

These provisions confer extraordinary powers on the IRS and must be used judiciously. When a jeopardy or termination assessment is made, the taxpayer is entitled to due process. See § 11.4, *infra*, for a further discussion of jeopardy and termination assessments and the procedure for obtaining a hearing.

§ 7.2   Statutes of Limitations on Assessment

When is it too late for the Service to notify a taxpayer that additional tax is due for a taxable year? The answer to this question depends on whether and when a return was filed (or deemed filed), the types of errors or omissions in the return, and the taxpayer's intent in filing the return (that is, whether the taxpayer willfully intended to evade tax).

As in any area of the law, familiarity with the statutes of limitations is essential to proper handling of a tax controversy. The rules governing the time in which tax assessments may be made or claims for refund of overpayments must be filed are complex, technical and often confusing. This section will discuss the general 3–year statute of limitations on assessment of tax deficiencies and the exceptions to this general rule, as well as rules relating to extension of the statutory time limits and mitigation of the statute of limitations.

A.   *General Rule: 3–Year Statute of Limitations*

The general rule is contained in I.R.C. § 6501(a), which requires that tax must be assessed within three years after the return is filed. Thus, the important starting point for the running of the statute of limitations is the point at which the return is filed, because the statute commences on the day after the date the return is filed.

B.   *When Return Is Deemed Filed*

There are three general dates on which a return is deemed filed. Under the general rule, a return is filed on the date it is received by the IRS. Emmons v. Commissioner (Tax Ct.1989). Under I.R.C. § 7502, a return that is mailed on or before the due date is timely filed, even though it is not received until after the due date. Thus, the date of mailing (as evidenced by the postmark) is the date of filing, if the return is filed on or before the due date. This is known as "the mailbox rule." Returns filed early (before the due date) are treated as filed on the due date, for statute of limitations purposes. I.R.C. § 6501(b)(1). This is known as "the early return rule."

To illustrate: a return mailed on March 8 that is due on April 15 is treated as filed on April 15. A return that is mailed on April 25 and due on April 15 is considered filed when the Service receives it. A return due on April 15 and postmarked on that date is considered filed on April 15, even though the IRS does not receive the return until after April 15.

If the due date falls on a Saturday, Sunday or legal holiday, then the return is timely filed if it is mailed on the next succeeding day that is not a Saturday, Sunday or legal holiday. I.R.C. § 7503.

For example, if the due date is April 15, and April 15 is a Sunday, then mailing the return on Monday, April 16 will constitute timely filing.

In 1992 Congress extended the mailbox rule of section 7502 to include the postmarks of foreign governments, thus permitting taxpayers to comply with the timely filing requirement by mailing their returns from a foreign country. Until 1997, however, the mailbox rule did not apply to returns sent by private delivery services such as Federal Express. Now, under section 7502(f), the mailbox rule has been extended to private delivery services designated by the IRS as acceptable. For a list of the private delivery services that may be used in compliance with section 7502(f) *see* Notice 2004–83, 2004–52 I.R.B.1030.

C.   *No Time Limit if No Return Filed*

If no return is filed, then there is no time limit on assessing and collecting the tax. I.R.C. § 6501(c)(3). Thus, failure to file a return in 1955 could result in assessment and collection in 2005.

Significantly, this exception to the general 3–year statute of limitations can apply in situations in which the taxpayer actually a filed a form with the Service that he thought constituted a tax return, but which did not comply with all requirements. A tax return must be made "according to the forms and regulations prescribed by the [Commissioner]," and "the information required by such forms or regulations" must be furnished. I.R.C. § 6011(a). Although the Supreme Court has held that "perfect accuracy or completeness is not necessary to rescue a return from nullity," Zellerbach Paper Co. v. Helvering (S.Ct.1934), some errors or omissions can be fatal. For example, a return that is not signed by the taxpayer under penalties of perjury does not constitute a "return" and thus does not commence the statute of limitations. Campise v. Commissioner (Tax Ct.1980) (unsigned return did not start statute of limitations); Sommer v. Commissioner (Tax Ct.1983) (failure to comply with requirement of I.R.C. § 6065 that returns be signed "under penalties of perjury," by striking out those words on the Form, resulted in no "return" deemed filed). Unfortunately, the Service does not notify the taxpayer that no "return" has been filed in such cases.

The Tax Court summarized applicable Supreme Court precedent as creating a four-part test for determining whether a document constitutes a "return" that will commence the running of the statute of limitations:

First, there must be sufficient data to calculate the tax liability; second, the document must purport to be a return; third, there must be an honest and reasonable attempt to satisfy the requirements of the tax law; and fourth, the taxpayer must execute the return under penalties of perjury. Beard v. Commissioner, 82 T.C. 766, 777, 1984 WL 15573 (Tax Ct.1984), aff'd, 793 F.2d 139 (6th Cir.1986).

Any document that satisfies this test will start the statute of limitations to run, despite the fact that the Service must return the document to the taxpayer for additional information. Blount v. Commissioner (Tax Ct.1986) (rejecting the Service's claim that an individual's Form 1040 did not constitute a "return" because the taxpayer failed to attach a Form W–2). On the other hand, there are numerous cases holding that "tax protestor" returns containing insufficient data on which to calculate the tax did not constitute "returns" and thus did not start the statute of limitations. These cases resulted in the "protestors" being subjected to penalties under I.R.C. § 6651 for failure to file a return. See Chapter 10 for a discussion of civil penalties.

If a delinquent return is filed, the statute of limitations will begin to run on the date that the return is received by the Service, provided the return is not fraudulent. Bennett v. Commissioner (Tax Ct.1958); Rev.Rul. 79–178, 1979–1 C.B. 435. Thus, if a taxpayer mailed his 2002 return on April 15, 2005, and the return was received by the Service on April 18, 2005, the 3–year statute of limitations would begin to run on April 18, 2005 (i.e., April 19 would be day 1), assuming that the return is not fraudulent, as discussed in the next Section.

D. No Time Limit for Fraudulent Return

Another exception to the general 3–year statute of limitations is contained in I.R.C. § 6501(c)(1), which permits assessment and collection "at any time" for "a false or fraudulent return with the intent to evade tax." A similar exception is contained in I.R.C. § 6501(c)(2), which provides for an unlimited time for assessment in "case of a willful attempt to defeat or evade tax." The Government has the burden of proving fraud, but if the taxpayer has been convicted of criminal fraud (attempted tax evasion under I.R.C. § 7201, discussed in Chapter 18), then the taxpayer will be collaterally estopped to challenge an assessment made after the 3–year statute of limitations has expired. See § 15.2 for a discussion of collateral estoppel in tax cases.

If a taxpayer files a fraudulent return but later files a nonfraudulent amended return, should the filing of the amended return start the statute of limitations? Because the filing of a nonfraudulent return after failing to file a return at all does trigger the statute of limitations, it would seem that correcting a fraudulent return by filing an amended, nonfraudulent return would have the same effect. However, the U.S. Supreme Court has held that the filing of a nonfraudulent amended return does not cure the filing of the fraudulent return, and that tax may be assessed at any time on the basis of the original fraudulent return. Badaracco v. Commissioner (S.Ct.1984).

Addressing the discrepancy in treatment for non-filers who file late versus those who repent and correct their fraudulent returns, the *Badaracco* Court stated that "Congress intended different limitations results." The Court reasoned that "a tax-payer's later repentance" does not cure or eliminate the original fraud. The Court also found it significant that the Code does not explicitly provide for the filing of amended returns, which the Court described as a "creature of administrative origin and grace." In dissent, Justice Stevens argued that our system of voluntary compliance will be undermined by the Court's decision, which in effect punishes those who try to correct their past fraudulent conduct. According to Justice Stevens, "the Court believes that taxpayers should be advised to remain silent, hoping the fraud will go undetected, rather than to make full disclosure in a proper return."

E.   6–Year Time Limit for Substantial Omissions of Gross Income

A further exception to the 3–year statute of limitations is the 6–year time limit for omissions from gross income of an amount that is more than 25% of the gross income stated in the return. I.R.C. § 6501(e). In other words, if the return omits gross income items that exceed 25% of the reported gross income, then the IRS has 6 years, rather than the usual 3 years, in which to assess a deficiency. "Gross income" is defined very broadly in I.R.C. § 61 and cases interpreting it to include every kind of addition to one's wealth (including, for example, illegal income from drug dealing or bribes). Section 6501(e) also applies to omissions of more than 25% of total gifts and gross estate assets.

The special 6–year time limit applies only if the item of gross income is completely omitted from the return; if the taxpayer includes the item but merely miscalculates or understates it, the general 3–year statute of limitations will apply. The Colony, Inc. v. Commissioner (S.Ct.1958). If the omission is serious enough to cause the return to be "false or fraudulent" or the result of a "willful attempt to defeat or evade" tax, under I.R.C. §§ 6501(c)(1) or (2), then there is no time limit on assessment of the tax. Regs. § 301.6501(e)–1(d).

Assume that a taxpayer has omitted a substantial item of gross income, thus triggering the special six-year statute of limitation. May the IRS then assert additional deficiencies that are unrelated to the omission and ordinarily would be time-barred? The Tax Court has held that the IRS may assert those additional deficiencies, thus allowing them to be "piggy-backed" onto the substantial omission after the general three-year statute of limitation has expired. Colestock v. Commissioner (Tax Ct.1994).

F. *Extension by Agreement*

Under I.R.C. § 6501(c)(4), the statute of limitations can be extended by written agreement between the taxpayer and the Service entered into before the time for assessment has expired. Why would a taxpayer ever enter into such an agreement? The answer is that the Service frequently requests such extensions when the statute of limitations is about to expire and it has not completed its examination or the matter is under administrative review. If the taxpayer refuses to execute a consent form, the Service might simply issue a notice of deficiency (resolving any questions in its own favor and asserting a maximum tax liability), which will force the taxpayer either to pay the disputed amount or file a Tax Court petition within 90 days of issuance of the notice. Although it is the announced policy of the Service to request consents to extend the statute of limitations only in unusual circumstances, such requests occur frequently.

There are two basic types of consents: the "regular" consent, Form 872, which extends the statute of limitations to a specified date; and the "special" or "restricted" consent, Form 872–A, which keeps the limitations period open for up to 10 years. Before the end of the 10–year period, either the taxpayer or the Service may terminate the special consent, but regardless of which party terminates, the Service has 90 days to assess a tax deficiency.

The method of termination varies slightly depending upon the party that is terminating. The taxpayer can terminate a Form 872–A consent only by filing a Form 872–T with the I.R.S. office that is handling the case. Grunwald v. Commissioner (Tax Ct.1986); Rev.Proc. 79–22, 1979–1 C.B. 563. The termination is effective only when the Service receives the executed Form 872–T. On the other hand, the Service may terminate a Form 872–A consent by mailing either a Form 872–T or a notice of deficiency to the taxpayer. Note that although a taxpayer's Form 872–T is not effective until actually received by the Service, the Service's termination is effective upon mailing.

Section 6212 provides that a notice of deficiency shall be mailed to the taxpayer's last known address. (See Chapter14, § 14.2, *infra* for a discussion of the "last known address" requirement for deficiency notices.) If a notice of deficiency is not mailed to the taxpayer's last known address, can it nevertheless serve as a valid termination of a special consent to extend the statute of limitations? The Tax Court, ruling in favor of the taxpayer by strictly construing the termination requirements against their drafter, the Government, decided in a reviewed decision that such a notice could serve as a valid termination. Roszkos v. Commissioner (Tax Ct.1986). (See § 14.2.E, *infra*, for a discussion of reviewed Tax Court decisions). The court reasoned that although the deficiency notice had been improperly addressed, it nevertheless had the potential to advise the taxpayer of the intended termination, and the taxpayer had actually learned of the notice in time to file a timely petition in the Tax Court. Although the court had ruled earlier that an improperly addressed notice of deficiency would not support a valid assessment because the notice did not comply with the statutory requirement of being mailed to the taxpayer's last known address, the court in *Roszkos* concluded that the improperly addressed notice terminated the Form 872–A.

The Service appealed the decision to the Ninth Circuit, which took the somewhat unusual step of reversing a reviewed Tax Court decision. The Ninth Circuit ruled that when the Service terminates a Form 872–A consent by mailing a notice of deficiency, the termination is invalid and ineffective if it is not mailed to the taxpayer's last known address, as required by section 6212. Roszkos v. Commissioner (9th Cir.1988); *accord* Holof v. Commissioner (3rd

Cir.1989). The Ninth Circuit held that the improperly addressed notice did not terminate the Form 872–A consent, and thus the later assessment was not time-barred.

G. *Summary*

To summarize, the time limits for assessing a deficiency in tax are as follows:

—general rule: 3 years from date return is filed or date actually received by IRS, if later;

—6 years from date return is filed for substantial omission of gross income (i.e., omission of item(s) of income constituting 25% or more of total);

—if statute of limitations was extended by consent, on or before 6 months after expiration of extended period.

—no time limit for fraudulent returns (even if the taxpayer later files a nonfraudulent amended return);

—no time limit if no return is filed, but if the taxpayer eventually files a return, the time limit is three years from the date the IRS receives the return.

CHAPTER 8

OVERPAYMENTS: ADMINISTRATIVE REFUNDS

§ 8.1 What Is An Overpayment?

An overpayment of tax is simply when the amount paid exceeds the amount owed. Before an overpayment can arise, there first must be a payment of tax. Occasionally, there may be a question as to whether a remittance is a payment or a deposit. Under some circumstances, a taxpayer may make a deposit against the tax owed in order to stop the running of interest. The issue of whether a remittance constitutes a payment or a deposit is an important one because the 2–year statute of limitations runs from the date the tax is paid (see § 8.3, *infra*), while a deposit has no effect on the statute of limitations. The taxpayer is entitled to recover a deposit at any time without following the specific procedure for a refund, although the taxpayer is not entitled to interest on a deposit.

An overpayment can occur in any of several ways: (1) by overwithholding of tax on wages or salary, (2) by inadvertent error in calculating the tax liability, (3) by carrybacks from other taxable years, (4) by a payment made after the close of the statute of limitations (I.R.C. § 6401), and (5) by a judicial determination. In (1) through (4), the Service either will refund the amount of the overpayment on its own, or the taxpayer will have to file a claim for refund. This Chapter will discuss the administrative claim for refund, while Chapter 14 will discuss the refund suit. *See also* § 9.1 for a discussion of the *Lewis v. Reynolds* case defining an overpayment.

§ 8.2 The Refund Claim

Once a tax has been assessed and collected, the Service has no authority to refund or credit the amount of any overpayment (except in the case of a math error on the return) unless the taxpayer files a claim for refund. I.R.C. §§ 6511(b)(1) and 6514. Claims for refund of taxes overpaid for the current year are made routinely by individuals on Form 1040. Claims for refunds of income taxes overpaid in previous years are made by individuals on Form 1040X and by corporations on Form 1120X. All claims for refunds of taxes other than income taxes must be made on Form 843. Claims for refund of taxes overpaid in previous years must "set forth in detail each ground on which a credit or refund is claimed and facts sufficient to apprise the Commissioner of the exact basis thereof." Reg. § 301.6402–2(b)(1). Because the refund claim will serve as the basis of any subsequent suit on the claim, it should be carefully drafted to comply with all requirements in the Regulations and to specify the exact amount to be refunded. Once the statute of limitations for making a refund claim has expired (see § 8.3, *in-*

fra), the taxpayer may not amend the claim to cure a defect or add new issues or grounds. *Id.*

A. *Informal Refund Claims*

If the statute of limitations for filing a formal refund claim has expired, it is still possible that some communication from the taxpayer to the Service might qualify as an informal but valid refund claim. An informal claim will be upheld as valid if it is in writing sufficient to apprise the Service of the grounds of the claim, the taxable year involved, and that a refund is being sought. A Form 870 can serve as informal refund claim, for example. An informal claim that is timely filed but inadequately specific can be cured retroactively by a subsequent formal claim filed after the statute of limitations has expired but before the Service rejects the informal claim. American Radiator & Standard Sanitary Corp. v. United States (Ct.Cl.1963).

B. *Waiver of Defects in Refund Claims*

Claims for refund that satisfy requirements imposed by statute, but that do not satisfy requirements imposed by the Regulations, are sometimes upheld as valid on the theory that the Service has waived its right to insist on strict compliance. Failure to comply with statutory requirements (such as the statute of limitations), however, can never be waived by the Government. On the other hand, if the defect in the formal or informal refund claim pertains only to requirements imposed by the Regulations, it has been held that the Government waiver may occur as late as during the trial of the case. United States v. Smith (5th Cir.1969) (defects waived when Government failed to object to introduction of evidence that cured the defects). The taxpayer bears a considerable burden in establishing that the Service has waived its right to demand strict compliance. The Supreme Court has held that the taxpayer's "showing should be unmistakable that the Commissioner has in fact seen fit to dispense with his formal requirements and to examine the merits of the claim." Angelus Milling Co. v. Commissioner (S.Ct.1945).

C. *Filing the Claim*

Refund claims are filed with the IRS Service Center in the region in which the tax was paid. A separate claim must be filed for each taxable year and for each type of tax. The taxpayer bears the burden of establishing that the claim was timely made. Under § 6402(a), the IRS will refund or credit the amount of an overpayment to the person who made the overpayment. In *United States v. Williams* (S.Ct.1995), the U.S. Supreme Court held that the taxpayer who paid the tax in order to remove a lien against her property was entitled to the refund even though she was not the party against whom the tax was assessed. The Court did not decide the extent to which a party who volunteers to pay a tax assessed against someone else is entitled to seek a refund of the overpayment. Refund claims generally are nonassignable.

The Service Center generally will process and refund (or credit against an existing tax liability) any claimed overpayment for the current year prior to any audit or other action, but claims for refund of taxes overpaid in previous years are usually examined by the Compliance Team of the Operating Division. If the Government either denies the claim for refund, by issuing a statutory notice of claim disallowance under I.R.C. § 6532(a)(1), or six months passes in which the refund claim is not granted, the taxpayer may then file a refund suit in the U.S. district court. See § 14.3, *infra,* for a discussion of refund suits. Taxpayers who do not wish to pursue an administrative appeal may expedite the process by requesting in writing that their claim for refund be immediately rejected. The Service will issue a notice of claim disallowance promptly after receiving such a request.

§ 8.3 When the Refund Claim Must Be Filed

A claim for a refund of overpaid taxes must be filed on or before the *later* of the following:

—3 years from the date the return was filed; or

—2 years from the date the tax was actually paid.

I.R.C. § 6511(a). If the statute of limitations has been extended by agreement between the Service and the taxpayer, the refund claim may be filed any time within six months after the extended period has expired. I.R.C. § 6511(c)(2). The time of filing determines the amount of the refund because under § 6511(b), the amount of the refund or credit cannot exceed the portion of the tax paid within that period.

To illustrate: On April 15, 2000, taxpayer mails his 1999 return, which reflects $8,000 of total tax due and paid. On March 1, 2002, a deficiency of $2,000 plus interest is assessed, and on May 1, 2002, the taxpayer pays the deficiency.

The return was deemed filed on April 15, 2000, the due date, because it was mailed on that date. See § 7.2.B, *supra*. The deficiency assessment was made within the 3–year time limit. If the taxpayer believes that any of the total of $10,000 tax paid plus interest is actually an overpayment, he may file a refund claim on or before April 15, 2003 (the 3–year period from the date the return was filed). If he does not file the claim within that period, he may file on or before May 1, 2004 (2 years from the date the asserted deficiency was paid), but the amount of his refund is limited to the amount he paid within the 2–year period preceding the claim ($,2000).

In the example above, if a Form 872 consent had been executed on March 1, 2001 extending the time limit to April 15, 2004, and if the deficiency had been assessed and paid on the dates above indicated, then a refund claim could be timely filed on or before October 15, 2004 (6 months from the expiration of the extended period for assessment). If filed on or before October 15, 2004, the claim would be valid and within the statute of limitations as to all $10,000 in tax plus interest paid.

See I.R.C. § 6511(d) for exceptions to the time limit on filing claims for refunds.

In summary:

–claim for refund of overpaid tax must be filed on or before later of: 3 years after return filed or 2 years after tax paid. § 6511(a).

–suit for refund of overpaid tax must be filed no earlier than: 6 months from date of filing refund claim (with no response from IRS) or date of notice of disallowance. § 6532(a)(1). *See* further discussion, Chapter 14, § 14.3.B, *infra*.

–suit for refund of overpaid tax must be filed no later than: 2 years from date notice of disallowance issued or 2 years from date statutory notice of disallowance was waived. § 6532(a)(3).

CHAPTER 9

REMEDIES TO ABSOLVE THE HARSHNESS OF THE STATUTE OF LIMITATIONS ON ASSESSMENTS AND CLAIMS FOR REFUND

Because the statutes of limitations are strictly construed and cannot be waived, it is possible that unfairness could result either to the taxpayer or to the Government if the other party manipulates the time bars and takes inconsistent positions. Where possible, courts have construed the statutory provisions to provide a fair and just result. Where it has not been possible to construe the statutes in this manner, the courts have employed equitable doctrines such as recoupment and the legal remedy of setoff (or offset) to prevent harsh and unfair treatment that would result from application of the statutory time bar (in the case of equitable recoupment) and failure to offset claimed overpayments of tax with underpayments for tax years not barred by the statute of limitations (offset). In addition, since 1938 there have been mitigation provisions in the Code itself. These statutory mitigation provisions, I.R.C. §§ 1311–1314, override and displace the judge-made doctrines in cases in which the statutory provisions apply. The judicially-created equitable doctrines continue to apply to cases that are not covered by the statutory provisions.

§ 9.1   Statutory Offset

Statutory offset arose in the case of *Lewis v. Reynolds* (S.Ct.1932), in which the administrator of an estate filed a refund suit against the Service to recover an alleged overpayment. The estate initially had filed a return claiming a deduction for attorney's fees and state inheritance taxes. Several years later, the return was audited and the Commissioner disallowed all deductions except the attorney's fees and assessed a deficiency. The estate paid the deficiency and then filed a claim for refund of this amount. The Commissioner conceded the substance of the estate's argument, that the denial of the state inheritance taxes had been improper, but he also stated that the attorney's fees had been improperly allowed. Although the statute of limitations on assessment had run, the Commissioner denied the estate's claim on the ground that the amount of the attorney's fees exceeded the amount of the inheritance tax deduction; therefore, there was no overpayment.

The U.S. Supreme Court agreed with the Commissioner, holding that while no new assessment could be made since the statute of limitations had expired, the taxpayer could not obtain a refund if there was no overpayment for that taxable year. Since the amount of tax that had been paid by the estate was less than the amount that was properly owed, the estate was not entitled to a refund.

§ 9.2 Statutory Mitigation Provisions

In 1938 Congress added the statutory mitigation provisions, sections 1311–1314, to the Code. These provisions are quite technical, but have a simple goal. They are designed to permit a taxpayer or the government to take a qualified "peek" into a time-barred year in order to use an inconsistent position to offset or increase the current tax liability. In other words, if there is an adjustment to an item on a return in a current year that is inconsistent with the treatment of that item in an earlier year, the mitigation provisions allow the earlier year to be opened to adjust the treatment of the earlier item in order to make it consistent with the current treatment. The effect of the adjustment, however, occurs in the current year. These provisions can be used either by taxpayers (to decrease their current tax liability) or by the IRS (to increase the taxpayer's current tax liability). In either case, the party seeking to take advantage of mitigation must show that the other party took a position in an open year that is inconsistent with the position taken by that party in a now-closed year.

Most courts and commentators have concluded that the statutory mitigation rules apply only to income taxes, *see, e.g.*, Provident National Bank v. United States (E.D.Pa.1981) and Hall v. United States (10th Cir. 1992), but some courts have applied the rules outside the income tax context. *See*

Chertkof v. United States (4th Cir.1982). It is clear that the mitigation provisions do not apply to employment taxes. I.R.C. § 1314(e).

There are four requirements for obtaining relief under the statutory mitigation rules:

1. There must be a 'determination' that an error was made concerning the proper treatment of an item. (§ 1313).

2. The operation of any law or rule of law must prevent correction of the error. (§ 1311(a)).

3. The "determination," coupled with the erroneous inconsistent treatment, must result in one of seven "circumstances of adjustment" listed in section 1312.

4. The party in whose favor the "determination" is made must have maintained an inconsistent position with respect to the "determination" in a year that is now barred from litigation. (§ 1311(b)).

The statutory mitigation scheme basically permits refunds or assessments that would otherwise be barred by the statute of limitations or other rule of law (such as res judicata, discussed in Chapter 15). The statutory scheme depends on the existence of a "determination" that establishes the correct treatment of an item and thereby establishes that the prior, inconsistent treatment of the (otherwise time-barred) item was erroneous. In other words, either the taxpayer or the Service treated an item in one way, and it was later decided by a "determination" for a different tax year that a different treatment of that item was correct. The statutory mitigation scheme then allows the prior year to be reopened to correct the earlier, incorrect treatment.

"Determination" is defined in section 1313(a) as including only the following:

—a court order or decision that is final;

—a closing agreement made under I.R.C. § 7121 (*see* Chapter 6);

—final disposition of a claim for refund;

—an agreement entered into pursuant to section 1313(a)(4) (which should be entered into on Form 2259, Agreement As To Determination Pursuant To Section 1313(a)(4), and is intended to expedite the claim for an adjustment of the prior year's tax liability).

The court that makes the "determination" may not also order the adjustment for the prior and inconsistent year; only after a final determination (in any of the four forms described above) may the taxpayer or the Government seek an adjustment for the prior year under I.R.C. § 1311.

Only certain, defined types of errors ("circumstances of adjustment," in the statutory language) are eligible for statutory mitigation. These are listed in section 1312 as follows:

—double inclusion of an item of gross income (§ 1312(1));

—double allowance of a deduction or credit (§ 1312(2));

—double exclusion of an item of gross income (§ 1312(3));

—double disallowance of a deduction or credit (§ 1312(4));

—errors concerning the basis of property after prior erroneous treatment (§ 1312(7));

—correlative deductions and credits between certain related corporations (§ 1312(6)), and correlative deductions and inclusions between a trust or estate and its beneficiaries (§ 1312(5)).

To illustrate the first "circumstance of adjustment" listed above, the double inclusion of an item of gross income, assume that a cash basis taxpayer erroneously includes in income for 2002 accrued rents receivable that are actually received in 2003 and 2004. After the statute of limitations expires on the 2002 return, the Commissioner assesses a deficiency for 2003 and 2004, the years in which the rent should have been included in income. If the Tax Court sustains the deficiency, section 1311 will permit the 2002 return year to be "opened" to correct the erroneous inclusion of the rent in income. See Reg. § 1.1312–1(b), Ex. (1).

The most unsettled of the circumstances of adjustment is section 1312(7), which permits mitigation if there has been an error concerning the basis of property. The statutory language permits an adjustment if "[t]he determination determines the basis of property, and in respect of any transaction on which such basis depends," there occurred any of several errors specified in the statute. Courts have interpreted the phrase "in respect of any transaction on which such basis depends" very narrowly to deny relief. The Tenth Circuit has held that the mitigation provisions do not apply if a taxpayer fails to take depreciation deductions to which she was entitled, and, upon sale or other disposition of the property, the Commissioner reduces her basis in the property (thereby increasing the amount of taxable gain) by the amount of depreciation that was allowable. The court reasoned that the failure to take depreciation deductions is not a "transaction" within the meaning of the statute. Gardiner v. United States (D.Utah 1975).

Similarly, the Seventh Circuit, in *O'Brien v. United States* (7th Cir.1985), denied relief through the mitigation provisions in a case involving a dispute over the valuation of stock. The stock was valued in 1974 for estate tax purposes at $215 per share, but the Commissioner asserted a higher value. The executor petitioned the Tax Court to resolve the dispute. In 1975 the corporation was liquidated, and the recipient of the stock, the decedent's son, reported his taxable gain using the $215 basis established by the estate tax return. In 1980 the Tax Court ruled that the stock's basis was $280 per share. The son then filed a refund claim to recover the overpayment from his 1975 return, asserting that the basis he had used to compute his taxable gain had been determined to be erroneous by the Tax Court's 1980 decision. The court denied relief, ruling that the error had not occurred "in respect of" the father's death and the son's acquisition of the stock, but instead had occurred "in respect of" the subsequent liquidation of the corporation. The court further held that because the son was not a party to the Tax Court estate tax litigation, he was not a taxpayer with respect to whom that determination was made, thus further foreclosing him from relief under section 1312(7).

Once it has been determined that an adjustment is warranted, the method of making the adjustment depends on whether the effect of the adjustment is a tax deficiency or a tax overpayment. In either case, the adjustment will bear interest and be subject to additions to tax under the laws governing deficiencies and overpayments for the year to which the adjustment relates. If the adjustment results in a tax deficiency (that is, it is in the Government's favor), then it is to be assessed and collected the same as any other deficiency: the Commissioner must issue a "notice of deficiency" and the taxpayer may contest the asserted deficiency in the Tax Court, or pay the deficiency and file a claim for refund. If the adjustment results in a tax overpayment (that is, it is in the taxpayer's favor), then the taxpayer must file a claim for refund, unless the Government refunds the amount without the filing of a formal claim. If the claim is denied or is not acted on in six months, the taxpayer may then sue for a refund.

The statute of limitations on the making of an assessment or claiming a refund resulting from the adjustment begins to run on the date the "determination" is made (often the date the court decision becomes final), and it expires one year after the determination is made. Therefore, for example, if the determination is an agreement between the taxpayer and the Commissioner (as contemplated in section 1313(a)(4)), and if the adjustment is in the Government's favor, then the Commissioner has one year from the date of the agreement to mail a notice of deficiency; if the agreement results in an overpayment, rather than a deficiency, the taxpayer has one year from the date of the agreement in which to file a claim for refund.

§ 9.3 Equitable Recoupment

The doctrine of equitable recoupment in federal tax cases permits the bar of the statute of limitations to be avoided in certain circumstances in which equity demands relief. The doctrine was first applied by the Supreme Court in 1935 in *Bull v. United States* (S.Ct.1935), and was subsequently refined in *Stone v. White* (S.Ct.1937), *Rothensies v. Electric Storage Battery Co.* (S.Ct.1946), and *United States v. Dalm* (S.Ct.1990).

Equitable recoupment is permitted only when the same transaction or taxable event has been subjected to two taxes based on inconsistent legal theories. The doctrine is properly invoked only when the prior treatment cannot be challenged because of the statute of limitations, while the present claimed treatment is not time-barred. United States v. Dalm (S.Ct.1990). The doctrine permits the court to examine the transaction or event as a whole to determine a fair result. The doctrine is designed to prevent unjust enrichment of either the taxpayer or the Government. Thus, a taxpayer may invoke the doctrine to avoid unfair double taxation, and the Government may invoke the doctrine to prevent unfair tax avoidance.

§ 9.4 Equitable Tolling

What if a taxpayer has overpaid his taxes, but because of severe problems (such as a disability or duress) does not discover the error until after the period for filing a refund claim has expired? If neither the statutory mitigation provisions nor the doctrine of equitable recoupment applies, does the taxpayer have any recourse? The Supreme Court in *United States v. Brockamp* (S.Ct.1997) held that the doctrine of equitable tolling of the statute of limitation does not apply to section 6511's limitations on filing refund suits. The court reasoned that if Congress wished to make equitable exceptions to the time requirements, it could do so. Part of the Taxpayer Bill of Rights Act 3 enacted by Congress in 1998 is an amendment to section 6511 that provides for equitable tolling of the statute of limitation on filing refund claims in certain circumstances involving medically determinable physical or mental impairments. IRC § 6511(h).

CHAPTER 10

CIVIL PENALTIES AND INTEREST

The Code contains two types of penalties to aid the IRS in its enforcement of the law: civil penalties, discussed in this Chapter, and criminal penalties, discussed in Chapter 18. The same action or omission can trigger both the imposition of a civil penalty and a prosecution under one or more of the criminal penalty provisions. Conviction of a tax crime does not bar the assessment of a civil penalty; in fact, conviction of a tax crime can collaterally estop the taxpayer from challenging civil penalties that contain the same elements as the criminal provision.

Studies conducted during 1988–89 by the IRS, the Tax Section of the American Bar Association and other groups concluded that the civil penalty system was unfair, unduly harsh and complex, and ineffective in its principal purpose of promoting voluntary compliance. As a result, the civil penalty system was completely overhauled by the "Improved Penalty Administration and Compliance Tax Act" ("IM-PACT"), which was enacted in late 1989 and is effective generally for returns due after December 31, 1989.

Despite the overhaul of the civil penalty system effected by IMPACT, Congress remains dissatisfied with the system. As part of the Taxpayer Bill of Rights Act 3, Congress directed the Joint Committee on Taxation and the Treasury Department to conduct separate studies reviewing the administration and implementation by the IRS of the penalty and interest provisions of the Code and to make legislative recommendations "to simplify penalty or interest administration and reduce taxpayer burden." (Act § 3801). The 1998 Restructuring and Reform Act also made several important changes to the penalty system. It suspended the accrual of interest and penalties after one year (18 months for taxable years beginning before January 1, 2004) if the IRS fails to send a notice of deficiency within one year (or 18 months until 2004) of the later of the date the return was due or the date the return was filed. IRC § 6404(g). The 1998 Act also requires that all non-computer generated penalties be approved in writing by the supervisor of the IRS employee recommending the penalty, and further requires that each notice of penalty sent to a taxpayer must contain information about the type of penalty, the Code section authorizing it, and a computation of the amount of the penalty. IRC § 6751 (applicable to notices issued and penalties assessed after December 31, 2000).

§ 10.1 Delinquency Penalties

Section 6651(a)(1) imposes a penalty of up to 25% of the net tax due for delinquency in filing a return.

The penalty is imposed at the rate of 5% per month, subject to the 25% ceiling. In addition, § 6651(a)(2) imposes a separate penalty of up to 25% of the net tax due for delinquency in paying tax. This failure to pay penalty is imposed at the rate of 0.5% per month. The 5% failure to file penalty under § 6651(a)(1) will be offset by the 0.5% failure to pay penalty under § 6651(a)(2) when the two penalties run together. I.R.C. § 6651(c). Since the § 6651(a)(1) penalty reaches its maximum at 5 months (5% per month up to 25%), while the § 6651(a)(2) penalty reaches its maximum at 50 months (0.5% per month up to 25%), there will be a 2.5% reduction in the § 6651(a)(1) penalty for the 5 months that the two penalties run together. Thus, a taxpayer who nonfraudulently fails to file a return and pay the tax due in a timely fashion is subject to a maximum penalty under section 6651 of 47.5% of the net tax due: 25% maximum for delinquent filing less 2.5% (§ 6651(a)(1)), and 25% maximum for delinquent payment (§ 6651(a)(2)).

A fraudulent failure to file a return is subject to a penalty of 15% per month, up to a maximum of 75% of the net tax due. I.R.C. § 6651(f). Under section 7454(a), the burden of proving fraud is on the IRS. If the IRS does not sustain its burden, its ability to impose any penalty for the failure to file depends on the contents of the notice of deficiency. If in the notice of deficiency the IRS determines the basic section 6651 penalty in the alternative to the fraud penalty, then the court may consider imposition of the section 6651 penalty, and the taxpayer would bear the burden of proof. On the other hand, if the notice of deficiency does not contain an assertion of the section 6651 penalty, but the IRS asserts the section 6651 penalty in its answer or other pleading, then the court may consider the section 6651 penalty, but the burden of proof with respect to the penalty will be on the IRS. If the IRS fails to sustain its burden of proving fraud and fails to assert the section 6651 penalty, either in the notice of deficiency or in its answer, then the court may not consider the section 6651 penalty and the taxpayer will not be liable for any failure to file penalty. H.R.Rep. 101–247, 101st Cong., 1st Sess. 1402 (1989).

Note that the IRS is given ample opportunity to assert the basic section 6651 failure to file penalty in the alternative to the increased penalty for fraudulent failure to file. The legislative history is somewhat unclear, however, on whether the IRS may successfully assert the basic penalty in the alternative in a pleading other than its answer. Congress' failure to include the phrase "or other pleading" in its description of the consequences of failure by the IRS to assert the basic penalty in either the notice of deficiency or its answer, while including the phrase in an example in which the court could consider the basic penalty, leaves it uncertain whether asserting the basic penalty in the alternative in a pleading other than the IRS answer will permit the court to consider imposition of the basic penalty.

Both the section 6651(a)(1) and the section 6651(a)(2) penalties apply to the "net tax due." This is the amount of tax owing, less any amounts paid or withheld before the due date, less any credits allowable. Thus, if a taxpayer whose total tax due and owing is $10,000, but whose employer withheld $8,000 in federal income taxes, failed to file a return and pay the $2,000 net tax due, he would be subject to a maximum penalty under section 6651 of $950 (47.5% of the $2,000 net tax due).

Both the failure to file and the failure to pay penalties are subject to the statutory defenses of "reasonable cause" and absence of "willful neglect." The Supreme Court has held that the duty to file and pay is personal and nondelegable, and reliance on an attorney to file an estate tax return does not constitute "reasonable cause." United States v. Boyle (S.Ct.1985). The *Boyle* Court distinguished the reliance on an advisor as to questions of law (including whether a return must be filed) from the case before it (in which the executor was aware of the duty to file an estate tax return but relied on his lawyer to file it timely). According to the Court, "one does not have to be a tax expert to know that tax returns have fixed filing dates and that taxes must be paid when they are due." Thus, if the necessity to file a return is not a matter of common knowledge and the taxpayer relies on the advice of counsel that no return need be filed, this can satisfy the "reasonable cause" standard.

The Internal Revenue Manual, section 20.1.1.3.1.2, lists other defenses the Service will recognize as satisfying the reasonable cause standard, including the following:

—death or serious illness of the taxpayer or a member of his immediate family;

—destruction by fire or other casualty of the taxpayer's residence, business premises or business records;

—through no fault of the taxpayer, he is unable to obtain records necessary to complete the return.

There are other circumstances listed, and even if the taxpayer's situation is not squarely covered by one of the exceptions listed in the IRM, the taxpayer should submit a request for abatement of the delinquency penalty with the delinquent return or in response to the deficiency notice, describing reasons why it would be unfair to impose the penalty. See § 10.7, *infra*.

What about the person who lacks the funds to pay his tax? Regulations state that a failure to pay will be considered due to reasonable cause if the taxpayer shows that he exercised ordinary business care and prudence in providing for payment of his taxes but was still unable to pay the tax or would suffer undue hardship if forced to pay the tax. Reg. § 301.6651–1(c)(1). The Regulations further state that the Service will consider all the facts and circumstances, including the amount of the taxpayer's expenditures in relation to his income. A lavish or extravagant lifestyle, or living beyond your means, does not constitute "reasonable cause" for failing to pay a tax.

Another typical situation in which the section 6651 penalties are assessed is in the case of "protest" returns. Tax returns are not considered "returns" (and thus no return is deemed filed) if they do not contain sufficient information to compute the tax due. "Protestors" who file incomplete returns are subject to the failure to file and failure to pay penalties of section 6651. See § 5.1, *supra*, for what constitutes a "return."

Section 6654 imposes a separate penalty for failure to pay, or for underpayment of, estimated taxes. The penalty also applies to underwithholding of federal income tax from wages. Unless the taxpayer falls within one of the four exceptions to liability described in section 6654(d), imposition of the penalty is mandatory. Reasonable cause and lack of willful neglect are irrelevant.

§ 10.2   Accuracy Penalties

The numerous accuracy-related penalties under pre–1990 law were repealed and their replacements consolidated into a single penalty of 20% of the underpayment attributable to the penalized conduct. The 20% penalty of section 6662 applies to each of the following: negligence or disregard of rules or regulations; any substantial understatement of income tax; any substantial valuation overstatement; any substantial estate or gift tax valuation understatement; and any substantial overstatement of pension liabilities. These provisions and the civil fraud penalty are discussed in separate subsections below.

The 20% penalty of section 6662 and the civil fraud penalty of section 6663 are subject to a uniform reasonable cause exception contained in section 6664(c). Under this provision, no penalty should be imposed if the taxpayer establishes that there was reasonable cause for the underpayment and the taxpayer acted in good faith. Congress identified several purposes behind the new standardized exception, including simplifying administration of the penalties, enhancing public understanding of the required standard of behavior, and providing greater judicial review of IRS impositions of penalties.

Section 6664(a) contains a definition of the term "underpayment" that is applicable to all the accuracy-related penalties and is intended to simplify and coordinate, rather than to change, the pre–1990 rules. Under this section, an underpayment is the amount by which the correct tax exceeds the sum of the amount shown as due on the taxpayer's return plus amounts not shown that were previously assessed or collected over the amount of any rebates made. A "rebate" is a credit or refund.

Finally, the accuracy-related penalties can be imposed only if a return was filed.

A.   *Negligence or Disregard of Rules and Regulations*

Section 6662(c) continues the prior law's definitions of negligence and disregard. "Negligence" "includes any failure to make a reasonable attempt to comply" with the Code, and "disregard" "includes any careless, reckless or intentional disregard."

When the Service imposes a negligence penalty, the penalty is presumptively correct and the taxpayer bears the burden of proving (by a preponderance of the evidence) both that he was not negligent and that he did not carelessly, recklessly or intentionally disregard rules and regulations. As discussed below, however, when the Commissioner asserts the fraud penalty, the burden of proving fraud is on the Commissioner. If the Commissioner asserts only the fraud penalty and fails to carry his burden of proof, the court may not impose the negligence penalty, even if it finds that the taxpayer was negligent, unless the Commissioner asserts negligence in the alternative to fraud. For this reason, the Service usually will assert the negligence penalty in the alternative when it asserts the fraud penalty.

Although it is impossible to generalize about the types of conduct that a court will find negligent, the following summary reflects common situations.

1. Inadequate Books and Records. The negligence penalty is often sustained in cases in which the taxpayer carelessly kept his records and made no attempt to keep or preserve accurate records.

2. Reliance on Advisors. The negligence penalty will be sustained if the taxpayer failed to give accurate and complete information to the advisor, but good faith and reasonable reliance after full disclosure rebuts the negligence claim.

3.   Good Faith But Mistaken View of the Law. If the underpayment is due to a taxpayer's mistaken but honestly held interpretation of the tax laws, the negligence penalty usually will not be sustained, particularly if the issue is complex and the taxpayer attempted to comply with the Code.

The legislative history indicates that Congress believed the standardized reasonable cause exception could benefit taxpayers who may have been subject to the negligence penalty under pre–1990 law. First, a complete and specific disclosure of a nonfrivolous return position (similar to that required to avoid the substantial understatement penalty of section 6662(d)) will generally demonstrate that the taxpayer did not intentionally disregard rules or regulations. Merely completing a tax form will not satisfy the disclosure requirement, however. Instead, the disclosure must be complete, specific and identified as being made to avoid the accuracy-related penalty. H.R.Rep. 101–247, 101st Cong., 1st Sess. 1393 (1989). Second, a good-faith challenge to a regulation, identified as such in a disclosure statement, will not subject the taxpayer to the negligence penalty. Frivolous challenges will not be immune to the negligence penalty, however. In addition, failure to keep proper books and records, as under pre–1990 law, will subject the taxpayer to the negligence penalty even if complete disclosure is made. *Id.*

B. *Substantial Understatement Penalty*

The most controversial penalty contained in the Code is the penalty for substantial understatement of tax. This penalty was enacted in 1982, and the penalty rate was established then at 10% of the underpayment of tax. In 1986, the rate was raised twice, first to 20%, then to 25%. After 1990, the penalty rate is 20% of the underpayment of tax. The penalty is imposed if there is a "substantial understatement" of tax liability, which is defined to mean that the correct tax liability exceeds the reported liability by the greater of 10% of the correct tax or $5,000 ($10,000 for corporations). To illustrate: if an individual's correct tax liability for 2005 is $25,000, but he reports a total tax liability of $15,000, then a "substantial understatement" exists because his understatement ($10,000) exceeds the greater of $2,500 (10% of total tax liability) or $5,000. For individuals, $5,000 is the minimum understatement that will trigger the penalty.

Critics of the substantial understatement penalty describe it as a "no fault" or strict liability penalty because it is imposed automatically if a substantial understatement exists. Unlike the negligence penalty or the civil fraud penalty, which penalize taxpayers for careless or fraudulent behavior, this penalty can be imposed upon taxpayers who make honest and reasonable efforts to comply with the Code but whose tax liabilities are increased after audit.

There are ways to avoid the penalty, however. In situations not involving "tax shelter" items, the penalty should not be imposed if the taxpayer either discloses the relevant facts on or with the return and the position has a reasonable basis, or substantial authority exists for the position. Disclosure usually should be made on Form 8275 (issued for this purpose) or on a statement attached to the return explaining the facts and identifying the attachment as a disclosure under section 6662. Disclosure of a frivolous (or even a non-frivolous) position for which there is no reasonable basis will not shield a taxpayer from the penalty.

Because disclosing an uncertain item can trigger an audit, taxpayers are reluctant to do so. If no disclosure has been made, the penalty can be avoided only if "substantial authority" for the position exists. Types of authority upon which a taxpayer may rely include the Code and Regulations (including proposed and temporary Regulations), revenue rulings and procedures, court cases, congressional intent as reflected in committee reports, General Explanations of tax legislation prepared by the Joint Committee on Taxation (the "Blue Book"), and private letter rulings, technical advice memoranda and other statements of position issued by the IRS. On the other hand, conclusions reached in legal treatises, periodicals or opinions are not "authority." Reg. § 1.6662–4(d)(3)(iii).

Once the allowable sources of authority have been identified, the taxpayer then must determine whether the authority supporting his position is "substantial." According to the Regulations, "[t]here is substantial authority for the tax treatment of an item only if the weight of the authorities supporting the treatment is substantial in relation to the weight of authorities supporting contrary positions." Reg. § 1.6662–4(b). Furthermore, the taxpayer's jurisdiction is to be ignored: if the federal district court in the taxpayer's district has ruled favorably on the issue, this does not constitute substantial authority. Only if the Circuit Court of Appeals to which an appeal would lie has ruled in favor of the taxpayer's position will precedent in the taxpayer's jurisdiction constitute substantial authority. *Id.*

For "tax shelter" items, avoiding the penalty is even more difficult. The broad statutory definition of "tax shelter" can subject many items to the section 6662(d) tax shelter rules. "Tax shelter" for section 6662(d) purposes is defined to mean "a partnership or other entity, any investment plan or arrangement, or any other plan or arrangement, if the principal purpose of such partnership, entity, plan, or arrangement is the avoidance or evasion of Federal income tax." As discussed above, it is perfectly legal to plan or arrange to "avoid" income taxes, and a seemingly infinite number of actions or plans are designed to do exactly that. Nonetheless, if the plan or arrangement is principally motivated by a desire to decrease or avoid tax, then it is a "tax shelter" for purposes of section 6662(d).

In the case of an individual taxpayer, the substantial understatement penalty for "tax shelter" items may be avoided if there is substantial authority for the position and the taxpayer reasonably believed when he filed his return that the position taken was "more likely than not" the proper treatment of the item. Disclosure of the item on or with the return will not preclude the penalty. A taxpayer's belief that the position was "more likely than not" proper will be "reasonable" only if he performs the analysis required by the Regulations and concludes that there is a greater than 50% likelihood that his position will be upheld in litigation, or if he relies in good faith on the "unambiguous" opinion of a professional tax advisor that the chances are greater than 50% that the position would be upheld in litigation. In the case of a corporate taxpayer, the substantial authority and disclosure defenses are not available to avoid the substantial understatement penalty for a tax shelter item. Instead, a corporate taxpayer must demonstrate reasonable cause for the understatement and that it acted in good faith.

The Service may waive the penalty if the taxpayer shows that he acted in good faith and that there was reasonable cause for the understatement. I.R.C. § 6664(c). Under recently issued Regulations, a taxpayer's failure to disclose a reportable transaction is "strong indication that the taxpayer failed to act in good faith." Reg. § 1.6663–4(d). See discussion of reportable transactions, § 3.4.B, *supra*. In addition, the penalty will not be imposed if the taxpayer files an amended return either disclosing the item in question or showing additional tax due.

If there is an understatement attributable to a reportable or listed transaction that was not disclosed, the accuracy penalty increases to a rate of 30% for transactions in taxable years ending after October 22, 2004, unless the taxpayer can demonstrate reasonable cause and good faith. I.R.C. §§ 6662A; 6664(d).

C. *Valuation Penalties*

Individuals, closely held corporations, and personal service corporations are subject to penalty under section 6662 for underpayment of income tax based on inflated property valuations. Individual partners are subject to the penalty for overvaluations by partnerships. A similar penalty is imposed under section 6662 for understatements of estate or gift tax due to valuation understatements. The amount of the penalty depends on the degree of the valuation error.

The 20% penalty applies only to valuation overstatements of 200% or more. Section 6662(h) provides for a 40% penalty for "gross" valuation overstatements, defined as those exceeding 400% of the correct value or adjusted basis. Under section 6662, the penalty is to apply only if the underpayment attributable to the valuation overstatement exceeds $5,000 ($10,000 for corporate taxpayers).

For valuation understatements in connection with estate or gift tax, the threshold for imposition of the 20% penalty is a $5,000 underpayment. The uniform 20% penalty will apply to all valuation understatements except those representing only 25% of the correct amount. Such understatements are subject to the special 40% penalty of section 6662(g) for "gross" misstatements of value.

For substantial overstatements of pension liabilities, the uniform 20% (or 40% for "gross" misstatements) penalty of section 6662 will be imposed only if the overstatement exceeds 200% (150% under former law) of the correct amount. The threshold underpayment triggering the penalty is $1,000.

§ 10.3　Civil Fraud Penalty

Section 6663 imposes a penalty of 75% of the understatement of tax liability due to fraud. This penalty may not be combined with the accuracy penalty of 6662, and may be imposed only if a return was actually filed.

A. *Definition of "Fraud"*

Unlike section 6662, which defines the terms "negligence" and "disregard," section 6663 does not define "fraud." Courts have long recognized that the essence of fraud is the taxpayer's state of mind. Precisely what state of mind the Government must prove has been variously described, but most definitions require a motivation or intent to evade a known tax. According to the Tax Court, fraud is the intent "to evade taxes known to be due and owing by conduct intended to conceal, mislead, or otherwise [to] prevent the collection of taxes, [where] there is an underpayment of tax." Nelon v. Commissioner (Tax Ct.Memo.1997).

"Fraud" for purposes of the civil penalty under section 6663(b) is synonymous with tax evasion, the "willful attempt in any manner to evade or defeat any tax," under the criminal fraud provision, section 7201. In fact, prior to 1954 the civil fraud penalty was phrased in terms of "intent to evade tax," rather than the current "fraud." Moreover, the voluminous cases interpreting the term "willfully" under the tax criminal sections are instructive and applicable also in the definition of civil fraud. Both civil fraud and criminal evasion depend on the taxpayer's state of mind. To be liable for either the civil or criminal fraud penalty, the taxpayer must intend to evade a tax known to be due.

The existence of fraud is a question of fact to be determined by the entire record. By itself, an understatement of income, even if it is substantial, does not establish fraud. The Government must establish additional facts sufficient to convince the trier of fact that the taxpayer understated his income (or overstated his deductions) with the intent to evade tax. Over the years, many commentators and courts have compiled lists of "badges of fraud," based on the substantial body of case law. Typical situations in which the fraud penalty has been upheld include the following:

—taxpayer was convicted of criminal evasion under I.R.C. § 7201. Such a conviction will collaterally estop the taxpayer from challenging the civil fraud penalty;

—pattern of underreporting income (or overstating deductions) over several years;

—secret bank accounts or unexplained deposits;

—falsified or inadequate books and records;

—undisclosed sources of income from outside the taxpayer's regular business, including undisclosed illegal income;

—willful failure to file tax returns, coupled with some other indication of fraudulent intent;

—concealment of assets;

—dealings in cash.

Obviously, this list is not exhaustive, and other facts can support imposition of the fraud penalty.

Perhaps the most difficult issue in tax fraud litigation is the line between tax avoidance (which is legal) and tax evasion (which is illegal and will subject the taxpayer to possible civil and criminal penalties). Judges and scholars from Justice Holmes in a famous 1916 case to the present day have attempted to minimize the analytical problems involved by simply declaring the rule to be obvious: tax avoidance is the attempt to avoid taxes in a legal manner, while tax evasion (or fraud) is the attempt to evade taxes in an illegal fashion. In practice, though, the distinction is not easily drawn.

In the absence of a fairly clear "badge of fraud," such as a failure to file returns or falsification of books and records, it is difficult to predict whether a taxpayer's conduct will subject him to prosecution for criminal evasion, or instead to imposition of the civil fraud penalty or the less severe negligence penalty. According to the Internal Revenue Manual:

The major difference between civil and criminal fraud is the degree of proof required to establish fraud on the part of the taxpayer. Criminal fraud requires sufficient evidence to prove guilt beyond a reasonable doubt. Civil fraud requires clear and convincing evidence of tax evasion. The civil fraud penalty may be imposed upon a taxpayer whose criminal case verdict was not guilty. If the taxpayer has been convicted of criminal tax evasion under IRC section 7201, the civil fraud penalty should be asserted for the same tax year. However, the criminal case conviction does not mean the civil penalty will be automatically sustained. [IRM § 20.1.5.12.5]

The IRS itself sometimes misjudges completely whether a given situation warrants prosecution or the imposition of the fraud penalty. *See, e.g.,* Estate of Spruill v. Commissioner (Tax Ct.1987) (valuation dispute; IRS had sought criminal prosecution, but Justice Department declined to prosecute; Tax Court refused to uphold civil fraud penalty).

Generally, if it appears that the taxpayer honestly believes that his position is allowable under the Code, the taxpayer should not be subject to the civil fraud penalty, even if his position is not upheld. This is because the taxpayer lacks the intent to evade a tax believed to be owing, which is the essence of fraud. On the other hand, where the position or scheme is so clearly contrary to existing authority that the taxpayer's claim of good faith belief is not credible, then the fraud penalty probably will be upheld, particularly if the taxpayer attempted to conceal or misrepresent his actions. Among other important factors, the taxpayer's education and profession will influence the court. For example, an experienced tax attorney whose return contains a position that is clearly contrary to existing authority is much more likely to be subject to the civil fraud penalty than is a person without such education and experience. Again, the key is the particular taxpayer's state of mind and intent. Knowledge of the intricacies of the tax laws can render incredible a taxpayer's claim that he honestly and in good faith believed he was complying with the Code when he takes a highly questionable or clearly erroneous position on his return.

Defense considerations should begin with the proposition that even gross negligence is not fraud. Thus, ignorance of the law or incompetence in keeping books and records generally does not constitute fraud. Similarly, mental or physical illness can vitiate the fraud penalty, as can good faith reliance on an attorney or other tax advisor after full disclosure of relevant facts. For a more detailed discussion of the state of mind requirements for fraud, see Chapter 18, § 18.1.A.(1), *infra*, concerning the "willfulness" requirements of the criminal tax sections and common defenses predicated on the absence of willfulness.

B. Burden of Proof

The Government bears the burden of proving fraud by "clear and convincing evidence." Although I.R.C. § 7454(a) is frequently cited as the source of this standard, neither the statute nor its legislative history recite the clear and convincing evidence standard. Nonetheless, this standard has been applied at least since 1939. The Commissioner can satisfy this burden by showing that the taxpayer intended to evade taxes known to be due by conduct designed to mislead, conceal or otherwise prevent collection of the tax. Once the Commissioner has proved that any portion of an underpayment of tax is attributable to fraud, the entire underpayment is treated as due to fraud and the burden shifts to the taxpayer to establish (by a preponderance of the evidence) that any portion of the underpayment is not attributable to fraud. I.R.C. § 6663(b).

Can a taxpayer thwart the Commissioner's imposition of the fraud penalty by filing a Tax Court petition challenging the asserted deficiency and the fraud penalty, and then simply failing to appear at trial? The Tax Court, in a reviewed decision with five dissents, held that in such a case, if the Government's specific allegations of fact, taken to be true by the taxpayer's default, are sufficient to establish fraud, then the fraud penalty will be sustained. Smith v. Commissioner, (Tax Ct.1988) (reviewed).

C. Statute of Limitations

As discussed in § 7.2.D, *supra*, there is no time limit on assessing tax deficiencies (and the civil fraud penalty) when the return is fraudulent. I.R.C. § 6501(c)(1). If any portion of any return is fraudulent, both a tax deficiency and the fraud penalty may be assessed at any time. This is true even though the taxpayer later repents (or simply gets cold feet) and files a nonfraudulent amended return for the year. Badaracco v. Commissioner (S.Ct.1984) (discussed in § 7.2.D., *supra*). On the other hand, if the Commissioner asserts the fraud penalty after the normal 3–year statute of limitations has expired, and the court refuses to uphold the fraud penalty, then the asserted tax deficiency (as well as the penalty) will be time-barred.

D. *Persons Liable for the Penalty*

Common relationships that could give rise to liability for the fraud penalty by someone other than the taxpayer himself include spouses, shareholders and corporations, partners and partnerships, executors and estates, and trustees and trusts. In the case of spouses filing joint returns, the fraud of one spouse may not be imputed to the other spouse. I.R.C. § 6663(c). If the spouses file separate returns, fraud by one certainly should not be attributed to the other, absent knowledge of and participation in the fraud.

In the case of closely-held corporations, it may be difficult to distinguish between the personal benefit sought by the owner-officer and the benefit to the corporation resulting from a fraudulent return. In such situations, should the penalty be asserted against the corporation (the "taxpayer"), or against the controlling shareholder, or both? Generally, the acts of a corporate officer can be imputed to the officer's "principal," the corporation. Thus, it is no defense for the corporation against which a civil fraud penalty has been asserted to claim that it is not responsible for the officer's actions, particularly when the officer is a controlling shareholder and the corporation received a benefit (lower tax liability) as a result of the officer's actions. However, if it can be shown that the corporation did not benefit from the officer's conduct, and that the officer was acting principally to benefit himself, then the officer's fraud should not be imputed to the corporation. For example, some courts have held that the fraud penalty should not be sustained against the corporation if the officer who prepared the return has embezzled corporate funds and attempted to conceal his embezzlement by preparing and signing false corporate returns.

Similarly, where partners in a general partnership participate in fraudulent reporting, the fraud penalty can be upheld against the partners. The partnership would not be liable for the fraud penalty, as partnership returns are informational only. For example, in a law partnership, if the partners each know of and acquiesce in underreporting of income (or overstatement of expenses), each partner can be held liable individually for the civil fraud penalty. To hold otherwise would ignore the fact that partnerships are not recognized as legal entities for purposes of the federal income tax system. Instead, they are treated as "conduits" whose income and deductions flow through directly to the partners.

A deceased taxpayer who filed a fraudulent return during his lifetime will not be relieved of the tax fraud penalty by his death. The civil fraud penalty may be asserted against his estate, since the civil fraud penalty is an "addition to tax," and thus is remedial rather than penal in nature. Simply stated, the civil fraud penalty survives the death of the taxpayer.

Likewise, the civil fraud penalty survives the bankruptcy of the taxpayer. Exceptions exist, and both the Bankruptcy Code and cases under section 6663(b) should be consulted in cases of bankruptcy.

E.   Collateral Estoppel

If a taxpayer has been convicted of a tax crime, such as willful failure to file a return or willful attempt to evade taxes, can he successfully defend an assessment of civil tax penalties relating to the same actions? In some circumstances, the doctrine of collateral estoppel will prevent the taxpayer from contesting the civil penalty. Although it might at first seem that any criminal conviction should be a sufficient basis for automatic civil penalties, the same principle concerning the nature of the issue decided in the criminal case will determine whether the taxpayer is collaterally estopped in the civil penalty action.

For many years the Government succeeded in collaterally estopping taxpayers from denying that tax underpayments were due to fraud when the taxpayers had been convicted of willfully failing to file returns under I.R.C. § 7203 or filing returns containing false statements under I.R.C. § 7206(1). But courts now have recognized that the elements of civil fraud under I.R.C. § 6653(b) are not identical to the issues involved in section 7203 or 7206(1) prosecutions, and have held that such convictions do not collaterally estop taxpayers from contesting the civil fraud penalty. Kotmair v. Commissioner (Tax Ct.1986) (conviction under section 7203 does not bar taxpayer from contesting civil fraud penalty); Wright v. Commissioner (Tax Ct.1985) (reviewed) (section 7206(1) conviction does not collaterally estop challenge to civil fraud penalty). Where the elements of the offense are identical, however, the taxpayer is estopped to challenge the civil penalty. Thus, conviction under section 7201, involving a willful attempt to defeat or evade tax, will collaterally estop denial of the fraud in a civil fraud case, since the elements of civil fraud (see I.R.C. § 6663(b) and discussion, § 10.3.A, *supra*) are identical to the necessary elements of criminal fraud (or attempted evasion) as contained in section 7201.

Because conviction of a criminal charge involving the same issues as the civil penalty can collaterally estop the taxpayer from challenging the civil penalty, it would seem that acquittal of the criminal charge would exonerate the taxpayer from the civil penalties. This is not the rule, however, for the reason that acquittal means nothing more than that the Government failed to meet its elevated standard of proof ("guilt beyond a reasonable doubt") in the criminal case. In civil fraud cases, the standard of proof the Government must satisfy is the more lenient "clear and convincing evidence" test. Significantly, a plea of *nolo contendere* to a criminal fraud charge does not bar the taxpayer from contesting a civil fraud penalty. *See, e.g.*, Mickler v. Fahs (5th Cir.1957) (going even further and forbidding use of taxpayer's plea of *nolo contendere* to impeach taxpayer).

§ 10.4   Frivolous Returns

Section 6702 authorizes the Service to impose a $500 penalty on anyone who files a return that does not contain sufficient information on which the correctness of the tax liability can be judged or that contains information that on its face indicates that the tax liability shown on the return is incorrect. For the penalty to be imposed, the taxpayer's conduct must be based on a frivolous position or a desire to delay or impede the administration of the tax laws. This penalty, which is clearly aimed at "tax protestors," is to be imposed in addition to other penalties. Moreover, it can be imposed even if the taxpayer does not have any tax liability.

§ 10.5   Failure to Make Timely Deposits of Tax

Under pre–1990 law, failure by an employer to make timely deposit of taxes withheld from employees' wages subjected the employer to a penalty equal to 10% of the underpayment, unless the underpayment was due to reasonable cause and not to willful neglect. IMPACT amended section 6656 to provide a four-tiered penalty, with the amount of the penalty increasing as the length of the delinquency increases. The purpose of the change is to provide an incentive to employers to correct any underpayments as quickly as possible.

For deposits of taxes required to be made after December 31, 1989, the section 6656 penalty is as follows: 2% of the underpayment if full payment is made within 5 days of the due date; 5% of the underpayment if full payment is made within 6 to 15 days of the due date; 10% of the underpayment if the delinquency continues more than 15 days after the due date, but full payment is made within 10 days of the first delinquency notice sent to the taxpayer under section 6303; and 15% of the underpayment if full payment is not made within 10 days after the first delinquency notice. Congress believed that the single 10% penalty under former law was too harsh for depositors who corrected their delinquencies quickly, but not harsh enough for depositors whose delinquencies continued more than 10 days after the date of the first delinquency notice. As was true under pre–1990 law, no penalty is to be imposed under section 6656 if the delinquency is due to reasonable cause and not to willful neglect.

§ 10.6 Failure To Make Timely Estimated Tax Payments

Self-employed taxpayers and those who derive income not subject to withholding are responsible for estimating the amount of tax liability that will be due and making estimated tax payments to cover this amount. Estimated tax payments for calendar year taxpayers are due by April 15, June 15, September 15 and the following January 15. Thus, when the return is due, the tax liability should have been paid in full or substantially paid. If the tax liability is underpaid, an estimated tax penalty will be imposed under section 6654 (section 6655 for corporate taxpayers). This penalty may be avoided if the taxpayer's total combined annual tax payments from all sources (withholding, estimated payments, and any amounts credited from the previous year's refund) are equal to the lesser of (1) 90 percent of the tax due or (2) 100 percent of the tax shown on the return for the preceding taxable year (110 percent for taxable years 2003 and after if the taxpayer's adjusted gross income exceeds $150,000 ($75,000 for married taxpayers filing separately)). Also, no estimated tax penalty will apply if the tax owed (reduced by payments made during the taxable year, including withholding) is less than $1,000.

Taxes collected through withholding are applied evenly to the 4 installments unless the taxpayer elects to have the amount credited to the period in which it is actually withheld. An underpayment of estimated tax in any of the quarters is considered a separate infraction of the revenue laws for that quarter. Any overpayment of tax may be credited against the following year's estimated tax.

The amount of the penalty is equal to the amount of interest that would be payable on the underpayment. See discussion of interest on underpayments in § 10.8, *infra*. The amount of the underpayment is the excess of the amount of the required installment over the amount (if any) of the installment paid on or before the due date. The penalty runs from the installment due date to the earlier of (1) the date a payment (or portion of a payment) is received or (2) the 15th day of the 4th month following the close of the taxable year. I.R.C. § 6654(b)(2). The reasonable cause defense applies only to a very limited extent, although the Service may grant a waiver of the penalty if it determines that it would be equitable to do so.

§ 10.7 Abatement of Penalties and Other Additions To Tax

Under section 6404 of the Code, the Service must abate (1) interest on erroneous refunds of less than $50,000 until the date the Service demands repayment; (2) penalties or additions to tax attributable to erroneous written advice furnished by IRS personnel in an official capacity in response to a specific, written request by the taxpayer; and (3) penalties or additions to tax attributable to the failure of the IRS to notify the taxpayer of the deficiency and additions within 18 months of the later of the original due date of the return (without regard to extensions) or the date a timely return is filed. The Service has discretion to abate penalties and other additions to tax attributable to (1) a mathematical error made by an IRS employee in assisting a taxpayer with the preparation of his return; (2) unreasonable errors and delays by IRS employees in performing a ministerial or managerial act that occurs through no fault of the taxpayer; and (3) where the amount in question is too small to warrant administration and collection costs.

An abatement is not binding on the Service and conveys no rights to the taxpayer. The Tax Court has jurisdiction to review a denial of a request for abatement.

§ 10.8   Interest on Deficiencies and Overpayments

The Government must pay interest to taxpayers who have overpaid their taxes, and taxpayers must pay interest to the Government for underpayments (deficiencies) of taxes. The principle is simple: the Government must compensate the taxpayer for its use of his money, and the taxpayer similarly must compensate the Government for his use of its funds. From 1987 to 1998, however, the interest rates taxpayers had to pay to the Government were higher than the rate the Government paid to taxpayers.

A.   *Interest on Deficiencies*

Interest on a tax deficiency begins to accrue on the due date of the tax return. If civil penalties are assessed, the taxpayer also must pay interest on the penalties. Interest on the negligence and fraud penalties, the substantial understatement penalty (§ 6662(d)), the valuation penalties, and the delinquent filing penalty begins to accrue on the due date of the return. I.R.C. § 6601(e)(2)(B).

The interest rate for underpayments is the short-term Federal rate plus 3 percentage points (2 percentage points for corporations), adjusted quarterly. I.R.C. § 6621(a)(2). Thus, for example, if the short-term Federal rate is 3%, the interest rate applicable to underpayments would be 6%. Rates are determined in the first month of each calendar quarter, to become effective the first day of the next calendar quarter. I.R.C. § 6621(b).

B. Interest on Overpayments

Interest on overpaid taxes begins to accrue on the date of overpayment. I.R.C. § 6611(b). The date of overpayment for taxes withheld from wages or for estimated taxes is the date the return is due. I.R.C. § 6611(d). Thus, if in 2002 a taxpayer's employer withheld $10,000 in federal income taxes, and on March 1, 2003 the taxpayer filed a return showing a total tax liability of $8,000, interest on the $2,000 overpayment would begin to accrue on April 15, 2003 (the due date of the return). If the Government refunds the overpayment within 45 days of the date the return is due, however, no interest is payable. I.R.C. § 6611(e).

Prior to 1999, the interest rate the Government was required to pay on overpayments of tax (the short-term Federal rate plus 2 percentage points) was lower than the rate the taxpayer was required to pay on deficiencies (the short-term Federal rate plus 3 percentage points). I.R.C. § 6621(a)(1) and (2). For post–1998 overpayments, however, the interest rate is the same as for underpayments—the short-term Federal rate plus 3 percentage points. I.R.C. § 6621(a)(1)(B).

C. Netting of Overpayments and Underpayments

If the taxpayer has overpaid for one taxable year and underpaid for another, the taxpayer and the government will be mutually indebted to one another. Under § 6621(d), there is no interest owed (net rate will be zero) on equal amounts of overpayment and underpayment that run simultaneously, provided none of the years in question is barred by the statute of limitations. This applies to any taxpayer and to any tax, whether from the same taxable year or different taxable years. Thus an overpayment of excise tax may be netted against an income tax deficiency. This broad offset is called "global netting."

CHAPTER 11

THE COLLECTION PROCESS

Before discussing the process of assessment and collection, it is helpful to review how a tax dispute can lead to a situation in which the Government can seize a taxpayer's property and potentially ruin his credit by filing notice of a federal tax lien. Recall from the discussion in Chapter 7 that a tax generally must be assessed within three years after the return is filed. Remember also that the issuance of the statutory notice of deficiency (the 90–day letter) tolls the statute of limitations on assessment and begins the 90–day period during which the taxpayer must either pay the tax or file a Tax Court petition for redetermination of the deficiency. If the taxpayer does neither (that is, he neither pays the tax nor files a Tax Court petition), then the IRS may assess the tax after the 90–day period has expired, but it must do so before the statute of limitations on assessment (generally three years from the date the return was filed) has expired. If the taxpayer files a Tax Court petition and litigates the dispute and loses, the tax may be assessed 60 days after the judgment becomes final, although the taxpayer may postpone the assessment by posting a bond and filing an appeal. Finally, if a return is filed acknowledging tax liability but full payment is not made, the tax can be assessed promptly after the IRS receives the return.

If the taxpayer loses a civil or criminal fraud case, the taxpayer also may make the acquaintance of the Area Collection Division. In civil fraud cases, there is no time limit on assessing the tax (I.R.C. § 6501(c)) or the civil penalty. Moreover, a taxpayer who has been convicted of tax evasion is certain to face assessment of tax and civil penalties at a time when he may be least able to pay.

§ 11.1   Assessment, Notice and Demand

As discussed in Chapter 7, an assessment of tax is merely the recording of the liability of the taxpayer on an official list. I.R.C. § 6203. The date that this tax is recorded is the date of assessment, and it triggers two new statutes of limitations: the Government has 60 days from the date of assessment in which to notify the taxpayer of the assessment and demand payment, and it has ten years from the date of assessment in which to collect the tax.

The Government may not begin enforced collection activities unless and until it has notified the taxpayer of the assessment and demanded payment. The Code directs the IRS to make the notice and demand "as soon as practicable" and in no event later than 60 days after the date of assessment. I.R.C. § 6303(a). The notice is to be delivered to the taxpayer's residence or his usual place of business, or mailed to his "last known address." (See § 7.1.A, *supra*, for a discussion of § 6212(b) and the "last known address"—the same principles apply in the notice and demand context.) The taxpayer usually is given ten days from the date of the notice and demand in which to pay the tax. In practice, the grace period usually is much longer than ten days because IRS computers are programmed to send a series of notices at intervals of three to five weeks warning the taxpayer that if payment is not made a Notice of Federal Tax Lien may be filed and there may be a levy made against the taxpayer's bank accounts, wages and other property.

While the IRS usually sends a notice and demand within 60 days after an assessment, occasionally it does not. If it fails to comply with § 6303, Reg. § 301.6303–1 provides that the assessment is not invalidated. The majority of courts to consider the issue agree but also have held that the IRS may not use the summary collection process (see § 11.2, *infra*). Instead, it must enforce its claim judicially. See § 11.3, *infra*. It is unclear, however, whether the right to use the summary collection process may be revived if the IRS ultimately sends a notice and demand. *See* Blackston v. United States (D. Md.1991) (holding that the government must use the judicial collection process).

§ 11.2   The Federal Tax Lien

A.   *Creation and Validity*

If the taxpayer neglects or refuses to pay the tax within the ten-day grace period, a general assessment lien (usually called a "general tax lien" or "federal tax lien") arises automatically at the time of assessment against "all property and rights to property, whether real or personal." This lien attaches to all property belonging to the taxpayer as of the date of assessment or subsequently acquired by the taxpayer during the existence of the lien. I.R.C. §§ 6321, 6322. The effect of the general tax lien is dramatic: once it arises, no further action is required before the Government can seize the taxpayer's property by levy.

The general tax lien is the foundation of the entire collection process. It is critical, therefore, that the IRS strictly comply with the statutory prerequisites: timely assessment, timely notice and demand, and the passage of the ten-day grace period prior to enforced collection activities. If any of the three prerequisites has not been met, the lien does not arise by operation of law and the taxpayer can bring a suit to enjoin collection. I.R.C. § 6213(a). The mere existence of the lien does not transfer title or constructive possession of the taxpayer's property to the Government, however. Instead, the IRS must either levy against the property, or bring a civil action to collect the tax.

B.   *Scope of the Lien*

The tax lien attaches to all property or rights to property, whether real or personal, tangible or intangible, belonging to the taxpayer on the date of assessment or acquired after assessment but during the existence of the lien. State law governs the nature and extent of a taxpayer's interest in property, although the federal tax lien is not affected or limited by state law provisions exempting certain property from creditors' claims. For example, although state law may provide a homestead exemption making one's home immune from creditors' claims, the taxpayer's home is subject to the federal tax lien and can be seized and sold to satisfy the tax debt.

In fact, the Supreme Court has held that a state homestead exemption does not protect from sale a home owned and occupied by a widow, even though she was not responsible for any of the taxes owed by her deceased husband, who owned an interest in the home prior to his death. United States v. Rodgers (S.Ct.1983). Thus, although the widowed Mrs. Rodgers did not owe any federal taxes, and although state law provided a homestead exemption, the Court held that the home, in which she and her children were living, could be ordered sold by a court in a proceeding brought by the Government under section 7403. Section 7403 permits a court to order property subject to a federal tax lien to be sold to satisfy the tax debt. According to the Supreme Court, section 7403 empowers the court to order that the entire property be sold, not just the delinquent taxpayer's interest in the property. After the property is sold, the nondelinquent spouse is entitled to complete compensation (from the sale proceeds) for the loss of her homestead estate. A judicial determination that certain property is subject to a federal tax lien, however, does not require the court to order a forced sale under section 7403. The *Rodgers* Court stated that courts have limited discretion to refuse to order a sale, and it remanded the case to the lower court to consider four factors in balancing the competing interests of the Government and the nondelinquent spouse.

In 1998 Congress addressed the *Rodgers* situation in the Taxpayer Bill of Rights Act 3 by amending section 6334(a)(13) (exemptions from levy). Under the 1998 amendment no seizure of a dwelling that is the principal residence of the taxpayer, the taxpayer's spouse or minor child is allowed without prior judicial approval. In addition, if the IRS intends to seek judicial approval to levy on the home, it must provide notice of the judicial hearing to the taxpayer and family members residing there. At the hearing, the IRS must demonstrate that all legal requirements pertaining to the levy have been met, the tax liability is owed, and there is no reasonable alternative for the collection of the tax debt. The 1998 amendment is effective for collection actions initiated more than 180 days after July 22, 1998, the date of enactment.

Obviously, the scope of the federal tax lien is very broad. It literally covers all types of property or rights to property of the delinquent taxpayer, regardless of where the property is located or who currently possesses the property, unless the property is specifically exempted from coverage. *See* United States v. Craft (S.Ct.2002) (allowing seizure of property held in a tenancy by the entirety).

C.   *Duration of the Lien*

The tax lien continues in existence until the tax liability is satisfied or "becomes unenforceable by reason of lapse of time." I.R.C. § 6322. The period of the lien is linked to section 6502 of the Code, which provides that the IRS must either levy on the taxpayer's property, or bring a civil action to collect the tax, within ten years after the date the tax is assessed. This ten-year period may be extended by agreement between the taxpayer and the IRS.

D. Notice of the Lien—Due Process Rights

Filing a notice of a tax lien can have a devastating impact on the taxpayer. Many taxpayers must borrow funds to pay their tax debts, and filing a notice of the lien may hamper the taxpayer's ability to obtain the necessary funds. Congressional hearings in 1997 and 1998 focused in part on tax liens filed erroneously, and the problems caused by such errors. Congress addressed these concerns in its 1998 enactment of Taxpayer Bill of Rights Act 3, which contains provisions providing "due process" in the collection process. For collection activities initiated more than 180 days after the date of enactment of TBOR 3 (July 22, 1998), the IRS must follow formal procedures giving the taxpayer notice and hearing rights in connection with the filing of a notice of a federal tax lien or an intent to levy on such a lien. See § 11.3.B *infra*, for a discussion of the administrative levy.

New Code sections 6320 and 6330 establish the new due process procedures. Both sections recite that, "[t]o the extent practicable, a hearing under this section shall be held in conjunction with a hearing under [the other] section." This means that the IRS should give the taxpayer written notices of both its filing of the lien and its intent to levy on it. The notice of filing of the lien must be given to the taxpayer within five business days of the filing, and the notice of intent to levy must be given not less than 30 days before levy. IRC §§ 6320(a)(1), 6330(a)(1). In both cases, notice may be given in person, or left at the taxpayer's dwelling or usual place of business, or sent by certified or registered mail to the taxpayer's last known address. I.R.C. § 6330(a)(2).

Notices under both sections must state the amount of the unpaid tax and inform the taxpayer of the right to request a hearing within 30 days. Lien notices also must describe the administrative appeals process and the procedures relating to the release of liens. Levy notices must describe the IRS's proposed actions and the taxpayer's rights. If the taxpayer requests a hearing, the hearing will be conducted by an Appeals officer not previously involved with the taxpayer's case. Timely request for a hearing postpones any collection activities until the Appeals officer issues a determination. At the hearing the taxpayer may raise "any relevant issue relating to the unpaid tax or the proposed levy," including such matters as request for innocent spouse relief or for an offer in compromise or installment agreement. IRC § 6330(c). The Appeals officer's determination must include consideration of "whether any proposed collection action balances the need for efficient collection of taxes with the legitimate concern of the person that any collection action be no more intrusive than necessary." *Id.*

If the decision of the Appeals officer is adverse to the taxpayer, the taxpayer may seek judicial review by filing a Tax Court petition (or in a district court, if the Tax Court lacks jurisdiction over the underlying tax liability) within 30 days of the Appeals officer's decision. Collection activities continue to be suspended if the taxpayer files a timely request for judicial review.

E.   *Priority of Claims*

The priority of a federal tax lien is governed by Code sections 6321–6323, as well as by provisions in the Bankruptcy Code. The general rule is "first-in-time-is-first-in-right," so a non-tax lien that is perfected prior to a federal tax lien would have priority over the tax lien. The federal tax lien arises automatically and attaches to the taxpayer's property without having to be filed. But the priority of the lien depends upon whether and when the Service has filed a notice of its lien. If the notice has not been filed, the tax lien is invalid against judgment creditors, purchasers from the taxpayer, and holders of mechanics liens or security interests. I.R.C. § 6323(a). If the notice has been filed, the tax lien takes priority over subsequently perfected security interests or liens under the general rule. But there are some exceptions to the general rule. First, if the earlier filed non-tax lien is "inchoate," the later federal tax lien takes priority over the non-tax lien. A lien is inchoate if it is indefinite as to the property subject to the lien, the amount of the lien, or the lienor. An example of an inchoate lien is a prejudgment attachment lien. Until a judgment determines the amount of the lien and the property subject to the lien, the prejudgment attachment lien is merely an "unperfected, inchoate interest in the property." United States v. Dishman Independent Oil, Inc. (6th Cir.1995). Second, there are ten categories of liens listed at section 6323(b) that will take priority over a prior tax lien. These are referred to as "superpriorities." They include mortgagees and purchasers of motor vehicles without notice of the federal tax lien, as well as purchasers of property at retail and casual purchasers of household property. The 10 superpriorities identified in section 6323(b) afford protection (or priority) to the listed interests, regardless of whether the interest arises after the federal tax lien is recorded.

In addition, special rules may apply to insolvent taxpayers. If the taxpayer has declared bankruptcy, the priority of competing claims is determined under the Bankruptcy Code instead of under the federal tax provisions. If the taxpayer is insolvent but has not declared bankruptcy, claims of the government may receive special priority under the Federal Insolvency Statute (31 U.S.C. § 3713). This statute provides that claims of the federal government are entitled to priority when (1) an insolvent debtor transfers property in a collective creditor proceeding outside of bankruptcy and (2) when the estate of a deceased debtor has insufficient assets to pay the claims of all creditors. Thus, when an insolvent debtor dies, commits an act of bankruptcy, or voluntarily assigns property, the Federal Insolvency Statute provides that the government shall be paid first. But does the Federal Insolvency Statute take priority over the Federal Tax Lien Act (FTLA) (I.R.C. § 6323)?

In the case of *United States v. Estate of Romani* (S.Ct.1998), the issue was whether the Federal Insolvency Statute applied to grant priority to a later-filed tax lien over an earlier judgment lien perfected under state law. Under the FTLA, the judgment lien clearly had priority because it was a choate lien that had been perfected before the notice of tax lien was filed. The question was whether the FTLA trumped the Federal Insolvency Statute. The U.S. Supreme Court held that the FTLA had priority over the Federal Insolvency Statute because the FTLA was the later enacted statute. The Court also noted Congress's "strong condemnation of secret liens," a policy that would be frustrated if the Federal Insolvency Statute took priority over the FTLA.

Although the *Romani* decision left the government's priority under the Federal Insolvency Statute in doubt, the Seventh Circuit in *Straus v. United States* (7th Cir.1999) declined to read *Romani* so broadly and instead held that "a general federal priority rule should give way to a specific, inconsistent provision in a later federal statute." *Id.* at 865–66. Thus, the Federal Insolvency Statute applies to give the government priority unless a creditor with a competing claim can establish that there is "a specific, inconsistent provision in a later federal statute."

F. Releasing the Lien

The Code requires the IRS to release a federal tax lien promptly when the underlying tax has been paid, or has been bonded or becomes uncollectible. I.R.C. § 6325. Prior to the passage of the Taxpayer Bill of Rights Act in 1988, the Code provided no means of compelling the IRS to comply with the statutory rules governing release of liens. For damages arising after 1988, Code section 7432 permits a taxpayer to obtain damages for the improper failure by the IRS to issue a certificate evidencing the release of the lien. Section 6325 requires the Service to issue such a certificate within 30 days after it determines that the tax has been paid, bonded or become uncollectible. Section 7432 authorizes civil damages (with no upper limit on the amount recoverable) for the Service's negligent or knowing failure to comply with section 6325. The measure of damages is the "actual, direct economic damages sustained," plus "the costs of the action," less any amount by which the taxpayer could reasonably have mitigated the damages.

The Taxpayer Bill of Rights Act of 1988 also added new Code section 6326, which provides for administrative appeal of erroneously recorded liens. As under prior law, the IRS is not required to notify a taxpayer of its intent to record a tax lien, so the damage to the innocent person caused by the filing of the lien cannot be avoided. Section 6326 requires the Service to release a lien that was filed erroneously within 14 days and to issue a certificate of release of lien that contains a statement that the lien was filed erroneously. Apparently, damages under section 7432 are not available, since section 7432 permits recovery only for failure to release liens as required by section 6325. However, damages presumably could be recovered under new section 7433, discussed in section 11.3.E, below.

§ 11.3 Judicial and Administrative Collection Procedures

Because delinquent taxes are a debt owed to the Government, the United States may bring any type of civil action available to other creditors. In addition, the Code gives the IRS the power to collect delinquent taxes by administrative levy, and it also provides special rules for civil suits involving tax liens. The existence of a valid tax lien is a prerequisite to all of the enforced collection methods.

A. *Government Suits Involving Tax Liens*

The types of civil actions the Government may bring to collect taxes are limited only by the Constitution. This is because the grant of jurisdiction to the United States District Courts is broad, as exemplified by the power granted under the All–Writs statute at section 7402(a) of the Code, "to make and issue in civil actions, writs and orders of injunction, and of *ne exeat republica*, orders appointing receivers, and such other orders as may be necessary and appropriate for the enforcement of the internal revenue laws." The writ of *ne exeat republica*, mentioned in the statutory language, prohibits a taxpayer from leaving the country. Other types of civil actions include suits to foreclose the federal tax lien, suits to reduce the tax assessment to judgment, actions to open safe-deposit boxes or to enter the taxpayer's property to seize property to satisfy the tax debt (conducted *ex parte*, with the taxpayer having no right to intervene), actions for the appointment of a receiver, and intervention by the Government in a civil action involving property subject to the federal tax lien that is the subject of the civil action.

Why would the Government ever file a civil suit to reduce the tax assessment to a judgment instead of using the summary collection process? The answer is that when the statute of limitations is about to expire, and it does not appear that the full tax can be collected through the administrative levy device, such a suit can be instituted to preserve the Government's right to collect the tax.

Similarly, a suit to foreclose a tax lien is usually brought when administrative levy is inconvenient or impossible, often because title to the property is disputed or there are multiple claims to funds the Government is seeking to seize. Such suits are actions *in rem*, and all persons claiming an interest in the property must be made parties. I.R.C. § 7403(b). An example of this type of suit is found in *United States v. Rodgers*, discussed in § 11.2.B, *supra*. In that case the Supreme Court held that a district court could order the sale of property sub-

ject to a federal tax lien, even though an innocent
third party also held an interest in the property.
The innocent third party was to be compensated
from the sale proceeds, however, for the loss of her
interest.

B. Levy

The federal tax lien is not self-executing, so the
IRS must enforce it either through a civil action or
an administrative levy. The normal method of enforced collection is through levy and sale. Section
6331 authorizes the Service to levy on all the taxpayer's property (or rights to property), except for
certain property exempted under section 6634.
Third parties who possess or control property on
which a levy has been made are obligated to surrender the property to the Government on demand.
I.R.C. § 6332. If the third party complies, she is
discharged of all liability to the taxpayer with respect to the property. If she refuses to comply, she
becomes personally liable for the lesser of the value
of the property or the amount of the tax liability,
and is subject to a penalty of 50% of the amount
recoverable (that is, 50% of the lesser of the tax
liability or the value of the property that she refused to relinquish to the Service). Also, the Sixth
Circuit has held that the ten-year statute of limitations that normally applies to collection actions does
not apply to third parties who refuse to honor a
notice of levy. Thus, there is no statute of limitations for collecting property from a third party who
refuses to surrender the property after receiving a

notice of levy. United States v. Weintraub (6th Cir.1979).

Although all property and rights to property of the taxpayer are subject to the federal tax lien, certain property is exempted from levy under section 6334. This section was amended by the Taxpayer Bill of Rights Acts of 1988, 1996 and 1998 to increase the types and value of exempt property. The following types of property (among others) are exempt: wearing apparel and school books; fuel, furniture, provisions and personal effects not exceeding $6,250 in value; weekly wages equal to the sum of the taxpayer's standard deduction plus his personal exemptions for the year divided by 52; certain public assistance payments; the taxpayer's principal residence, except when the IRS believes that collection of the tax is in jeopardy or when approved in writing by a federal judge. Other classes and types of property exempt from the levy are listed in section 6334.

Levy may be made at any time after the federal tax lien arises and before the statute of limitations on collection has expired. Recall that the tax lien arises when the following three events have occurred: the tax has been assessed, the Service has given notice of the assessment and demanded payment, and the ten-day grace period has passed, during which the taxpayer has neglected or refused to pay the tax. The Code section that authorizes levy, section 6331, states generally that levy "includes the power of distraint and seizure by any means." The absence of statutory restrictions on this broad power has led to many tales of abuse. This, in turn, has led Congress to amend the levy provisions in the Taxpayer Bill of Rights Acts to eliminate some of the problems.

Because the federal tax lien arises automatically, it is only fair that the IRS notify the taxpayer prior to levying against his property. Prior to the passage of the Taxpayer Bill of Rights Act of 1988, the Service was required to notify the taxpayer ten days before it levied. For post–1989 levies, the taxpayer had to be given 30 days advance notice. Post–1998 levies may be made only after the due process rules of section 6330 are followed. See § 11.2.D, *supra*, for a discussion of the due process rules. In 1996 Congress added section 7524, which requires the IRS to send taxpayers an annual reminder notice of their outstanding tax liabilities.

How the levy is made depends on the type of property involved. Tangible personal property may be physically seized, although entry into a taxpayer's home or business premises to seize property is prohibited without an appropriate court order. An automobile parked on public property (such as a street) may simply be towed away. Property held by third parties may be seized by serving notice of levy on the third party. For example, levy on bank accounts and safe deposit boxes is accomplished by serving notice of levy on the bank, and salary or wages can be seized (subject to the limitations for the exempt amount of wages discussed above) by serving notice of levy on the employer.

The effect of the levy is to transfer the taxpayer's interest in the property to the IRS and to give the IRS full legal right to the property seized. For property in the hands of third parties, the notice of levy creates a custodial relationship between the holder or custodian of the property and the IRS. Because the tax lien can attach only to the taxpayer's interest in the property, it follows that seizure of property can vest in the Government only the rights that the taxpayer had in the property. Thus, when seized property is sold, it is possible that the buyer will have less than perfect title to the property. For this reason, buyers purchasing at tax sales prefer to purchase property that is sold after an IRS civil action in which title to the property is settled.

One troubling question is whether funds held in a joint bank account may be seized by levy when only one of the co-owners is liable for delinquent taxes. This question can be of enormous practical significance to many people, including spouses and business co-owners, because the bank or financial institution is required to "freeze" the levied account for 21 days following receipt of the notice of levy. Thus, even if the levy is erroneous, funds of innocent parties will be tied up for at least 21 days. If the matter is not settled prior to the end of the 21–day period (usually by the payment of the delinquent tax), the bank must turn over to the IRS all the funds in the account. The Supreme Court held in 1985 that the Service can levy on joint accounts in which the delinquent taxpayer has the right, under state law, to withdraw all amounts in the account.

United States v. National Bank of Commerce (S.Ct. 1985). The Court reasoned that the levy statute, section 6331, is a "provisional remedy," that authorizes the levy subject to postseizure administrative or judicial proceedings (under sections 6343(b) and 7246) to determine the rights of innocent third parties.

C. Installment Agreements

Prior to passage of the first Taxpayer Bill of Rights Act in 1988, the use and availability of installment agreements were not uniform. The 1988 Act gave the IRS statutory authority to enter into written installment payment agreements with taxpayers and required the IRS to include a clear description of this potential solution in its notice of intent to levy. IRC § 6159. In 1998, Congress concluded that installment agreements still were not being used in appropriate cases, so it amended section 6159 to add new section 6159(c), which requires the IRS to enter into agreements to accept payment of tax liability in installments if:

1.   The aggregate tax liability is $10,000 or less;

2.   The taxpayer has not, in the preceding five years, failed to file any federal income tax return, failed to pay any federal income tax liability, or entered into an installment agreement for payment of any income tax liability;

3.   The IRS has determined (based on information provided by the taxpayer at the request of the IRS) that the taxpayer is financially unable to pay the tax liability when due;

4. The agreement provides for full payment of the tax liability within three years; and

5. The taxpayer agrees to comply with the Internal Revenue Code during the time the agreement is in effect.

D.   *Offers in Compromise*

Some taxpayers are simply unable to pay their tax liabilities, and an installment payment plan cannot help. In such cases, an offer in compromise (OIC) under section 7122 might be appropriate. The IRS views the offer in compromise as a legitimate collection alternative that should be utilized in appropriate cases in which there is genuine doubt about either the taxpayer's liability for the tax or the taxpayer's ability to pay. Most offers in compromise involve doubts about the taxpayer's ability to pay.

To begin the process, the taxpayer must complete a Form 656 and provide the required documentation to give the IRS the information necessary to analyze the taxpayer's financial situation. The taxpayer also must execute a consent extending the statute of limitations on assessment of the tax. The IRS will consider a number of factors, principally the taxpayer's net realizable equity in assets and his present and prospective income. If the IRS accepts the offer, the taxpayer's debt is extinguished upon his compliance with the terms of the offer. Offers involving more than $50,000 in tax liability must be reviewed by the Office of the Chief Counsel.

As part of the 1998 Taxpayer Bill of Rights Act 3, Congress amended section 7122 by adding a new subsection (c) establishing standards for IRS evaluation of offers. This new section requires the IRS to develop and publish schedules of national and local allowances designed to ensure that taxpayers entering into OIC agreements have an adequate means to provide for basic living expenses. In addition, the IRS must determine, on the basis of each taxpayer's facts and circumstances, whether the use of such schedules is appropriate. The IRS is barred from using the schedules to the extent use of the schedules would deprive the taxpayer of adequate living expenses. Moreover, the IRS may not reject an offer from a low-income taxpayer solely on the basis of the amount of the offer. Under the 1998 TBOR, the IRS cannot turn down a taxpayer who is contesting his liability for the asserted tax simply because it cannot locate his return for verification. Also under this Act, such taxpayers are not required to provide a Form 433—A financial statement.

The 1998 Act also prohibits the IRS from levying on the taxpayer's property during the period the offer is pending and for 30 days after the offer is rejected. Levy is also prohibited during the period an installment agreement offer is pending or in effect or for 30 days after it has been rejected or terminated.

E. Civil Damages

Prior to the passage of the first Taxpayer Bill of Rights Act in 1988, there was no statutory mechanism for recovery of civil damages from the Government for improper collection activities. The 1988 Act added new Code section 7433, which authorizes suit against the Government for damages resulting from the reckless or intentional disregard by IRS employees of any federal tax statute or regulation. Unlike section 7432, discussed in § 11.2.F, *supra*, this section places a ceiling of $100,000 on the maximum amount recoverable, and it provides for damages in favor of the Government if the court finds that the suit is frivolous. Therefore, if a taxpayer suffers damages from the Government's failure to release a lien, suit should be brought under section 7432, rather than section 7433, to take advantage of the former's potential for unlimited damages against the Government and lack of exposure to potential damages against the taxpayer in the event the suit is determined to be groundless.

Suit under section 7433 must be brought within two years after the right of action accrues, and no damages will be awarded unless the taxpayer has exhausted her administrative remedies. While the statute does not specify the administrative remedies that must be exhausted, the taxpayer probably must notify the IRS of the improper activities and demand that it cease those activities and entertain any good faith settlement offer.

F.   *Sale of Seized Property*

Section 6335 requires the IRS to deliver a notice of seizure to a person whose property has been seized. The notice must specify the amount of tax that is due and describe the property seized. In addition, the IRS must deliver to the taxpayer and publish a notice of sale, identifying the property to be sold and the time, place and manner of sale. The sale generally must take place not less than ten nor more than forty days after the notice is published. For perishable goods or goods whose value will substantially decrease if they are not sold immediately, the sale may take place more quickly. The IRS must set a minimum sale price, and if that minimum price is not bid, it may either buy the property for that price or return the property to the taxpayer.

To avoid loss of his property, the taxpayer may pay the tax plus costs incurred by the IRS after the levy and prior to the sale. I.R.C. § 6337(a). When such payment is made, the IRS must return the property to the taxpayer. If such pre-sale payment is not made, the taxpayer may not recover his personal property from the buyer after the sale, but real property may be redeemed (by paying the buyer the same amount the buyer paid plus interest) within 180 days from the sale date.

As mentioned above, the taxpayer whose property has been seized now has the right to request that the IRS sell the property within 60 days, and the IRS must comply unless doing so would not be in the Government's best interest. I.R.C. § 6335, as amended by the Taxpayer Bill of Rights Act of 1988. As a result, taxpayers have a mechanism to prevent their property from languishing unsold for months or years after seizure.

§ 11.4 Jeopardy and Termination Assessments

In cases in which extraordinary collection action is required, the Service may make a jeopardy or termination assessment. According to the Regulations, circumstances that justify a jeopardy or termination assessment include the following:

(i) The taxpayer is or appears to be designing quickly to depart from the United States or to conceal himself.

(ii) The taxpayer is or appears to be designing quickly to place his property beyond the reach of the Government either by removing it from the United States, by concealing it, by dissipating it, or by transferring it to other persons.

(iii) The taxpayer's financial solvency is or appears to be imperiled. [Reg. §§ 1.6851–1(a)(1), 1.6861–1(a).]

Particularly the third circumstance, that the taxpayer's financial solvency appears imperiled, grants enormous discretion to the IRS to bypass the normal collection rules and safeguards. For that reason, Congress amended section 7429 in 1998 to require that IRS Counsel first review and approve any proposed jeopardy assessment, termination assessment or jeopardy levy.

For jeopardy and termination assessments the requirement that no assessment can be made until the statutory notice of deficiency has been sent and remained unanswered for 90 days is waived. Instead, the Service is required simply to send the deficiency notice at a later time, which will give the taxpayer an opportunity to contest the asserted deficiency in the Tax Court. When a jeopardy or termination assessment is made, the IRS must notify the taxpayer and demand immediate payment of the assessed tax. In addition, under section 7429, it must give the taxpayer a written statement explaining the basis of the assessment within five days after the assessment. If the taxpayer wishes to contest the assessment, he must petition the IRS for administrative review within 30 days of the notice. If the IRS finds that the assessment is excessive or inappropriate, it may abate all or part of the assessment.

If the taxpayer is not satisfied with the administrative review, he may bring a civil action in the United States District Court, which must determine whether the IRS acted reasonably in making the assessment and whether the amount assessed is appropriate. Suit must be brought within 90 days (formerly 30 days, prior to amendment as part of the Taxpayer Bill of Rights Act of 1988) after the IRS notifies the taxpayer of its decision or 16 days have passed in which no IRS decision is made on the taxpayer's request for review. The IRS has the burden of proving the reasonableness of the assessment, but the taxpayer bears the burden of proving that the amount assessed is excessive. I.R.C. § 7429(g).

Before levying on the taxpayer's property following an assessment, the IRS normally must wait 10 days after notice and demand has been made. In addition, the IRS normally may not levy until 30 days after issuing its notice of intent to levy. These delay periods do not apply to jeopardy and termination assessments, and the IRS may immediately seize the taxpayer's property. Although prior to 1988 a taxpayer could obtain administrative and judicial review of jeopardy and termination assessments, no such review was available to challenge the decision to levy. The Taxpayer Bill of Rights Act of 1988 amended section 7429 to provide that if the Service levies on property within 30 days after it has given notice of the assessment and demand for payment under section 6331(a), then it must furnish the taxpayer (within 5 days after the levy) a written statement of the information upon which it relied in making the levy. The taxpayer may then (within the same time periods for challenging the assessment) demand administrative and judicial review of the jeopardy or termination levy. Thus, for post–1989 jeopardy and termination assessments and levies, section 7429 now affords the same protections for both the assessment and the levy. The 1988 change may not provide any real additional protection, however, because presumably any jeopardy or termination assessment that is found to be reasonable would automatically and necessarily validate a prompt levy. Note also that levies made more than 30 days after the notice and demand are outside the scope of section 7429 and thus no administrative or judicial review is provided.

Finally, Code section 6867 provides an important mechanism for assessing tax against persons in possession of large amounts of cash. Under that section, the IRS may make a jeopardy or termination assessment against any person in physical possession of more than $10,000 in cash or cash equivalent, if the person denies ownership of the funds and the true owner of the funds does not claim them and submit to IRS procedures for determining the amount of tax that may be due.

Section 6867 was used successfully by the Service in a case involving a Miami "bag man" whose job was to receive large amounts of cash and convert them to money orders or cashier's checks for less than $10,000 and then to deposit the checks or money orders in various bank accounts. The purpose of this scheme was to "launder" illegally obtained funds by depositing them in banks so as to avoid the restrictions imposed on deposits of more than $10,000 cash. When the sheriff stopped the person, he had in his possession $175,000 in cash, cashier's checks and money orders. A termination assessment against the possessor of the cash was upheld by the Eleventh Circuit, even though it was undisputed that the possessor was not the true owner of the cash. The true owner's (a foreign corporation) acknowledgment of ownership was found insufficient because it failed to submit to IRS examination. Matut v. Commissioner (11th Cir. 1988).

Congress enacted section 6867 in the belief that a person in possession of large amounts of cash who denies ownership but refuses to identify the true owner is most likely trying to conceal illegal income, whether it be his own or that of a principal (such as an employer). The effect of section 6867 is to create a presumption that collection of tax is in jeopardy any time a person in possession of more than $10,000 in cash or cash equivalent denies ownership of the funds and fails to identify the true owner. Under section 6867 the funds are deemed to be gross income of the person in whose possession they are found. The IRS may immediately assess a tax at the highest rate against the possessor and seize the funds to satisfy the assessed debt. If the true owner never identifies himself and acknowledges ownership, the assessment will be upheld. The possessor, however, has no standing to challenge the assessment. Morgan v. United States (9th Cir.1992).

CHAPTER 12

BANKRUPTCY PROCEEDINGS

When a debtor cannot resolve her financial difficulties on her own, she may seek help from the Bankruptcy Court. Under the recently enacted Bankruptcy Abuse Prevention and Consumer Protection Act of 2005 (hereinafter referred to as the "2005 Bankruptcy Act"), before a debtor can file bankruptcy, she will have to go through consumer credit counseling at her expense to attempt to work out a repayment plan that satisfies her creditors. During this time, which may take several months, interest and late charges on her debts will accumulate. If it is determined that she cannot pay her debts, then she will be allowed to file bankruptcy. A bankruptcy action is begun by the filing of a petition with the Bankruptcy Court and it has a profound effect on collection actions. When the petition is filed, two things happen automatically: (1) creditors are stayed or enjoined from taking any further collection action and (2) a bankruptcy estate is created which includes "all legal or equitable interests of the debtor in property as of the commencement of the case." 11 U.S.C. § 362(a)(6); § 541(a)(1).

§ 12.1   Types of Bankruptcies

An individual debtor typically files a bankruptcy petition under either Chapter 7 or Chapter 13 of the Bankruptcy Code, while a business debtor typically files under Chapter 11. Chapter 7 is a liquidating bankruptcy. If the debtor is a business, it ceases operations and terminates its business. If the debtor is an individual, his or her assets are sold to satisfy the claims of creditors and any remaining claims are discharged, subject to certain exceptions (see § 12.3.B, *infra*), and the debtor then receives a fresh start. Under Chapter 7, a trustee is appointed to protect the interests of the unsecured creditors. Secured creditors are protected to the extent of their collateral or security interest and do not require the protection of the trustee. If an asset is fully encumbered by the claims of secured creditors, the trustee generally has no interest in those assets because they are of no benefit to the unsecured creditors. The remaining property, subject to certain statutory exemptions, will be marshaled by the trustee and sold to satisfy the claims of the unsecured creditors. If property is subject to the claim of a secured creditor but is not fully encumbered by that claim, the property may be sold by the trustee to satisfy the claim of the secured creditor. Any amount remaining after that claim is satisfied is used to satisfy the claims of unsecured creditors.

Under the 2005 Bankruptcy Act, a new means test is applied to determine which debtors are eligible to file a petition under Chapter 7. If the debtor earns more than the median income for her state and can afford over the next 5 years to make payments of at least $10,000 or 25% of her nonpriority, unsecured debt up to a minimum of $6,000, whichever is less, she will not be eligible to file under Chapter 7 and instead must file under Chapter 13.

Chapter 13 is used by a small debtor who can afford to make monthly payments against her debts. The Chapter 13 debtor must file a plan with the Bankruptcy Court which must provide for full payment of all priority debts. Dischargeable debts that remain unpaid at the conclusion of the plan will be discharged and the debtor will no longer be liable.

Chapter 11 involves a reorganization of a business in an attempt to make the business profitable once again. The debtor/management continues to run the day-to-day business operations, but must seek approval of the Bankruptcy Court before any significant business decisions are made.

§ 12.2 The Automatic Stay

When a debtor files a bankruptcy petition, creditors (including the federal government) are automatically stayed from engaging in any further collection action. This allows all collection and enforcement activities to be brought into a single forum—the Bankruptcy Court. The 2005 Bankruptcy Act provides sanctions and damage awards for willful violation of the automatic stay. The stay does not apply to criminal proceedings, whether state or federal, or to proceedings over which the Bankruptcy Court has jurisdiction. The statute of limitations on assessment and collection is suspended while the stay is in effect, although the Service may assess a deficiency, issue a notice and demand for payment, and refile a Notice of Federal Tax Lien. No actual collection may occur during the pendency of the bankruptcy case, however, absent permission from the Bankruptcy Court. The tax lien does not attach unless the Bankruptcy Court has determined (1) that the tax liability is a nondischargeable debt and (2) the property to which the lien would attach has been transferred out of the bankruptcy estate to the debtor.

The Bankruptcy Court and the Tax Court have concurrent jurisdiction to determine the debtor's tax liability but the Bankruptcy Court decides which court will hear the case. If a Tax Court petition is filed before the bankruptcy petition, the bankruptcy petition will stay the proceedings in the Tax Court. Either the IRS, the bankruptcy trustee or the debtor/taxpayer may request that the stay be lifted in order for the Tax Court to hear the case. If the Bankruptcy Court grants the request and the case is heard by the Tax Court, the decision of the Tax Court is *res judicata*. If the request is denied, the stay remains effective until the case is closed or dismissed or the debtor is discharged, and during the pendency of the bankruptcy case the Bankruptcy Court may decide the case. The Tax Court, which retains jurisdiction over the claim until the case is decided by the Bankruptcy Court, may determine the liability for the nondischargeable claims at the close of the bankruptcy proceeding. If the debt-or/taxpayer receives a notice of deficiency prior to filing a bankruptcy petition, section 6213(f) sus-pends the 90–day period for filing a Tax Court petition for the period during which the taxpayer is prohibited from filing in the Tax Court and for 60 days thereafter.

§ 12.3　The Bankruptcy Estate

When a bankruptcy petition is filed, a bankruptcy estate is created that includes the debtor's legal and equitable interests as of the commencement of the case. Under Chapter 7, the property of the bank-ruptcy estate is held for distribution to creditors in accordance with the priority of their claims under the Bankruptcy Code. The filing of the bankruptcy petition is the demarcation point for determining the property that goes into the estate, because property acquired by the debtor before that point is part of the estate. Property acquired by the debtor after the petition is filed remains property of the debtor, while property that the estate acquires after the commencement of the case becomes property of the estate. Thus, income earned by the debtor after the petition is filed remains the property of the debtor. In some cases, it may be difficult to deter-mine whether property is acquired pre-petition or post-petition. A tax refund, for example, is part of the bankruptcy estate even though it may be re-ceived after the petition is filed, if the overpayment to which the refund relates was made with funds received before the petition was filed. Conversely, if the overpayment was made with funds received after the petition was filed that otherwise were not part of the bankruptcy estate, then the refund is not a part of the estate either. Property that the debtor holds in trust for another does not constitute an equitable interest and thus is not included in the estate.

A. *Priority of Claims in Bankruptcy*

Claims of creditors generally fall into three categories: secured, priority and unsecured. In general, secured claims are entitled to first priority because they are satisfied by specific assets (i.e., collateral). A tax lien is secured to the extent of the value of the property to which the lien attaches, provided that Notice of the Lien has been filed prior to the date of the bankruptcy petition. Even though the lien is perfected, a bankruptcy trustee may set aside certain transfers and liens such as fraudulent transfers and perfected liens that are subordinate to those claims having superpriority status. Thus, the tax lien must secure an allowed claim for taxes that is not avoidable by the bankruptcy trustee. Any non-tax secured claims allowed by the court that are senior to the tax claim will take priority over the secured tax lien.

Priority of claims determines the order in which the claims are satisfied and whether the claims are dischargeable. There are currently ten categories of priority claims under the Bankruptcy Code. 11 U.S.C. § 507(a). Under the 2005 Bankruptcy Act, domestic support obligations are elevated from seventh to first priority. Trustee fees also are accorded first level priority. Administrative expenses, including tax liabilities incurred during the administration of the bankruptcy estate are accorded second priority. Taxes that accrue during the ordinary course of business during the "gap period" between the commencement of an involuntary bankruptcy case and the appointment of a trustee are accorded third priority. Unsecured claims for income taxes withheld on wages and salaries earned within 180 days prior to the filing of the bankruptcy petition are entitled to fourth priority. Unsecured income tax or gross receipts tax claims that meet certain requirements (mostly pertaining to when the return was due, whether it was timely filed, and when the tax was assessed) are entitled to eighth priority and are nondischargeable. If a Notice of the Tax Lien is not filed before the bankruptcy petition, the tax claim is considered unsecured. Most other unsecured tax claims are dischargeable and are not entitled to priority.

Treatment of secured tax claims is determined under section 724(b) of the Bankruptcy Code. Under this provision, the satisfaction of secured tax claims is limited:

(1) senior secured nontax claims that are allowed by the court are satisfied first,

(2) priority claims in levels 1 through 7 then are satisfied to the extent of the amount of the tax claim,

(3) the difference, if any, between the amount of the tax lien and the amount of the claims in (2) will be paid to the holder of the tax lien,

(4) secured claims that are junior to the tax lien will be paid next,

(5) any amount remaining will be paid in satisfaction of the tax lien, if it was not fully satisfied under (3), and

(6) if there is any excess amount remaining, it will remain in the estate.

Section 724(b) at first blush provides an odd distribution scheme. But the rationale behind this scheme rests on three considerations: (1) if the tax claim is allowed in full, secured creditors will bear the burden of the debtor's unpaid tax liability, (2) some of the priority claims are subject to dollar limitations on the amount of recovery, so it is fair to subject the Government to a limitation as well, and (3) the tax lien survives the bankruptcy and can be satisfied from later acquired property of the debtor. *See* § B., *infra*.

Some claims are entitled to "superpriority" status. If there is more than one claim holder in a particular category (under 11 U.S.C. § 724(b)), the distribution is made in the order it otherwise would have been made. This means that the superpriorities discussed in § 11.2.E., *supra* (discussing § 6323(b) of the Internal Revenue Code), may apply to provide priority over a senior secured claim. Otherwise, if no claim within the category is entitled to superpriority, the claims will be satisfied in accordance with seniority.

Interest on the tax claim assumes the same priority as the underlying tax liability, provided the interest arises pre-petition. Post-petition interest on the tax claim is allowed only if the claim is "oversecured," which means that the collateral securing the claim must be greater than the amount of the claim. Interest is determined under the bankruptcy laws and not under the tax laws.

> **Example:** A debtor files a bankruptcy petition on July 1, 2005. He has property valued at $20,000 that is subject to a $14,000 secured lien for unpaid federal income taxes, which includes $1,000 in interest that accrued pre-petition, $8,000 in claims attributable to first through seventh priority under § 507 of the Bankruptcy Code, and a $4,000 secured nontax lien that is junior to the tax lien. Under § 724(b), the $8,000 of priority claims will be allowed first in full. The excess of the difference between the amount of the federal tax lien and the amount of the priority claims ($6,000) will be allocated to the federal tax claim. The junior nontax lien then will be satisfied in full, and the remaining $2,000 will be allocated to the federal tax lien.

The priority of penalties depends upon when they accrued and whether they are compensatory or punitive. A compensatory pecuniary loss penalty is entitled to seventh order priority and is not dischargeable. A punitive, nonpecuniary loss penalty that is incurred more than three years before the bankruptcy petition was filed is dischargeable and may be avoided by the trustee. If the punitive penalty was incurred within two years of the petition, it is not dischargeable and is entitled to be paid after the priority claims and after the general, unsecured claims.

B. *Discharge of Liabilities*

Discharge is the release of the debtor from personal liability for her debts. The 2005 Bankruptcy Act clarifies that taxes arising from the failure to file a return, the filing of a late return, or the fraudulent filing of a return are not dischargeable, regardless of whether the debtor files under Chapter 7 or Chapter 13. As before, those tax claims entitled to priority under 11 U.S.C. § 507(a) also are nondischargeable. The 2005 Act expands the list of nondischargeable debts to include those incurred to pay state and local taxes; those incurred by reason of death or injury caused while operating a motor vehicle, vessel or aircraft while intoxicated; and those incurred to pay fines and penalties.

Note that even though a debtor may receive a discharge from personal liability, any lien against the debtor's property continues as a valid encumbrance. This should be borne in mind when considering the "fresh start" after bankruptcy. Another consideration is that under the 2005 Act, proof of completion of a financial management course is a prerequisite for discharge. Moreover, before a discharge can occur in a Chapter 7 case, the debtor must file his or her most recent federal income tax return with the Bankruptcy Court and must provide the return to any creditor who timely requests it.

Debtors sometimes file for bankruptcy under multiple Chapters. For instance, a common ploy is to file under Chapter 7 to eradicate the unsecured debts, then subsequently file under Chapter 13 to deal with the secured debts (which usually includes a mortgage) through monthly payments without the threat of late fees or enforced IRS collection action. This is commonly referred to as a "Chapter 20." Under the 2005 Bankruptcy Act, this type of multiple filing is discouraged through expansion of the time period between filings. Thus, a debtor who receives a discharge under Chapter 7 cannot refile under Chapter 13 within 3 years from the Chapter 7 discharge. Further, the Supreme Court has held that the 3–year lookback period for determining when taxes are nondischargeable under section 507(a)(8)(A)(i) is tolled during the pendency of any prior bankruptcy petition. Young v. United States (S.Ct.2002).

§ 12.4 A Comparison of Bankruptcy and Other Alternative Forms of Tax Payment

Other forms of alternative methods of paying tax debts were discussed previously in Chapter 11, *supra* (*see* § 11.3.C and § 11.3.D). Like bankruptcy, these methods also apply to taxpayers who are experiencing financial exigencies that make it difficult to pay their taxes. The taxpayer/debtor must give careful consideration to whether to file bankruptcy or to use one of the alternative payment methods. While much depends on the individual facts of the particular case, there are certain comparisons that can be made. For instance, after the 2005 Bankruptcy Act, bankruptcy becomes a much more complex and expensive process:

- Some debtors may not be eligible for bankruptcy, particularly after the 2005 Act, because Chapter 7 now has a means test and Chapter 13 also has jurisdictional limitations.

- The result of the 2005 Act is that the onset of the bankruptcy action may be delayed while the debtor is required to seek credit counseling. Since the automatic stay does not apply during this period, collection action can commence and late fees and interest will accumulate. Under an offer in compromise, the debtor begins to pay immediately on the tax debt.

- The offer in compromise addresses only the federal tax debt. Frequently, the debtor has other debts as well. In this case, the debtor would be better advised to consider a bankruptcy petition in order to obtain a fresh start.

- Chapter 7 allows a debtor to wipe out dischargeable debts that exceed the value of the nonexempt assets. Except for liens on the property itself, the debtor is free and clear of the debts that are discharged and may keep certain exempt property. By contrast, Chapter 13 requires debtors to repay their debts over time under a debt repayment plan. Under this plan, however, some debts may be discharged and the debtor may be able to avoid late fees and some interest. An offer in compromise is similar to a Chapter 13 bankruptcy except that the debtor is dealing with the IRS and not with the Bankruptcy Court. Note, however, that if the debts are primarily nondischargeable (and remember that the 2005 Act has expanded the list of nondischargeable debts), it will be more difficult for a debtor to wipe out debts and start afresh. Thus, the debtor may be better advised to forego bankruptcy in favor of an offer in compromise.

- If the debtor is married with jointly owned property but is solely liable for the debt, such property generally is exempted from the bankruptcy estate. In an offer in compromise, however, at least half of the equity in the property must be considered in the offer. *See also* discussion of *Rodgers v. United States*, in § 11.2.B, *supra*. Thus, the debtor in such a case would be better advised to consider bankruptcy.

CHAPTER 13

THIRD PARTY LIABILITY

In some circumstances, a person other than the "taxpayer" can be liable for a tax plus penalties for its nonpayment. Spouses who file joint returns, transferees and fiduciaries of the taxpayer, as well as "responsible persons" of business entities, and even lenders to and sureties of a business can be held liable for substantial tax liabilities, penalties and interest. This chapter explores the liability of third parties for the taxpayer's actions.

§ 13.1 "Innocent Spouse" Rules

Since 1948 married couples have been permitted to combine their income and deductions and pay their taxes under a different and lower rate. In exchange for the right to file a "joint" return, married couples are jointly and severally liable for the accuracy and payment of amounts shown on the return. In a society in which divorce is common and tax laws are increasingly complex, it is not surprising that "innocent" spouses seek relief from the harsh rule of joint and several liability. The innocent spouse relief rules first became part of the Code in 1971 under former sections 6013(e) and 6653(b)(3), and were subsequently amended in 1984 and again in 1998. Section 6013(e) provided relief for an innocent spouse from tax liabilities, interest and penalties under certain conditions. Section 6663(c) relieved a spouse from liability for the civil fraud penalty when the fraud was attributable only to the culpable spouse, even if relief from liability under section 6013(e) was not available.

Prior to the enactment in 1971 of the first innocent spouse relief statutes, the only way to escape joint and several liability was to establish that the return in question was not a "joint return" because the spouse's signature on the return resulted from mistake, duress or fraud. This defense, which hinged on the absence of intent to make a joint return, remained important because the first requirement for relief under section 6013(e) was that a joint return must have been filed. Thus, a spouse who did not qualify for relief under section 6013(e) still could prevail by establishing that she was not jointly and severally liable because no joint return had been filed.

A. Pre–1998 Rules

As originally enacted in 1971, the requirements for innocent spouse relief under section 6013(e) were as follows:

1. A joint return was filed.

2. There was an omission from gross income that exceeded 25% of the income shown on the return.

3. The spouse seeking relief neither knew nor had reason to know of the omission.

4.   The innocent spouse did not significantly benefit from the tax understatement and thus should not be held personally liable.

Importantly, if the tax deficiency (and interest and possibly penalties) was due to overstating deductions rather than understating income, no relief was available, regardless of how innocent the spouse might be.

To remedy some perceived problems with the 1971 rules, Congress amended the innocent spouse rules in 1984. The first and third requirements of the 1971 rules were kept intact, and the fourth was changed to require relief if, in view of all the facts and circumstances, it would be inequitable to hold the innocent spouse personally liable. Congress also added the following new provisions:

1.   There could be no relief unless the tax understatement exceeded $500.

2.   The deficiency must have been due to "grossly erroneous items," which was defined to include any omission from gross income and erroneously claimed deductions and credits for which there was "no basis in fact or in law."

3.   If the tax understatement was due to erroneously claimed deductions, no relief was available unless the tax understatement exceeded a certain percentage of the innocent spouse's income for the year before the deficiency notice was mailed. The percentage varied, depending on the innocent spouse's income. If her adjusted gross income was $20,000 or less, then the tax liability from which

she was seeking relief must have exceeded 10% of that income. If her adjusted gross income in the year before the deficiency notice was mailed was more than $20,000, then the tax liability must have exceeded 25% of that income.

To illustrate this third rule, basing relief on the innocent spouse's income, assume that John and Mary were divorced in 1987, but filed a joint return in 1986. John fabricated numerous expense items and overstated his business deductions on the 1986 return, a fact that Mary neither knew nor had reason to know. The 1986 return was audited, and in March of 1990 a deficiency of $5,000 was asserted based on the overstated deductions. If Mary otherwise qualified for innocent spouse relief but her adjusted gross income for 1989 was $21,000, she could be held liable for the entire deficiency because the $5,000 deficiency was only 23% of her adjusted gross income for the previous year. Because her adjusted gross income exceeded $20,000, no relief was available unless the deficiency exceeded 25% of that income. Had her adjusted gross income been $20,000 exactly, she would have qualified for relief, since the $5,000 deficiency exceeded 10% of that income.

While application of the "ability to pay" limitation was straightforward (if arguably harsh and arbitrary), construing the term "grossly erroneous items" had proved difficult for the courts. As mentioned above, the statute defined the term to include any omission from gross income, but only those deductions and credits for which there was "no basis in fact or law." I.R.C. § 6013(e)(2)(B). The Tax Court had construed the term to mean groundless, phony, frivolous or fraudulent, and had refused relief where the position taken on the return was disallowed by the court but was not blatantly "phony." *See, e.g.*, Douglas v. Commissioner (Tax Ct.1986) (denying relief to widow who could not substantiate claimed deductions pertaining to deceased spouse's employee business expenses and alimony payments).

B.   *1998 Amendments*

The Taxpayer Bill of Rights Act 3 significantly changed the innocent spouse rules in an attempt to make the remedy less complicated and more readily available to those who truly need it. The 1998 amendments created a new section 6015, under which there are three basic ways a taxpayer may obtain relief from joint and several liability: (1) through liberalized traditional innocent spouse rules; (2) through a new procedure for electing separate liability; and (3) through a new rule permitting equitable relief under certain circumstances.

Under the first avenue for relief, section 6015(b), taxpayers can be relieved of liability for any tax understatement, not just one that is "substantial." In addition, the item causing the understatement need only be erroneous, not "grossly erroneous" as under prior law. The new rule also permits apportioned liability under which a spouse may be relieved of liability for a portion of a tax understate-

ment even if the spouse knew or had reason to
know of other understatements of tax on the same
return. For example, if the spouse knew or had
reason to know that deductions were erroneously
overstated, but did not know that the other spouse
had income that was not reported, the spouse claiming relief is relieved of liability for the tax on the
erroneously unreported income.

The second type of relief, described in section
6015(c), was completely new. It allows a qualified
taxpayer to elect (in addition to relief under the
newly-liberalized innocent spouse rule described
above), to have his or her liability for any deficiency
limited to the portion of the deficiency attributable
to the items allocable to the electing spouse. Generally items of income and deduction are allocated as
if the two spouses had filed separate returns. To
qualify to make the election, the taxpayer must be
(at the time of election) either: (1) no longer married to, (2) legally separated from, or (3) living apart
for at least twelve months from, the person with
whom the electing spouse filed the joint return. The
burden is on the electing person to establish that he
or she meets these qualifications.

The election may not be made in certain circumstances. First, it is unavailable if the IRS demonstrates that assets were transferred between the
spouses in a fraudulent scheme in which both
spouses participated. In such a case, neither spouse
is eligible to make the election and joint and several
liability will apply to each spouse. Second, if the IRS
proves that the electing spouse had actual knowl-

edge (not just reason to know) that an item on a return is incorrect, the election will not apply (and joint and several liability will remain) with respect to the portion of the deficiency attributable to that item. Third, the portion of the tax deficiency for which the electing spouse is liable is increased by the value of any "disqualified assets" received from the other spouse. Disqualified assets include any property or property right transferred to an electing spouse for the principal purpose of tax avoidance. A rebuttable presumption of tax avoidance intent applies to any property transfers made less than one year before the date of the notice of proposed deficiency. This presumption may be rebutted by a showing that the principal purpose for the transfer was not tax avoidance. The presumption does not apply to transfers pursuant to a divorce or separate maintenance decree.

The third avenue for relief lies in a new "catch-all" provision, section 6015(f), authorizing equitable relief in circumstances to be defined by the IRS. This provision is designed to provide relief for spouses whose joint returns reflect a tax liability, but the tax was not paid with the return and the innocent spouse did not know or have reason to know that the guilty spouse used the funds for his or her own benefit instead of paying the tax liability. Relief under this provision is also to be available in situations in which relief would be equitable but is not specifically provided for in other sections. One of the factors that courts have considered under section 6015(f) is whether the "innocent spouse" significantly benefitted from the under-statement. *See, e.g.,* Cheshire v. Commissioner (5th Cir.2002) (denying relief on the ground that the spouse benefitted by receiving more in the divorce settlement).

A taxpayer seeking relief under any of these three routes must affirmatively elect within two years from the date on which the electing person is aware that collection activities have begun. For this pur-pose, Notice of Intent to Levy would constitute collection activities against the electing spouse, but simply mailing the notice of deficiency or the de-mand for payment does not amount to collection activities.

If the IRS denies requested relief, the taxpayer may petition the Tax Court within 90 days of the date the denial was mailed by registered or certified mail. IRC § 6015(e). In addition, the taxpayer may petition the Tax Court if the IRS has taken no action within six months from the date the request for relief was filed. *Id.* Filing a Tax Court petition for review of the IRS's denial of relief has the effect of tolling the statute of limitations on collection and prohibiting enforced collection efforts.

§ 13.2   Transferees and Fiduciaries

Section 6901 authorizes the IRS to assess and collect taxes from "transferees" and "fiduciaries" of the taxpayer who incurred the tax liability. Rules governing the extent of liability and time limits on imposing the liability differ for the two types of third parties.

A.   Transferees

"Transferee" is defined in section 6901(h) to include donees, heirs, legatees, devisees and distributees. Regulations give as examples shareholders of dissolved corporations, successors of corporations, and assignees or donees of insolvent persons. Courts have expanded the definition to include one who takes or receives property from the taxpayer without adequate consideration to the detriment of creditors. The basis of transferee liability is that the transferee has acquired assets of the taxpayer and is liable either at law because of a deemed "assumption of the contract," or in equity because of actual or constructive fraud.

Corporate successors and distributees are a significant class of transferees. For example, the surviving corporation in a merger will be liable at law either on a theory of assumption of the taxpayer-corporation's liabilities or simple transferee liability as a matter of law, because most states' merger statutes provide that the surviving corporation is liable for the debts of the disappearing corporation in a merger. Similarly, the buyer of a corporation's stock will become liable at law, and even a buyer of a corporation's assets can be liable as a transferee for tax deficiencies of the selling corporation on a theory of express or implied assumption of the seller's liabilities.

Transferee liability in equity is based on the law of fraudulent conveyances. The Government must establish that the transferor was insolvent at the time of transfer and that the transfer was made for less than full and adequate consideration.

The transferee is liable retroactively for the transferor's tax liability for the year of the transfer, regardless of whether the transferee knew of the tax liability. Although statutory deficiency notices are normally presumed correct and the burden is therefore on the petitioner to overcome this presumption, the burden is on the Government in Tax Court cases to prove that the third party is a transferee within the meaning of section 6901. I.R.C. § 6902(a). Section 6901 itself is merely procedural, and state law controls on the issues of the existence and extent of transferee liability. Commissioner v. Stern (S.Ct.1958).

A 1988 Tax Court memorandum decision, *Hunt v. Commissioner* (Tax Ct.Memo.1988), illustrates these principles. Brenda Powers Hunt made loans to her brother, James Powers, from 1964 through 1979. Brenda's funds were used to make the down payment and monthly mortgage payments on his house, as well as his child support payments. In 1979, after Brenda requested repayment, James transferred title to the house to her by warranty deed. Brenda was unaware at the time that her brother had failed for several years to file federal income tax returns.

The IRS assessed James' tax liabilities against Brenda as a transferee in equity. Brenda defended on the basis that the conveyance of title to the house was in satisfaction of $29,000 of debts to her, and supported this by the real estate transfer tax receipt for $29, reflecting transfer for $29,000 consideration. Under applicable state law (Georgia), creditors can recover property transferred by a debtor if the transfer is without valuable consideration and the transferor is insolvent at the time of transfer. However, transfers of property between related parties in satisfaction of pre-existing indebtedness are considered made for valuable consideration. The court held that the IRS had failed to sustain its burden of proving both that James lacked sufficient assets to pay his tax liabilities at the time of transfer and that Brenda was liable as a transferee under state law.

A transferee who is found to have assumed the transferor's liability by a deemed assumption of contract is liable for the unpaid taxes of the transferor accrued to the date of the transfer to the extent of the amount for which he is deemed to have contracted. A transferee whose liability is based on actual or constructive fraud is liable to the extent of the difference between the fair market value of the property received and the consideration paid for it.

The statute of limitations for assessing transferee liability expires one year after the limitations period expires on assessing the transferor. I.R.C. § 6901(c)(1).

B. *Fiduciaries*

The term "fiduciary" is defined in section 7701(a)(6) as a "guardian, trustee, executor, administrator, receiver, conservator, or other person acting in any fiduciary capacity for any person." Fiduciary liability is narrower than transferee liability. It is based on the fiduciary's payment of debts of the taxpayer that did not have priority over the Government's claim for taxes. While a transferee may be liable to the extent of the value of the property received, a fiduciary can be liable only to the extent of debts actually paid by him that did not have priority over taxes.

The statute of limitations on assessment of tax based on fiduciary liability is the later of one year after the liability arises (that is, after debts are paid by the fiduciary) or the expiration of the statute of limitations on collection (not assessment) of the tax from the taxpayer. Because of the longer period of limitations for assessment of tax on a theory of fiduciary liability, the IRS sometimes will assess under this theory when the statute on assessment has expired against a transferee. In one such case, the Tax Court held that a sole shareholder of a dissolved corporation who received all of its assets and paid some of its debts, but not its taxes, was a transferee but not a fiduciary and was not liable for the corporation's taxes because the statute of limitations on assessment of transferee liability had expired. Grieb v. Commissioner (Tax Ct.1961).

§ 13.3   Trust Fund Taxes and Responsible Persons

An enormous potential liability for business managers, but one which they often do not know exists, is the 100% penalty under section 6672 for nonpayment of taxes withheld from employees' pay. "Responsible persons" are jointly and severally liable for the 100% penalty. Officers, directors or partners of firms with large payrolls can be personally liable for a penalty equal to 100% of the "trust fund taxes" withheld from employees' pay.

Sections 3102(a) and 3402(a) require employers to withhold from employees' wages both federal income tax and the employees' share of FICA (Social Security) contributions. Section 7501(a) requires employers to hold these monies "in a special fund in trust" for the United States until the employer actually pays them over to the Government. Hence, the term "trust fund taxes" means taxes withheld by the employer from the employees' wages and subject to the statutory requirement that they be held in trust for the Government. Under section 1462, an employee whose withheld taxes are not paid over to the Government is credited with the amount withheld and is not liable for such amounts even if the Government fails to collect them from the employer or its "responsible persons." To deter nonpayment of trust fund taxes, the Code imposes criminal penalties under sections 7201 and 7202, in addition to the 100% civil penalty of section 6672.

In a sense, the liability imposed under section 6672 is not really a penalty, but instead is a collection device under which the Government can recover delinquent trust fund taxes from those who are responsible for their payment. The distinction becomes important in bankruptcy proceedings, in which responsible persons seek to have their liability under section 6672 discharged. The courts have held that the liability is not dischargeable because it is a tax, rather than a penalty. The Government is entitled to only one recovery, and it cannot collect both the delinquent taxes and the 100% "penalty." In the alternative, some courts have held that the penalty is considered a pecuniary penalty since it is intended to compensate the government for the trust fund taxes that were not remitted.

A.   "Responsible Persons"

If the Service is not able to collect the trust fund taxes from the employer because the employer has no assets, then it will seek to identify as many responsible persons as possible and to hold them jointly and severally liable under section 6672. As discussed in § 13.3.D, *infra*, if the IRS is unable to collect the funds from responsible persons, it then may seek to impose liability for the unpaid taxes on lenders and sureties of the employer. Although any number of responsible persons or lenders may be liable for payment of the employer's withheld taxes, the Government is only entitled to recover the amount of the trust fund taxes, and must abate all remaining assessments when its right to retain the collected sums is established.

Courts have adopted the term "responsible person" as shorthand for the statutory description of persons liable under section 6672: any "person required to collect, truthfully account for and pay over any tax imposed." The Supreme Court interpreted this statutory language to mean that a person responsible for collecting the taxes can be liable for the penalty, even if he lacks authority to pay over the taxes when they are due. Slodov v. United States (S.Ct.1978). Thus, a person who is responsible for collecting and accounting for taxes, and who actually does so, can be liable for the 100% penalty if he terminates employment before the taxes are to be paid over and the employer fails to pay them when they are due. The issue in *Slodov* was whether a person who acquired control of a business that was delinquent in its payroll taxes could be held liable for the delinquent taxes. In other words, can a responsible person be held liable for tax liability incurred before he became a responsible person? The Supreme Court held that such a person could be liable for the taxes that were already delinquent when he assumed control, but found that the taxpayer in question was not liable because there were no funds available to pay the taxes when he assumed control. According to the Court, section 7501 does not impose a trust on after-acquired funds, and the section 6672 penalty cannot be imposed for use of after-acquired funds to pay creditors other than the Government.

"Person" is defined in section 6671(b) as "an officer or employee of a corporation, or a member or employee of a partnership, who as such officer, employee or member is under a duty to perform the act in respect of which the violation occurs." Expanding this statutory focus on "duty," some courts define their inquiry in terms of status, duty and authority. Mere status, without any actual duty or authority, will not render someone a "responsible person," although the Internal Revenue Manual states that the Service will ordinarily look to the president, secretary and treasurer of a corporate employer. IRM 5.7.3.3.1. The issue really is one of control. A person with significant control over the timing and amount of payments will be held responsible even if she claims lack of knowledge. Thus, a corporate president who claims the bookkeeper is completely responsible and that she had no idea the taxes were not paid will not escape liability. Section 6672 is not a strict liability penalty. The statute authorizes the penalty only against one who "willfully" fails to collect, account for or pay over the withholding taxes. Courts have found that mere negligence does not satisfy the "willfulness" standard, but voluntary, conscious and reckless disregard for an obvious or known risk is sufficient, even if the person lacked the specific intent to defraud the Government. Thus, a decision to pay other creditors rather than the trust fund taxes is willful conduct that will subject the responsible person to the 100% penalty. Some courts have held that the existence of "reasonable cause" for the failure may relieve a person from liability for the penalty. A responsible person bears the burden of proving lack of willfulness.

The broad sweep of section 6672, and the Government's zeal in attempting to collect under it, have produced numerous "horror stories." A good example of the breadth of the penalty's reach is a 1984 revenue ruling in which the IRS stated that a volunteer member of a board of trustees of a charitable organization may be liable for the penalty. Rev.Rul. 84–83, 1984–1 C.B. 264. In 1996 Congress enacted section 6672(e) which prohibits the IRS from assessing the responsible person penalty against an unpaid volunteer member of a board of directors (or trustees) of a tax-exempt organization if the person serves in an honorary capacity and has no knowledge of the unpaid tax.

The difficulty of applying the governing principles is well illustrated by *Roth v. United States* (11th Cir.1986). Roth was an employee-at-will of a small construction company in which Dobbins was the majority shareholder. Dobbins was the president and chairman of the board; Roth was not a director, but he did hold the title of executive vice-president and was authorized to sign company checks. At a time when the company was already delinquent in its payroll taxes, Dobbins ordered Roth not to pay the taxes then due. Roth obeyed, and the Government later assessed the 100% penalty against him, but did not assess a penalty against Dobbins. After a jury trial, the judge instructed the jury that it must relieve Roth of liability if it found that, although he was otherwise a responsible person, he was prevented by the president of the company from paying the payroll taxes. The Government objected to the instruction. The jury found that Roth was not liable for the penalty for any of the withheld taxes. The Government moved for a j.n.o.v., which the trial court denied.

On appeal, the Eleventh Circuit reversed and held Roth liable for the penalty for all the unpaid taxes (almost $23,000), including those he was ordered not to pay, even though his only escape from liability would have been to quit his job or disobey and risk being fired. In dissent, Judge Godbold thought it entirely possible that a properly instructed jury might find that, as a result of the president's order, Roth lacked authority to pay the taxes, and that, even if he did have authority, he did not act willfully or there was reasonable cause for his actions. For a factually similar case relieving an employee from liability under reasoning similar to Judge Godbold's, *see* Cellura v. United States (N.D.Ohio 1965).

B.   *Allocation of Partial Payments*

Employment taxes consist of two portions: (1) the employer's portion, which consists of the employer's share of FICA (Social Security) taxes plus the employer's share of FUTA (federal unemployment) taxes and (2) the employee's portion, which the employer is required to withhold and remit quarterly to the Government. The latter portion consists of income taxes and the employees' share of FICA and RRA (Railroad Retirement Act) taxes. It is only the second portion that constitutes trust fund taxes. The employer is directly liable for the first portion.

If a payment is made pursuant to a judicial action or an administrative action that results in a seizure of the property, such as a levy, it is considered a non-voluntary payment. If a non-voluntary partial payment of employment taxes is made, the Government may allocate the payment as it chooses. Generally, it will apply the payment first to the employer's portion of the unpaid taxes, rather than to the trust fund portion because it usually stands a better chance of collecting the trust fund portion since responsible persons remain liable for that portion. When employment taxes are not paid, it usually means that the employer is struggling financially and the Government's ability to recover the taxes from the employer is impaired. Thus, the Government will allocate the partial payment according to its own best interest. If a taxpayer makes a voluntary partial payment, the taxpayer has a right to direct the application of the funds and the Government must abide by the taxpayer's allocation. But if the taxpayer does not instruct the Government as to how the payment should be allocated, the Government may make whatever allocation it chooses.

C. Time Limits and Other Procedural Aspects

If the delinquent employer never filed a payroll tax return, then the section 6672 penalty may be assessed against the responsible person(s) at any time. If a return was filed, the penalty must be assessed within three years after the date of filing. I.R.C. § 6501(a). At least 60 days prior to assessment, the IRS must notify those the IRS has identified as responsible persons. Once the tax has been assessed, the Service must within 60 days from the date of assessment notify all those against whom the tax has been assessed and demand payment. I.R.C. § 6303(a).

Congress amended section 6672 in 1996 to require the IRS to issue pre-collection notices to persons the IRS has identified as responsible persons at least 60 days prior to any notice and demand for payment of the tax. This permits such persons to appeal that determination administratively. The 1996 amendments also create a new federal right of contribution among persons who are assessed the same penalty and permits such persons to bring separate federal actions against each other to determine each person's proportionate share of the penalty. IRC § 6672(e). These changes should alter the prior practice of the person with the most assets (rather than the greatest culpability) being responsible for paying the entire tax liability.

Recall from Chapter 8 (§ 8.3, *supra*) that the time limit in which a refund claim must be filed is the later of: (1) 3 years from the date the return was filed and the taxes paid, if paid at that time; or (2) 2 years from the date the taxes were paid, if paid later. Although most taxes must be paid in full before a refund suit can be maintained, the 100% penalty under section 6672 is a "divisible" liability. (See further discussion, § 14.3.A., *infra*). To qualify to litigate a refund claim based on section 6672, an alleged responsible person need only pay the payroll tax for one employee for one quarter, not the entire deficiency. Thus, a person against whom a section 6672 penalty has been assessed can gain access to a jury trial in a United States district court (or can invoke the jurisdiction of the Court of Federal Claims, a separate refund tribunal in which a jury trial is not available) without paying the entire assessed amount. In order to bring such a suit, the person first must post a bond in accordance with section 6672(c). After payment of the minimum amount, the refund suit must be filed within two years from the date of payment. The alternate 3–year rule is inapplicable because there was no return filed with respect to the payroll taxes by the person against whom the penalty is being asserted. Litigation in the Tax Court without first paying any part of the tax is not possible because the penalty is assessed without prior issuance of the statutory notice of deficiency, a prerequisite to Tax Court jurisdiction.

To illustrate: if a section 6672 penalty in the amount of $52,000 is asserted against a corporate officer, and on May 1, 1990 she pays an amount equal to the taxes of one employee for one quarter, she may file a refund claim on or before May 1, 1992. Her refund suit may then be filed within six months of the payment date (or the date the IRS issues a statutory notice of disallowance). The suit will be time-barred if not filed within two years of the earlier of these dates (passage of six months from date of payment or issuance of a notice of disallowance of the refund claim).

D. *Lender Liability*

Lenders and other creditors frequently exercise a significant amount of control over debtor-busi-

nesses. This control can result in liability for delinquent trust fund taxes under either section 6672 or
section 3505, a separate statutory provision aimed
directly at such creditors. Creditors will be subject
to the 100% penalty under section 6672 if, in their
efforts to protect their interests, they effectively
control the debtor by dictating which bills the debt-
or can pay and generally managing the debtor's
business. Merely pressuring the debtor to pay
amounts due to a bank or other creditor should not
expose the creditor to liability under section 6672,
but the question of control is an issue of fact and
there certainly is an increased risk for a lender who
becomes involved with the details of the debtor's
business in an attempt to improve the debtor's
financial health. At some point the degree of control
exercised by the lender or other creditor can render
it a responsible person under section 6672.

A separate source of lender liability is section
3505, which makes a lender liable for a debtor's
unpaid trust fund taxes in two different situations.
The first, covered by section 3505(a), makes the
lender liable for a penalty equal to 100% of the
unpaid payroll taxes if the lender pays the debtor's
wages directly and fails to pay the trust fund taxes
to the Government. This degree of control would
also justify the section 6672 penalty, but Congress,
in enacting section 3505 in 1966, sought to provide
bright-line standards for certain conduct of lenders.
Thus, where a lender or its agent pays the debtor's
employees' wages and fails to collect and pay over
the trust fund taxes, the lender will be subject to a

100% penalty under section 3505(a) without regard to the section 6672 factors of willfulness and "responsibility."

The second situation covered by section 3505 has generated significant litigation because it imposes liability under circumstances that section 6672 would not reach. Section 3505(b) imposes a penalty of 25% of amounts advanced to a debtor specifically for payrolls if the lender had actual notice or knowledge that the debtor did not intend to or would be unable to make timely payment of the trust fund taxes. A lending organization is deemed to have "actual notice or knowledge" if the person handling the account knew or would have known if due diligence had been exercised that payroll taxes were not being paid over to the Government. This section is not designed to make a lender a "super cop" required to scrutinize all borrowers' use of loaned funds, but neither will it permit a lender to hide behind labels or language in an agreement that does not reflect the parties' knowledge and intentions. For example, ordinary working capital loans are outside the scope of section 3505(b), unless the lender knows that the loan amounts to a "net payroll loan" (the funds being advanced are sufficient only to cover the net wages and not the "withheld" taxes) and that the borrower cannot timely make payment of its payroll taxes. The Government bears the burden of proving the purpose of the loan and the lender's notice or knowledge of the borrower's inability to pay the trust fund taxes.

Notice the difference in the amount of the penalties. Both section 6672 and section 3505(a) impose a penalty of 100% of the unpaid payroll taxes. Section 3505(b), however, provides for a penalty of 25% of the amounts advanced by the lender to the borrower for the purpose of payrolls. If the lender is not paying the employer's wages directly, and thus is not subject to the section 3505(a) penalty, may the Government proceed under section 6672, or must it seek only the lesser 25% penalty under section 3505(b)? Although there was some doubt about this in previous years, it now appears settled that the Government may assert the 100% penalty of section 6672, and it will be entitled to recover the full 100% if it establishes the requisite control and willfulness by the lender.

Important procedural differences also exist between sections 6672 and 3505. As discussed earlier, the Service must assess the section 6672 penalty against alleged responsible persons within three years after the payroll tax return is filed. Liability for the trust fund taxes is direct and personal against those who are responsible for its collection and payment, and the Government must give them notice of the assessment and make demand for payment within 60 days of the assessment. On the other hand, liability for unpaid payroll taxes under section 3505 may not be directly assessed against a lender. The Government instead must institute a civil proceeding for collection of the section 3505 penalty. Significantly, the Government may bring the civil suit against the lender any time within 10 years from the date the tax is assessed against the employer.

Because the IRS cannot assess the section 3505 penalty against a lender, and because it has 10 years in which to bring a civil action seeking to collect the penalty, there was a question whether the lender must be given notice of the assessment against the employer as a prerequisite for a later civil suit against the lender. The Supreme Court has held that section 6303(a) does not require the Government to notify a lender that is potentially liable under section 3505 when it assesses an employer. Jersey Shore State Bank v. United States (S.Ct.1987). It is thus possible for a lender to learn for the first time of its potential liability when a civil suit against it is filed under section 3505 for actions taken 10 years earlier involving employees and records that may no longer be available.

CHAPTER 14

CHOICE OF FORUM IN CIVIL TAX LITIGATION

§ 14.1 Introduction

When efforts fail to resolve a tax dispute administratively, the taxpayer must decide whether to pay the disputed tax (or abandon hopes of recovering a claimed refund), or to litigate the controversy. At this stage, the taxpayer enjoys an unusual and significant strategic advantage: the taxpayer in a civil tax controversy can select among three different courts, each with different procedures, precedents and levels of expertise. Although "forum-shopping" is present in other aspects of our judicial system, in no other type of case is one party favored with such broad discretion to select among several courts the forum that is most likely to rule in his favor.

The three available forums are the United States Tax Court, the United States district courts, and the United States Court of Federal Claims (formerly the Claims Court). To ensure that the proper forum is selected, one must be familiar with the most important features of each. For example, factors that may determine the appropriate selection include whether a jury trial is available, whether the taxpayer must first pay the disputed tax in order to litigate in that forum, the apparent expertise of the judges, and the precedents governing decisions in the tribunal.

Examples of how important the choice of forum can be abound. One of the most famous is *Estate of Carter v. Commissioner* (2d Cir.1971), in which a widow appealed from a decision of the Tax Court holding that payments made to her by her deceased husband's employer were taxable income to her, rather than a tax-free gift. The appellate court observed that if the widow had been able to pay the deficiency and thereby qualify to litigate the issue in United States district court, she would have won based on the precedents governing the court. But because she could not afford to pay the tax, her only choice was the U.S. Tax Court, which took a much more restrictive view of what constituted a tax-free gift. The appellate court reversed the Tax Court, stating that "[w]e cannot believe * * * the result should depend on whether a widow could afford to pay the tax and sue for a refund rather than avail herself of the salutary remedy Congress intended to afford in establishing the Tax Court and permitting determination before payment." The *Golsen* rule, discussed at section 14.2.D., *infra*, precludes a recurrence of this exact problem, but examples of the disastrous impact of improper or unlucky forum selection continue to occur. Thus, the best trial forum should be selected initially, if at all possible.

§ 14.2 United States Tax Court

As its name implies, the Tax Court hears only tax cases, and because of that fact, Tax Court judges are usually quite expert in tax matters. Thus, taxpayers who have the most complicated and technical issues often select the Tax Court for its supposed expertise. Most taxpayers, though, choose to bring suit in the Tax Court because it is the only forum with deficiency jurisdiction. That means that the taxpayer is not required to first pay the disputed tax in order to file suit (i.e., it is a "sue-first-pay-later" forum). For this reason, it is sometimes referred to as the "poor man's court." An irony is that while the Tax Court is the forum chosen by most taxpayers, statistics show that the taxpayer loses more often in the Tax Court than in the other forums. Of course, statistics do not take into account the legal issues involved or the merits of the cases. Also, because the taxpayer need not pay the tax to litigate in the Tax Court, more frivolous cases are docketed in the Tax Court than in the other forums.

Trial by jury is not available in the Tax Court. As a result, the Federal Rules of Evidence, which apply in Tax Court proceedings, are enforced much less stringently than in a jury trial in a U.S. district court. The Tax Court has its own rules of practice and procedure, which differ from the Federal Rules of Civil Procedure. Tax Court rules require the parties to cooperate generally to resolve factual disputes. For example, pretrial discovery is more limited by the Tax Court Rules than by the Federal

Rules of Civil Procedure, and Tax Court Rules require that the parties first engage in informal communication to attempt to reach the objectives of discovery before utilizing formal discovery procedures. T.C. Rule 70(a)(1).

Unlike the other available courts, the Tax Court permits non-lawyers to represent taxpayers in cases before it. Under Tax Court Rule 24(b), a taxpayer may represent himself in a Tax Court proceeding, and Rule 200 permits accountants and others, who pass an examination, to practice before the Tax Court. For obvious reasons, however, including most non-lawyers' lack of familiarity with litigation procedures and tactics, the taxpayer usually should be represented by an attorney. Note, however, that the Tax Court has held that it does not have the power to appoint counsel for indigent taxpayers.

The Tax Court is an Article I "legislative" court, which means that it was established pursuant to Article I of the U.S. Constitution, rather than Article III, which established many other federal courts. I.R.C. § 7441. This distinction has little practical effect in selecting the appropriate forum, except that the Tax Court's jurisdiction is strictly limited by statute. See § 14.2.A., *infra*, for a discussion of jurisdictional prerequisites. The main impact of Article I status is on the compensation and tenure of the judges. Tax Court judges serve for terms of 15 years, rather than for lifetime appointments (which is the case for U.S. district judges). I.R.C. § 7443. Tax Court judges must retire at age 70, I.R.C. § 7447, and they do not enjoy the protection that

Article III judges have from reduction in their compensation during their tenure. The Tax Court consists of 19 judges appointed by the President with the advice and consent of the U.S. Senate. I.R.C. § 7443. The Tax Court is based in Washington, D.C., but its judges travel throughout the country to hear tax cases. Thus, taxpayers often find the Tax Court to be as convenient as the U.S. district court. Moreover, while usually the taxpayer need not travel to Washington, D.C. for the trial of his case, he may choose to have the trial in Washington to avoid local publicity.

The court was established in 1924 as the Board of Tax Appeals. Decisions from the former Board of Tax Appeals are cited as "___ B.T.A. ___". In 1942 its name was changed to the Tax Court of the United States. In 1969 the court's name was again changed, this time to the United States Tax Court, and several significant changes were made: the court's status was changed from an agency of the Executive Branch that had functioned as a *de facto* court to an official Article I "legislative" court, and Tax Court judges were given expanded powers to enforce their orders by fine or imprisonment. Prior to 1969, Tax Court judges could not enforce their own contempt citations, but instead were required to petition the U.S. district courts for an enforceable contempt order.

The Supreme Court has ruled that the Tax Court is a "court of law" that is different from other legislatively-created tribunals (such as the SEC) because it exercises exclusively judicial power. Freytag v. Commissioner (S.Ct.1991). Following the decision in *Freytag*, the Tax Court ruled that its jurisdiction included the power to apply the doctrine of equitable recoupment, a power that formerly had been doubted. Estate of Mueller v. Commissioner (Tax Ct.1993). This decision was overruled on appeal, however. See Estate of Mueller v. Commissioner (6th Cir.1998). Currently, a conflict exists among the circuits as to whether the Tax Court has equity jurisdiction.

A. *Jurisdictional Requirements*

The Tax Court does not have jurisdiction over all controversies relating to federal taxes. Its jurisdiction is limited to specific statutory grants of jurisdiction, which include: income, estate and gift tax cases; windfall profits tax and certain excise tax cases; and some declaratory judgment and disclosure cases. Even if subject matter jurisdiction exists, Tax Court jurisdiction is further dependent on exact compliance with several statutory prerequisites: the Commissioner must "determine" that a tax "deficiency" exists, the IRS must mail a notice of deficiency to the taxpayer, and the taxpayer must file a petition in the Tax Court within 90 days of the mailing of the notice of deficiency. Once a taxpayer has invoked the Tax Court's jurisdiction by timely filing a petition, that election is irrevocable, and the taxpayer may not dismiss the petition and seek a refund trial. Estate of Ming, Jr. v. Commissioner (Tax Ct.1974).

There is no required form for the notice of deficiency, and any document that fairly informs the taxpayer that the Commissioner has "determined a deficiency" and that identifies the taxable year and the amount of the deficiency is usually upheld under I.R.C. § 6212(a). Although it might seem that the mailing of a notice of deficiency would be proof enough that the Commissioner had "determined" a deficiency, two cases have held that a notice of deficiency that was vague and bore no relationship to the return filed by the taxpayer did not comply with I.R.C. § 6212(a) because the Commissioner did not "determine" a deficiency as required by the statute. Scar v. Commissioner (9th Cir.1987); Campbell v. Commissioner (Tax Ct.Memo.1988). In both cases the deficiency notices stated that they were being sent "in order to protect the government's interest." The effect of these decisions is to discourage the Service from mailing hasty, last-minute notices based on little or no actual examination of taxpayers' returns.

In 1988 Congress enacted new I.R.C. § 7521, which requires that all deficiency notices mailed after Jan. 1, 1990 describe the basis for and identify the amounts sought as tax due, interest, penalties and additions to tax. Failure by the Service to comply with these requirements will not automatically invalidate the notice, however. In addition to notices of deficiency issued under I.R.C. § 6212, section 7521 also applies to the first notice of proposed deficiency (usually the "30–day letter," described in Section 6.2.B, *supra*), as well as to notices of assessment and demand for payment of tax that must be sent within 60 days after the tax is assessed and before collection procedures can be instituted. See Chapter 11 for a discussion of assessment and collection procedures.

The taxpayer initiates a suit in the Tax Court by filing a petition seeking a "redetermination" of the tax deficiency computed by the Service. The Commissioner of the Internal Revenue Service is the named respondent. The Commissioner is represented by attorneys from the Office of the Chief Counsel. In the other two available forums, the Government is represented by trial lawyers from the Tax Division of the Justice Department.

The petition may not be filed until the Service has issued the taxpayer a statutory "notice of deficiency" (known as a "90–day letter"). The notice of deficiency is sometimes referred to as the "ticket to the Tax Court" because Tax Court jurisdiction depends on its issuance. The taxpayer has 90 days from the date the notice of deficiency is mailed to the taxpayer's "last known address" to file the petition or pay the tax. If the taxpayer does neither, the Service will assess the deficiency and begin collection proceedings. Deficiency notices mailed after December 31, 1998 must specify the date determined by the IRS as the last day on which the petition may be filed. IRC § 6213, as amended by Taxpayer Bill of Rights Act 3 of 1998. Actual assessment of the tax (after which the Service can institute collection procedures) is barred during the 90 days after issuance of the notice of deficiency. If the taxpayer files a petition with the Tax Court during this 90–day period, the statute of limitations on assessment of the tax is suspended during the pendency of the case. I.R.C. § 6503(a)(1).

To summarize, the date of mailing of the notice of deficiency is important because mailing of the statutory notice (rather than the date the taxpayer receives the notice) triggers three separate but related statutory rules:

a. It suspends the statute of limitations on assessment of the deficiency. I.R.C. § 6503(a)(1).

b. It begins the 90–day statute of limitations in which the Tax Court petition must be filed. I.R.C. § 6213(a).

c. It bars the Service from any assessment or collection activity during the 90–day period and, if the taxpayer files a petition in the Tax Court during the 90–day period, it further bars assessment or collection activity until the decision of the Tax Court becomes final.

Because the Code focuses on the date of mailing of the notice of deficiency, rather than on the date the taxpayer actually receives it, it is important to retain the envelope in which the notice was mailed. The date on the notice itself may be different from the date the notice is mailed.

B. The Taxpayer's "Last Known Address"

What happens if the taxpayer never receives the statutory notice? Obviously, the taxpayer will not have had an opportunity to petition the Tax Court to review the deficiency, and often the taxpayer first learns of the problem when the Service begins collection activity by placing liens on the taxpayer's property and levying on his bank accounts. See Chapter 11 for a discussion of the tax collection process. The Code requires only that the Service mail the notice, and permits (but does not require) mailing by certified or registered mail. I.R.C. § 6212(a). The Code also states that the notice "shall be sufficient" if it is "mailed to the taxpayer at his last known address." I.R.C. § 6212(b). Because we live in such a highly mobile society, it is not surprising that many taxpayers receive notices of deficiency weeks after they are mailed, or never receive them at all.

If the taxpayer never receives the notice of deficiency, one course of action is to seek an injunction barring collection of the deficiency on the theory that the notice of deficiency was never mailed by the Service, and therefore the assessment and collection are barred under I.R.C. § 6213(a). This Code section is an exception to the general bar on suits to restrain assessment or collection of taxes, but winning such an action is quite difficult because there are detailed procedures outlined in the Internal Revenue Manual for keeping records of mailings of deficiency notices, and compliance with these procedures is proof of mailing. *See* Keado v. United States (5th Cir.1988).

More frequently, taxpayers have challenged the validity of the notice by claiming that it was not mailed to their "last known address." If the statute of limitations has not run, the Service may simply correct its error and reissue the notice to the correct address. If the statute of limitations has expired on the deficiency, then the taxpayer's success in challenging the validity of the notice depends on a number of factors. First, if the court finds that the notice was in fact mailed to the taxpayer's last known address, then the notice is valid despite the fact that the taxpayer never received it. In one case, for example, the notice was held valid despite evidence that there had been a fire in the post office that could have caused the taxpayer's alleged nonreceipt of the notice. Harrison v. Commissioner (Tax Ct.Memo1979).

Another factor that will affect the court's determination of whether the notice is valid is the taxpayer's actual receipt of the notice, despite the fact that it was not mailed to his "last known address." The Tax Court has held that if the taxpayer actually receives the notice without prejudicial delay, then the notice is valid even though it was not mailed to the taxpayer's last known address. Frieling v. Commissioner (Tax Ct.1983) (taxpayers timely filed Tax Court petition; notice held valid even though not mailed to last known address); Mulvania v. Commissioner (Tax Ct.1983) (notice actually received 16 days after it was mailed to former but not last known address held valid; petition filed more than 90 days after notice mailed dismissed for lack of jurisdiction). The court's reasoning in these cases was that mailing to the last known address is merely a "safe harbor" for the Government, and that the notice still may be valid even though it was not mailed to the last known address. Receipt of actual notice of the deficiency determined by the Commissioner, without prejudicial delay, is all that is required, according to the Tax Court. *See* McKay v. Commissioner (Tax Ct.1987).

Receipt of the notice of deficiency by the taxpayer's attorney or accountant, and the actions taken by the advisor, also can affect whether the notice is valid. For example, in *Mulvania v. Commissioner* (9th Cir.1985), the court held that a notice of deficiency that was not mailed to the taxpayer's last known address was invalid, even though a copy of the notice was received by the taxpayer's accountant. The accountant had informed the taxpayer of the notice approximately 45 days after he had received it. The accountant had a limited power of attorney authorizing him only to receive copies of correspondence. The Ninth Circuit held that "where a notice of deficiency has been misaddressed to the taxpayer or sent only to an adviser who is merely authorized to receive a copy of such a notice, *actual notice is necessary but not sufficient to make the notice valid.*" *Id.* (emphasis added). The court reasoned that the notice became "null and void" when it was returned to the IRS undelivered, and that "the taxpayer's actual knowledge did not transform the void notice into a valid one." *Id.*

Subsequently, however, the Ninth Circuit has held that actual notice is the central goal of section 6212(b)(1) and that delivery to the taxpayer of an exact copy of the notice of deficiency by the taxpayer's attorney is sufficient. McKay v. Commissioner, *supra* (9th Cir.1989). The *McKay* majority distinguished its earlier decision in *Mulvania* on the basis that the record in *Mulvania* contained no evidence that the taxpayer either received a copy of the notice or was informed of its contents. Thus, a notice of deficiency that is not mailed to a taxpayer's last known address, but of which the taxpayer is informed by his attorney or accountant without prejudicial delay, will be valid as long as the taxpayer receives a copy of the notice or is fully informed of its contents.

The dissenting judge in *McKay* argued that *Mulvania* was both correct and not distinguishable, and that the misaddressed notice should not be effective. According to the dissent:

> Until today's decision, the lines were drawn with clarity; if the IRS did not itself provide actual notice to the taxpayer or mail the notice to the taxpayer's last known address, the notice was invalid. We now depart from that line, and hold that in some circumstances notice can be provided by the taxpayer's own attorney, rather than the IRS. The inquiry now must shift from what IRS records show, to the nature of communications between tax advisors and clients. This decision * * * provides a disincentive for accurate record keeping on the part of the IRS, and will impede communication between tax advisors and their clients. [*McKay, supra,* at 1240, Schroeder, J., dissenting.]

The stakes in these cases can be quite high: if the court finds that the Service properly mailed the notice to the taxpayer's last known address, or that the taxpayer received the notice in time to file a Tax Court petition, then the taxpayer cannot litigate in Tax Court unless he actually files the petition within the 90–day period following mailing of the notice; on the other hand, if the court finds that the Service did not properly mail the notice to the taxpayer's last known address, and that the taxpayer did not actually receive the notice in time to file a Tax Court petition, then the notice is not valid and, assuming it was issued just prior to the expiration of the statute of limitations (as is usually the case), the Service will be time-barred from trying to assess and collect the tax.

Given these stakes, it is important to identify exactly what is a taxpayer's last known address. Unfortunately, there are no clear guidelines, and the courts are split concerning the effect of certain types of notice from the taxpayer. Although the Service generally may use the address shown on the return in question, that address may not be used if the taxpayer notifies the Service in a clear and concise manner that his address has changed. The IRS has issued guidance on how to provide it with clear and concise notification of change of address. See Rev. Proc. 2001–18, 2001–1 C.B. IV. Also, if the address on the return is incorrect, the taxpayer bears the burden of providing the correct address. Failure to carry this burden will result in a valid notice if mailed to the incorrect address, even though the taxpayer never receives the notice. *See* Armstrong v. Commissioner (10th Cir.1994).

C. *Small Tax Cases*

Taxpayers with asserted tax deficiencies of $50,000 or less for any taxable year have the option of electing the more informal procedures available under I.R.C. § 7463. The former $10,000 limit was increased to $50,000 as part of the Taxpayer Bill of Rights Act 3 of 1998. The purpose of this provision is to provide a simpler and less expensive alternative for taxpayers who do not have the funds or the desire to litigate their tax deficiency in a regular Tax Court trial. Tax Court Rule 177(b) requires that trial of small tax cases "be conducted as informally as possible consistent with orderly procedure," and further provides that any evidence deemed by the court "to have probative value" shall be admissible. Under Rule 177(c), neither briefs nor oral arguments are required in small tax cases.

Special trial judges, appointed by the Chief Judge of the Tax Court under Tax Court Rules 3(d) and 180–83, hear small tax cases. Under I.R.C. § 7463(b), decisions of the trial judge in small tax cases are final and nonappealable, and are not treated as precedent for any other case. A taxpayer electing small tax case procedures, therefore, gains the advantage of informality but forfeits both the opportunity to have his case tried by a regular Tax Court judge and his right to appeal an adverse decision.

The filing fee for both regular Tax Court petitions and those filed in small tax cases is $60. Small case procedure is not automatic; the taxpayer must request it and the Tax Court must approve it. I.R.C. § 7463(a).

D. Governing Precedent in Tax Court—The Golsen Rule

Appeals from Tax Court decisions are reviewed by the U.S. Courts of Appeals (other than the Court of Appeals for the Federal Circuit, discussed in § 14.4.A, *infra*), with venue generally determined by the taxpayer's residence. I.R.C. § 7482. Because the Tax Court's jurisdiction is nationwide, and because it is inevitable that the various Courts of Appeals will resolve some issues differently, the question arises as to how the Tax Court should decide a case in which the Courts of Appeals have rendered decisions that conflict with the precedent of the Tax Court. Should the Tax Court follow its own precedent, or the precedent of the majority of appellate courts, or the precedent of the Court of Appeals to which an appeal in the case before it would lie? After years of uncertainty, the Tax Court resolved this question in its 1970 decision in *Golsen v. Commissioner* (Tax Ct.1970), in which it declared that henceforth it would follow the governing precedent in the Court of Appeals to which the case before it is appealable. Although the court recognized that its decision could adversely affect the federal interest in uniform application of the tax laws, it concluded that efficient judicial administration required that it adopt the rule and that the court could foster uniformity by explaining why it disagreed with precedent it felt constrained to follow.

The effect of the *Golsen* rule can be illustrated by the following example. Assume that the issue involved is whether certain purported "interest" payments are deductible, and that the First, Second, Third and Tenth Circuits have held that such payments are not deductible, while the Fourth and Seventh Circuits have held that such payments are deductible. If an appeal in the case before the court would lie to the First, Second, Third or Tenth Circuit Court of Appeals, then the Tax Court must rule that the payment is not deductible. If appeal would lie to the Fourth or Seventh Circuit, the Tax Court would be required to hold such payments deductible. If appeal would lie to any other Circuit, the Tax Court could reach its own decision on the question because it would not be bound by any precedent in the Circuit.

E. *"Reviewed," "Regular," and "Memorandum" Decisions*

The precedential value of a Tax Court decision depends on whether the decision is reviewed by all 19 judges (a "reviewed" opinion, which has the greatest precedential value), or whether it is issued as a "memorandum" decision or what is known as a "regular" decision. The Chief Judge reviews all opinions of the Tax Court judges before issuance. The Chief Judge then decides whether the issue should be decided by all the judges (resulting in a "reviewed" decision). Both reviewed and regular decisions are published by the Tax Court and printed by the Government Printing Office in bound volumes designated as The United States Tax Court Reports. Such decisions, in which the Commissioner of Internal Revenue is the respondent, are cited as "___ T.C. ___."

Not all decisions of the Tax Court appear in the official Tax Court Reports, however. Decisions involving relatively settled legal principles are issued as "Memorandum Opinions" and are numbered serially each year in the form "T.C. Memo. 1990–1." Memorandum opinions have little precedential value and are not published in the official Tax Court Reports. Instead, they are printed by unofficial, commercial publishers and are made available to the general public.

In between "reviewed" decisions and "memorandum" decisions are what are often referred to as "regular" Tax Court decisions: those that have been reviewed by the Chief Judge and are published in the official Tax Court Reports, but are not reviewed by all 19 judges of the Tax Court. Such decisions usually involve some legal interpretation, unlike many "memorandum" decisions, but the issue is often less controversial or significant than is involved in most "reviewed" decisions. "Regular" Tax Court decisions have less precedential value than "reviewed" decisions but more than "memorandum" decisions.

In some cases, the Chief Judge may assign a case to a Special Trial Judge (STJ) that does not fall within the small case category. The Tax Court had taken the position from 1983 on that the report of the STJ was advisory only and did not have to be made available to the parties. The U.S. Supreme Court struck down this practice, though, in 2005, holding that the Tax Court's practice of withholding the report of the STJ "impedes fully informed appellate review of the Tax Court's decision." Ballard v. Commissioner (S.Ct.2005); Estate of Kanter v. Commissioner (S.Ct.2005).

§ 14.3 United States District Courts

The U.S. district courts have refund jurisdiction. Thus, in order to invoke the jurisdiction of the U.S. district court, the taxpayer must first pay the disputed tax and file a claim for a refund of the tax paid. I.R.C. § 7422(a); 28 U.S.C. § 1346(a)(1). Suit should be filed against the United States, rather than any Government officer or agent. Refund suits may be brought to recover any amount of tax allegedly overpaid, regardless of how small.

The U.S. district courts are the only tax forum in which a jury trial is available. This fact, coupled with the familiarity of the district court judges with local concerns, influences many taxpayers to choose the U.S. district court for litigation of their tax controversies. Attorneys from the Tax Division of the Justice Department represent the Government, except in the Southern District of New York and two California districts (where assistant U.S. attorneys represent the Government).

A. The "Full Payment" Rule

If the Service assesses a deficiency of $100,000 against a taxpayer, may the taxpayer pay only half the assessed deficiency (or perhaps even less) and file a refund suit? The applicable statute conferring concurrent jurisdiction on U.S. district courts and the Court of Federal Claims refers to "[a]ny civil action against the United States for the recovery of any internal-revenue tax alleged to have been erroneously or illegally assessed or collected, or any penalty claimed to have been collected without authority or any sum alleged to have been * * * wrongfully collected * * *." 28 U.S.C. § 1346(a)(1). This language would appear to permit a refund suit following partial payment. In a 1960 decision, however, the U.S. Supreme Court, after observing that the statute was ambiguous and the legislative history unhelpful, held that full payment of the entire tax assessed is a jurisdictional prerequisite to filing a refund suit. Flora v. United States (S.Ct.1960). The Service takes the position (Reg. § 301.6201–1(a)) that the *Flora* rule requires payment of all applicable interest and penalties, as well as the full underlying tax. There is a conflict among the courts on this issue, however, so the safest course to avoid problems concerning jurisdiction in a refund suit is to pay all interest and penalties.

An exception to the "full payment" rule exists for so-called "divisible" taxes. Income taxes, estate tax-

es and gift taxes are all non-divisible taxes that are
subject to the full-payment rule. Examples of divisible taxes that permit refund-suit jurisdiction without full payment of the entire amount assessed are
some excise taxes and penalties imposed on "responsible persons" under I.R.C. §§ 6671 and 6672
for failure to ensure that income taxes withheld
from employees' pay are actually paid to the Government. "Responsible persons" who wish to contest the penalty need only pay the full withheld
taxes of any one individual, rather than the total
amount withheld from all employees, to invoke jurisdiction. Steele v. United States (8th Cir.1960).
See § 13.3.A, *supra*, for a discussion of liability of
"responsible persons" under I.R.C. §§ 6671–72.

B.   When the Refund Suit Must Be Filed

There are two important time periods to consider
in determining a taxpayer's right to litigate a claim
for refund of overpaid taxes. The first is the date by
which a claim for refund must be filed. Because the
refund claim is a jurisdictional prerequisite to a
refund suit, untimely filing of the claim will preclude litigation of the controversy. The second time
limit to consider is the date by which the refund
suit must be filed. Untimely filing of the suit, even
if the claim was timely filed, also will deprive the
court of jurisdiction and subject the taxpayer's suit
to dismissal with prejudice. There are numerous
exceptions to the general statutory rules discussed
below, most of which permit claims for refunds
beyond the usual time period in situations in which

the taxpayer could not have known of his entitlement to a refund within the statutory period.

If a claim for refund is timely filed, but no refund is received, the next step is filing a suit for refund in either the U.S. district court or the Court of Federal Claims. The suit may not be filed until either 6 months have passed from the date the refund claim was filed, or the Service has disallowed the claim by issuing a statutory notice of claim disallowance under I.R.C. § 6532(a)(1). The refund claim is deemed filed when it is received by the Service. The refund suit must then be filed within 2 years from the date the IRS mailed the notice of disallowance. The taxpayer can waive the requirement of a statutory notice of disallowance by filing a Form 2297. If this course is followed, the 2–year statute of limitations begins to run on the date the form is filed. I.R.C. § 6532(a)(3). The taxpayer still must wait 6 months before filing the refund suit, however. Regs. § 301.6532–1(c). If the Service does not issue a statutory notice of disallowance, and if the taxpayer has not waived the notice requirement, the statute of limitations for filing the refund claim could remain open indefinitely.

To summarize: the refund suit will be premature if filed before 6 months after the refund claim was filed, unless the IRS issues a notice of disallowance prior to the passage of 6 months. The suit will be time-barred, unless it is filed within 2 years from either the date the IRS mailed the statutory notice of disallowance or the date the taxpayer filed a

Form 2297 waiving the statutory notice of disallowance.

A refund suit filed prematurely is subject to dismissal for lack of jurisdiction. Dismissal is without prejudice, and the taxpayer may simply refile the suit after the appropriate time has passed. Refund suits filed after the statute of limitations has expired are subject to dismissal with prejudice. Because the limitations periods are statutory, they may not be waived by the Service.

§ 14.4 United States Court of Federal Claims

The U.S. Court of Federal Claims exercises concurrent jurisdiction with the U.S. district courts over tax refund suits and about a quarter of its cases fall into this category. Because a significant portion of its docket consists of tax refund cases, Court of Federal Claims judges generally are viewed as having greater tax expertise than most U.S. district judges, but less than Tax Court judges. Some observers believe that Court of Federal Claims judges are more willing to decide a case on the equities involved than are Tax Court judges, who are sometimes described as inclined to adhere more faithfully to technical rules and to defer more to the views of the Service.

Like the Tax Court, the Court of Federal Claims is a "legislative court" that was established pursuant to Article I of the U.S. Constitution, although its precursor, the Court of Claims, was an Article III court. On October 1, 1982, the former U.S. Court of Claims was replaced by two new courts:

the U.S. Claims Court and the U.S. Court of Appeals for the Federal Circuit. The new Claims Court assumed most of the trial jurisdiction formerly held by the Court of Claims, including jurisdiction over tax refund suits. In 1992, the Claims Court was renamed the United States Court of Federal Claims.

The Court of Federal Claims consists of 16 judges appointed by the President with the advice and consent of the Senate. Since it is an Article I court, the judges of the U.S. Court of Federal Claims do not enjoy lifetime tenure or the other protections afforded Article III judges. Newly appointed Court of Federal Claims judges will serve for 15 years, while those who were Commissioners on the former Court of Claims will serve a total of 15 years from the date of their appointment as Court of Claims Commissioners. Court of Federal Claims judges may be appointed for a second term.

Like the Tax Court, the Court of Federal Claims is based in Washington, D.C., but it is authorized to hold sessions throughout the country. Court of Federal Claims rules permit great flexibility in scheduling for the convenience of the parties and witnesses. The judge may travel to several locations to hear evidence, and the trial may consist of a series of sessions. This flexibility can be especially important in complex cases with many witnesses scattered throughout the country.

Unlike the U.S. district courts, trial by jury is not available in the Court of Federal Claims, although Court of Federal Claims Rules, based on the Federal

Rules of Civil Procedure, afford the same discovery procedures available in the U.S. district courts. Because jury trials are not available, evidentiary rulings tend to be more relaxed than in U.S. district courts. Since the taxpayer must pay the disputed tax as a jurisdictional prerequisite, all the refund suit rules described in Section 14.3 of this Chapter are equally applicable to Court of Federal Claims actions. The United States is the named respondent in Court of Federal Claims tax refund actions. Attorneys from the Tax Division of the Justice Department represent the Government.

A. *Appeals*

The new Federal Circuit Court of Appeals (which resulted from a merger of the former Court of Claims and the U.S. Court of Customs and Patent Appeals) took over the appellate jurisdiction of the two merged courts, including jurisdiction over tax-refund suit appeals from the Claims Court. The Federal Circuit Court of Appeals is an Article III court on par with the other U.S. Courts of Appeals, but unlike the other Federal Courts of Appeals, the appellate jurisdiction of the Federal Circuit is defined by subject matter, rather than geography. Decisions of the Federal Circuit Court of Appeals are reviewable by the U.S. Supreme Court on petition for writ of certiorari. Prior to the 1982 reorganization, decisions of the Court of Claims were reviewable directly by the U.S. Supreme Court, because there was no intermediate appellate court.

B. *Governing Precedent in Court of Federal Claims*

The Court of Federal Claims is bound by precedent of the former Court of Claims, the U.S. Court of Appeals for the Federal Circuit and the U.S. Supreme Court. This can be especially significant if the issue involved has been decided adversely to the taxpayer in the regional Circuit Court of Appeals to which an appeal would lie in a particular case: in such circumstances, the taxpayer would be assured of losing both in U.S. district court and in the Tax Court (because of the *Golsen* rule, discussed at § 14.2.D., *supra*), and the Court of Federal Claims would offer the only realistic possibility of success (assuming there was no adverse precedent in the Court of Federal Claims).

§ 14.5   Strategic Considerations In Choosing A Forum

A. *Governing Precedent*

Although it is impossible to predict which factors will predominate in any given case, it is clear that some factors tend to be more important than others. The most important factor governing selection of the proper forum in any case will almost always be the governing precedents. Careful study of the precedents in the various courts and in the Circuit Courts of Appeals to which an appeal would lie (that is, the regional Circuit Court versus the Federal Circuit Court of Appeals) should be the first step. Attention should focus on cases involving the same or closely-related issues under the same or similar factual circumstances. Statistics revealing the total number of taxpayer victories versus the Government's winning percentage in general are of little or no meaning and simply cannot substitute for thorough research and analysis of pertinent precedent.

To analyze the importance of governing precedents, consider the following questions:

1. Has the U.S. Supreme Court ruled on the issue? If yes, then all available courts are bound to follow the Supreme Court's ruling. If the Supreme Court precedent is favorable to the taxpayer, victory in any forum should occur; if the precedent is adverse to the taxpayer, the Government should win in any forum. If no, then the following questions should be considered.

2. Has the taxpayer's Circuit Court of Appeals ruled on the issue? If yes, then both the Tax Court (by virtue of the *Golsen* rule, discussed at § 14.2.D., *supra*) and the U.S. district court are bound by that ruling. The Court of Federal Claims is not bound by it, however. If the decision is favorable to the taxpayer, either the Tax Court or the U.S. district court should be selected. If the decision is adverse to the taxpayer, both courts should produce the same defeat for the taxpayer. If no (the Circuit Court has not ruled on the question), then consider the following questions.

3. Has the Federal Circuit ruled on the issue? If yes, and if that ruling is favorable to the taxpayer, then the Court of Federal Claims should be selected. If the Federal Circuit has ruled adversely to the

taxpayer's position, the Court of Federal Claims should be avoided. If no (the Federal Circuit has not ruled on the issue), then consider the following questions.

4. Have any of the trial forums ruled on the issue? If yes, and if any has ruled favorably to the taxpayer's position, then that forum should be chosen. If any have ruled adversely to the taxpayer's position, that court (or courts) should be avoided. If no (that is, there is no precedent in any of the appellate or trial courts), then choice of forum will depend on factors other than precedent, such as the taxpayer's ability to pay the tax before litigating the issue, the desire to obtain (or avoid) a jury trial, and the desire to obtain (or avoid) judges with significant tax expertise.

B.   *Taxpayer's Ability to Pay the Tax; Interest Payable*

Another important consideration is the taxpayer's financial ability or willingness to pay the disputed tax before litigating the controversy. Although one's first impulse may be to select the Tax Court because it is the only forum that does not require prepayment of the full putative tax, the impact of interest must be considered. The Tax Reform Act of 1986 established a new method for determining the rates of interest on underpayments and overpayments. *See* § 10.8, *supra*, for a fuller discussion of interest. Basically, the system resulted in higher interest rates on underpayments (that is, interest the taxpayer must pay the Government) than on overpayments (interest the Government must pay when it refunds overpaid taxes). I.R.C. § 6621. Many observers believed the discrepancies in interest rates, depending on whether the taxpayer or the Government was the payor, were unfair so Congress eliminated the differences as part of the Taxpayer Bill of Rights 3 legislation of 1998.

There are procedures available to reduce the impact of interest rates on the choice of forum. Importantly, a taxpayer who wishes to try his case in the Tax Court but who also wants to avoid the cumulation of high interest on any potential tax finally determined to be owing may pay the tax after or even before (see Rev.Proc. 2005–18, 2005–13 I.R.B. 798 for procedures) filing the Tax Court petition. Thus, the taxpayer has the choice in Tax Court litigation to pay the tax or not. If the taxpayer pays the tax, plus interest to date and any penalties, but ultimately prevails, the Government must pay interest to the taxpayer on amounts found to have been overpaid. In addition to full payment of the tax, interest and penalties, the taxpayer may elect to post a cash bond and proceed with Tax Court litigation. Posting such a bond stops the running of interest against the taxpayer but will not require the Government to pay interest to the taxpayer should the taxpayer win.

C. *Tax Court Trap: Government May Assert Additional Tax Due*

Because the filing of a Tax Court petition suspends the statute of limitations on assessment of taxes, it opens the door to the Service to determine during the course of Tax Court litigation that taxes in addition to those identified in the notice of deficiency may be assessed against the taxpayer. There are many horror stories on this point. Consider, for example, the often-cited case of the taxpayer who litigated an asserted $16,000 tax deficiency in Tax Court and ultimately was held liable for a total underpayment of more than $1 million. Raskob v. Commissioner (B.T.A.1938).

If, after investigation, it is determined that there are additional "soft spots" in the taxpayer's returns (besides those already identified by the Service), then serious consideration should be given to permitting the statute of limitations to run by paying the asserted deficiency and filing a refund suit (which does not suspend the statute of limitations on assessment). Although the Government may raise new issues in a refund forum after the statute has run on assessment of additional deficiencies, these new issues cannot result in a net amount due the Government; they can only reduce the amount the Government must pay the taxpayer. *See* Lewis v. Reynolds (S.Ct.1932).

D. *Expense Involved*

Although the expense of the suit depends in large part upon the complexity of the issues, there are several statements that can be made in comparing the Tax Court and the Federal district courts. Generally, it is cheaper to file suit in the Tax Court because the Tax Court procedure is less formal than that of the Federal district courts. For instance, the parties will be required to engage in an informal stipulation process in the Tax Court prior to using the more formal discovery process under the Federal Rules. *See* The Branerton Corporation v. Commissioner (Tax Ct.1974). The evidentiary rules are more relaxed in the Tax Court than in the Federal district courts where the Federal Rules of Evidence are strictly adhered to. Also, the Tax Court Rules allow the taxpayer to be represented by a non-lawyer, such as an accountant, an actuary, or an enrolled agent, and in addition, there tend to be more *pro se* cases in the Tax Court than in the Federal district courts.

CIVIL TAX LITIGATION COMPARISON OF COURTS

	Tax Court	District Ct.	Claims Ct.
Must pay tax before filing suit	No	Yes	Yes
Jury trial available	No	Yes	No
Appeal from adverse decision to which court	U.S. Circuit Courts of Appeals; based on taxpayer's residence	Same as Tax Court	Federal Circuit Ct. of Appeals
Precedent followed	Circuit Ct. of Appeals to which appeal lies; based on taxpayer's residence	Same as Tax Court	Federal Circuit Ct. of Appeals; former Ct. of Claims
Established under Art. I or Art. III of U.S. Const'n	Art. I	Art. III	Art. I
Respondent (party against whom suit filed)	Commissioner of I.R.S.	United States	United States
Government represented by attorneys from	Appeals Division, Office of Chief Counsel; District Counsel	Tax Division, U.S. Dep't of Justice	Same as U.S. Dist. Ct.

CHAPTER 15

ADDITIONAL CIVIL LITIGATION CONSIDERATIONS

As mentioned in Chapter 14, the choice of forum is certainly a principal consideration in civil tax litigation. Other considerations include the three unrelated but important litigation concerns that are discussed in this chapter: (1) the allocation of burden of proof between the Government and the taxpayer; (2) the impact of res judicata and collateral estoppel in tax cases; and (3) recovery of attorneys' fees.

§ 15.1 Burden of Proof

The burden of proof contains two elements: the burden of persuasion and the burden of production. Burden of persuasion is the obligation to persuade the trier of fact, with the penalty for non-persuasion being defeat on the issue by the party bearing the burden. Burden of production refers to the obligation of the party bearing the burden to produce the necessary quantum of evidence. If the party fails to meet this burden, the judge may refuse to submit the issue to the jury. The burden of production may shift during a trial, but the ultimate burden of persuasion remains fixed. References to burden of proof in this chapter are to the burden of persuasion.

Historically and traditionally, the Commissioner's determination of tax liability enjoyed a rebuttable presumption of correctness. According to one court: "This presumption in favor of the Commissioner is a procedural device that requires the plaintiff to go forward with prima facie evidence to support a finding contrary to the Commissioner's determination. Once this procedural burden is satisfied, the taxpayer must still carry the ultimate burden of proof or persuasion on the merits. Thus the plaintiff not only has the burden of proof of establishing that the Commissioner's determination was incorrect, but also of establishing the merit of its claims by a preponderance of the evidence." Danville Plywood Corp. v. United States (Cl. Ct.1989).

Although the presumption of correctness was judicially created, its long-standing existence indicated Congressional approval. In 1998, Congress enacted an exception to this rule as part of the IRS Restructuring and Reform Act of 1998. The new provision, codified at IRC § 7491, alters what the legislative history refers to as "a fundamental element of the structure of the Internal Revenue Code." Although the new provision was touted by some of its supporters and some in the media as reversing the rule that "the taxpayer is guilty until proven innocent" (a statement that confuses criminal and civil liability), the exception it creates is actually fairly narrow.

Under section 7491, the Commissioner has the burden of proof in any court proceeding with respect to a factual issue if the taxpayer introduces credible evidence relating to the issue and meets four conditions:

1.   The taxpayer must comply with the substantiation requirements of the Code and Regulations (as under current law).

2.   The taxpayer must maintain records required by the Code and Regulations (as under current law).

3.   The taxpayer must cooperate with reasonable requests by the IRS for meetings, interviews, witnesses, information and documents.

4.   Taxpayers other than individuals must meet the net worth limitations that apply for awarding attorney's fees under section 7430. (No net worth limitations will apply to individuals.)

The third element, cooperation with reasonable requests from the IRS, is the most controversial. According to the legislative history:

Cooperation also includes providing reasonable assistance to the [IRS] in obtaining access to and inspection of witnesses, information or documents not within the control of the taxpayer....

A necessary element of cooperating with the [IRS] is that the taxpayer must exhaust his or her administrative remedies (including any appeal rights provided by the IRS). The taxpayer is not required to agree to extend the statute of limitations to be considered to have cooperated with the [IRS]. Cooperating also means that the taxpayer must establish the applicability of any privilege.

Critics of the new provision feared that audits would become more intrusive, with the IRS requesting more information from taxpayers in order to ensure that it could meet its new burden of proof.

Section 7491 also addresses the burden of proof in the context of reconstructed income and penalties. When the IRS uses statistical information to reconstruct a taxpayer's income, the IRS has the burden of proof with respect to the reconstructed income in any court proceeding relating to that income. In addition, the IRS now has the burden of establishing in any court proceeding the appropriateness of the imposition of any penalty. If the penalty would otherwise be appropriate but the taxpayer asserts a defense (of reasonable cause or substantial authority, for example), the taxpayer must establish that the penalty is inappropriate by proving that the defense applies.

A. Tax Court

Tax Court Rule 142(a) provides in part that "[t]he burden of proof shall be upon the petitioner, except as otherwise provided by statute or determined by the Court; and except that, in respect of any new matter, increases in deficiency, and affirmative defenses, pleaded in his answer, it shall be upon the respondent." Thus, the Government bears the burden of proof on all new issues and increases in deficiency (beyond that shown in the notice of deficiency).

B. *Refund Suits*

In refund suits, the taxpayer bears a double burden of proof. He must first establish that the Commissioner's assessment is wrong, and he must prove the exact amount of tax actually due (or that no tax is due and owing). This dual burden has its origins in the common-law assumpsit action for money had and received. The courts have viewed the statutory refund action as being similar to the assumpsit action, and thus have imported its burden of proof rules into refund actions. Lewis v. Reynolds (S.Ct. 1932) ("The action to recover on a claim for refund is in the nature of an action for money had and received and it is incumbent upon the claimant to show that the United States has money which belongs to him.").

The Government may attempt to offset the taxpayer's alleged overpayment of taxes with alleged underpayments on issues not raised in the refund complaint. In other words, once the refund complaint is filed, the Service is free to examine the returns in question, and those of other years, to attempt to reduce the taxpayer's recovery. If the Government attempts to offset a taxpayer's alleged overpayment of taxes with alleged underpayments in tax years not barred by the statute of limitations, then the burden of proof of the new issues depends on the type of tax involved in the proposed adjustment and whether it relates to the same tax year that is involved in the refund suit. If the proposed offsetting adjustment relates to the same type of tax (e.g., income tax or estate tax) in the same year, or a related type of tax that will affect the tax in issue and is in the same year, then the taxpayer will have the burden of proof on the issue, even though it was raised by the Government. On the other hand, if the proposed offset relates to a different and independent type of tax, or if it is for a year other than that involved in the suit, then the Government will bear the burden of proof on the issue. Missouri Pacific Railroad v. United States (Ct.Cl.1964).

As discussed in Chapter 9, it is possible for the Government to raise offset issues for years that are time-barred because the statute of limitations has expired. By utilizing the doctrine of equitable recoupment, the Government can resurrect transactions and issues that the taxpayer has entirely forgotten. On the bright side, such otherwise time-barred offsets cannot result in new and additional tax liability; they are limited solely to reducing the taxpayer's recovery in a refund suit.

Finally, the Service may issue a deficiency notice for the year or years in question after the taxpayer has filed a refund suit. The Government may assert the new deficiency as a counterclaim in the refund action. Except for issues of fraud, the taxpayer has the burden of proof on all issues raised in the Government's counterclaim. I.R.C. § 7422(e).

C. *"Naked Assessments"*

An exception to the general presumption of correctness of the Commissioner's determination of a tax deficiency has developed in a line of cases involving alleged illegal income. The Commissioner will determine a deficiency based on the taxpayer's involvement with an illegal activity, and will rely on the presumption of correctness of the deficiency determination. If the Commissioner cannot produce admissible evidence directly linking the taxpayer to the alleged illegal income, however, the deficiency determination is not entitled to a presumption of correctness and is considered arbitrary and unreasonable, to the extent that it is based on alleged illegal income. *See, e.g.,* Anastasato v. Commissioner (3d Cir.1986) (illegal commissions); Llorente v. Commissioner (2d Cir.1981) (drugs).

To illustrate these rules, the facts of *Llorente* are instructive. In that case the Service determined a deficiency in the taxpayer's income based on the expenditures method of reconstructing income. This method, which is discussed in § 18.1.A.(2), *infra*, basically identifies the taxpayer's expenditures for the year, compares them with his reported income, and assumes that the excess of expenditures over reported income is unreported income for the year. Among other expenditures alleged to have been made by Llorente, the Government asserted that he spent $54,000 to buy cocaine. The taxpayer denied buying cocaine or conspiring with others to do so.

The Government's principal witness, an undercover police officer, testified that he had seen the taxpayer in the presence of known cocaine dealers. He also testified that a confidential informant told him the taxpayer had gone with him and a known drug dealer to inspect a $54,000 cocaine shipment. In a reviewed decision, by a six-to-five vote, the Tax Court upheld the notice of deficiency, but it reduced the alleged cocaine expenditure from $54,000 to $18,000, on the theory that there was no evidence that the taxpayer intended to buy personally the entire $54,000 cocaine shipment. The Second Circuit reversed the portion of the Tax Court decision relating to the alleged expenditure for cocaine. According to the Second Circuit, a "mere peripheral contact with illegal conduct is insufficient" to link the taxpayer with actual illegal activity, and the Government must produce evidence directly linking the taxpayer with "some tax-generating acts, such as the purchase or sale of controlled substances." *Llorente* at 156. In other words, it is not enough to establish that the taxpayer knew or associated with drug dealers; the Government must prove that the taxpayer himself actually participated in buying and selling drugs if it is to satisfy its burden of going forward with the evidence in cases involving alleged unreported income. In *Llorente*, the Second Circuit ruled that the portion of the deficiency relating to the alleged cocaine purchase was arbitrary and unreasonable and that the taxpayer prevailed on that issue because the Service had failed to produce admissible evidence linking him with the alleged illegal activity.

§ 15.2   Res Judicata and Collateral Estoppel

Although an in-depth discussion of the principles of res judicata and collateral estoppel is inappropriate here, the effect of the doctrines in tax cases cannot be overlooked. The purpose of both doctrines is to provide finality for judicial decisions and to bar repetitious suits. The doctrine of res judicata, also known as "claim preclusion," bars relitigation of a claim after a final judgment on the merits has been issued in a suit involving the same parties or their privies. For tax cases, the Commissioner, the United States, and the district director (or division director) are considered identical parties. I.R.C. § 7422(c). Importantly, in tax cases, each taxable year generates a new and separate tax liability and cause of action. Res judicata thus bars a taxpayer from bringing suit with respect to tax liability for a year that was the subject of a prior suit. For example, if the taxpayer litigates an income tax deficiency for 1990 in the Tax Court, he cannot later file a refund suit for the same taxable year, even if the refund suit would involve issues not raised in the Tax Court proceeding. Res judicata would not bar the taxpayer from litigating the same issues that were raised in the Tax Court case for different tax years, however.

This does not mean that the taxpayer can litigate the same issues year after year. The doctrine of collateral estoppel, also known as "issue preclusion," bars the relitigation of issues actually litigated and necessarily determined in a prior suit. Application of the doctrine of collateral estoppel in tax cases is far more frequent than the use of res judicata, because the latter bars only relitigation of the same claim (which means tax liability for the same year) between the same parties or their privies. Recent decisions have defined and expanded the scope of the doctrine of collateral estoppel in significant ways.

A. Mutuality of Parties

Although res judicata applies only to claims involving the same parties or their privies, collateral estoppel can bar relitigation of an issue even if the parties in the subsequent suit are not identical to those in the first suit. The Supreme Court in 1979 abolished the mutuality of parties rule and declared that if a party "against whom estoppel is asserted had a full and fair opportunity to litigate," then that party can be collaterally estopped to relitigate the same issue in a subsequent proceeding, even though the other party to the litigation is different in the two proceedings. Parklane Hosiery Co. v. Shore (S.Ct.1979). In a case decided later that same year, the Supreme Court refined the *Parklane Hosiery* test by defining a three-pronged test for application of collateral estoppel: (1) whether the issues presented in the later case are substantially the same as those involved in the first case; (2) whether controlling facts or legal principles have changed significantly since the first judgment; and (3) whether other special circumstances warrant an exception to the application of the doctrine of collateral estoppel. Montana v. United States (S.Ct.1979).

Abolition of the mutuality of parties rule might prove to be a significant weapon for the Government in tax cases, as illustrated by the Tax Court's decision in *Meier v. Commissioner* (Tax Ct.1988) (reviewed). The taxpayer in *Meier* had been an unsuccessful defendant in a suit by his former employer, Hughes Tool Co., in an action for an accounting in which it was found that Meier had diverted his employer's funds for his own use and benefit. Hughes Tool Co. v. Meier (D.Utah 1977). The Commissioner sought to use the judgment against Meier in this litigation, to which the Service was not a party, to collaterally estop Meier from contesting that he had diverted his employer's income to his personal use and fraudulently failed to report the diverted funds as income. Applying the *Parklane Hosiery* standard, the Tax Court, in a reviewed decision with no dissent, held that Meier had "used all the legal and procedural means available to him to defend the accounting action." *Meier* at 289. Thus, he had a full and fair opportunity to litigate the issue of diversion of his employer's funds in the first action, and was collaterally estopped to deny the diversion in the Tax Court action. The Tax Court also upheld the fraud penalty of section 6653(b) on the basis of collateral estoppel, reasoning that the standard of proof required in the state accounting action was at least as stringent as the "clear and convincing" standard the Government must meet in proving fraud.

The IRS can be expected to monitor the dockets of federal and state courts to identify defendants who have been found liable for misappropriation of funds, or illegal income-producing activities, to assess tax deficiencies, penalties and interest based on facts that the defendant will be collaterally estopped to deny in a subsequent litigation of the tax issues.

B. *"Ultimate" Versus "Evidentiary" Facts*

Collateral estoppel may be applied in matters of law, matters of fact, and mixed questions of law and fact. Early case law limited applicability of collateral estoppel on questions of fact to "ultimate" facts. *See, e.g.*, Evergreens v. Nunan (2d Cir.1944). Judgment in one suit thus would not collaterally estop relitigation of an "evidentiary fact," as opposed to an "ultimate fact" or an issue of law. More recent commentary criticized this distinction as being difficult, if not impossible, to define and often out of line with the time and energy devoted by the parties to contesting the disputed fact.

The Tax Court first rejected the *Evergreens* analysis and adopted and amplified the *Montana* standards in *Peck v. Commissioner* (Tax Ct.1988), in which the court restated the *Montana* standards as five conditions necessary for application of collateral estoppel to factual issues in tax cases. Several months later, in the same reviewed *Meier* decision, *supra,* in which it first applied the *Parklane Hosiery/Montana* tests for nonapplication of the mutuality of parties rule, the Tax Court again rejected the *Evergreens* test of "ultimate" versus "evidentiary" facts and applied instead the three-pronged *Montana* test explained above.

For a discussion of collateral estoppel in civil penalty cases after criminal convictions, see § 10.3.E., *supra*.

§ 15.3 Attorneys' Fees

A. *Historical Development*

Prior to the enactment in 1980 of the Equal Access to Justice Act ("EAJA"), there was almost no opportunity for a taxpayer to recover litigation costs and attorneys' fees incurred in a tax dispute. The EAJA provided for recovery of costs in civil tax litigation, but it did not cover suits filed in the Tax Court.

In 1982, Congress added section 7430 to the Code. This section supersedes the EAJA for civil cases brought by or against the United States and involving the determination, collection or refund of any federal tax, interest or penalty. Under section 7430, a taxpayer who is a "prevailing party" in tax litigation may recover attorneys' fees and certain other costs. Not surprisingly, this provision has spawned substantial litigation and controversy, and Congress amended it in 1986, 1988, 1996, 1997 and 1998. These amendments have not resolved all the issues, however.

B. *"Prevailing Party"*

To be eligible to recover attorneys' fees, the taxpayer must be a "prevailing party." Prior to the 1988 amendment (effective for proceedings begun after November 11, 1988), this meant that the taxpayer had to prevail in the litigation. But for proceedings begun after November 11, 1988, costs also can be recovered if the taxpayer prevails at the administrative level.

The statute defines "prevailing party" as one who has substantially prevailed with respect either to the amount in controversy or to the most significant issue or set of issues. Until 1996 the taxpayer had the burden of proving that the Government's position was not "substantially justified." Now the government must prove that its position was substantially justified.

The IRS and the taxpayer may agree, particularly in cases settled out of court, that the taxpayer is the prevailing party. Caution is dictated, however. Tax Court Rule 231(a)(1) requires that the award for costs against the Government must be included in the decision stipulated by the parties for entry by the court. Apparently a subsequent motion for recovery of costs will not be entertained. If the case is tried, the court will determine whether the taxpayer is the prevailing party. If the case is settled administratively, the IRS will determine (subject to a right of appeal to the Tax Court by the taxpayer) whether the taxpayer is a prevailing party.

Finally, certain "wealthy" taxpayers cannot qualify for recovery of costs and fees, regardless of how unjustified the Government's position was. The Taxpayer Relief Act of 1997 amended section 7430 to increase the net worth limitations, which prohibit recovery by the following:

—an individual with a net worth of more than $2 million;

—a sole owner of an incorporated business with a net worth of more than $7 million; or

—a sole owner of an unincorporated business with more than 500 employees.

C. "The Position of the United States"

In addition to being a prevailing party, the court must find that "the position of the United States" was not substantially justified. One of the principal areas of controversy in applying section 7430 was whether "the position of the United States" includes only conduct and positions taken after litigation has begun, or instead includes positions and conduct at the administrative level. Congress amended section 7430 in 1986 to provide that "position of the United States" includes both the litigation position and "any administrative action or inaction by the District Counsel * * * (and all subsequent administrative action or inaction)." This definition was ambiguous, because it was unclear whether fairly minor involvement by the District Counsel should satisfy the definition, or whether the case must have been turned over to District Counsel for litigation in order to start the accruing of costs and fees.

In 1988 Congress again amended the definition. The meter now begins to run on potential recovery of fees and costs based on the position stated in the 90–day letter (the statutory notice of deficiency) or the Appeals Office decision, whichever is earlier. This means that a position stated in the notice of deficiency is deemed "the position of the United States," even if it is conceded by the Government at trial. Although this was an improvement over prior law, because it provides a bright line test for determining which positions count as "the position of the United States," the statute still did not protect taxpayers from fees and costs incurred during the audit, preparing the protest and at the Appeals level. The 1988 amendments had the unintended effect of discouraging taxpayers from incurring legal, accounting and other expenses at the administrative level, which undermined the mission of the Appeals Office by influencing taxpayers to postpone professional advice until there was a possibility of recovering fees and costs.

Congress rectified this problem by another amendment to section 7430 in 1998 as part of the Taxpayer Bill of Rights Act 3. Taxpayers may now recover administrative costs incurred from the date of the first letter of proposed deficiency which allows the taxpayer an opportunity for administrative review. In effect, taxpayers may now recover reasonable attorney's fees incurred after receipt of the "30–day letter." *See* section 6.2.B, *supra,* for a discussion of the 30–day letter.

The 1998 amendments also resolved uncertainty about whether the IRS's position should be deemed substantially justified if it has lost on the same issue in other courts. Some courts had found that the position of the United States was substantially justified even though the IRS had lost on the identical issue in other Circuits. The 1998 amendment provides that the court shall take into consideration whether the IRS has lost on the issue in other federal circuit courts of appeal. This change should facilitate recovery by taxpayers who are involved in a case of first impression within their Circuit, but whose issue has been resolved against the IRS in another Circuit.

D. Fees and Costs That Can Be Recovered

For cases subject to pre–1986 rules, there was a ceiling of $25,000 on the amount of reasonable litigation costs that could be recovered. Reasonable litigation costs were defined to include reasonable court costs, expert witness fees, attorneys' fees, and the costs of conducting any test or study necessary for the preparation of the case. In 1986 Congress removed the $25,000 ceiling but imposed statutory limits on the amount of attorneys' and expert witness fees. Expert witnesses may not be compensated at rates higher than the highest rate paid by the Government for its expert witnesses. Attorneys were limited to $110 per hour, unless the court determined that a higher rate was warranted based on some "special factor, such as the limited availability of qualified attorneys" for the type of case involved. I.R.C. § 7430(c)(1)(B)(iii). If the case is relatively straightforward, the tax expertise of the taxpayer's lawyer is not a special factor. A.O.D. 2002–06. In addition, the cost of any study, test, engineering project or other analysis can be recovered only if the court finds that the study was "necessary" for the preparation of the taxpayer's case.

In 1998 Congress raised the cap on attorney's fees to $125 per hour, indexed for inflation, for costs incurred and services performed more than 180 days after the date of enactment, July 22, 1998. The 1998 legislation also provides that the difficulty of the issues presented or the unavailability of local tax expertise are factors that may be considered in determining whether to award a higher hourly rate, thus overruling contrary provisions in the Regulations.

What about the lawyer who represents herself in a tax controversy? Can she recover legal fees for her own professional efforts? The answer appears to be "no." The Tax Court has ruled against such a recovery both by an attorney acting *pro se* and by an attorney's law firm in which he held an equity interest. Minahan v. Commissioner (Tax Ct.1987); Frisch v. Commissioner (Tax Ct.1986). Similarly, the Fourth Circuit has reversed a case that permitted an attorney/litigant to recover attorney's fees for successfully representing himself. The lower court awarded attorney's fees based on the fact that the taxpayer was required to forego other opportunities for fees because of the time involved in litigating his personal controversy. The Fourth Circuit, however, agreed with the Tax Court that foregone fees are not compensable. United States v. McPherson (4th Cir.1988).

As discussed above, the 1988 amendments expanded section 7430's applicability beyond pure litigation positions and costs to include certain conduct of the Government prior to litigation, and the expenses incurred by the taxpayer at certain administrative levels. These amendments apparently were intended to encourage wholehearted pursuit of administrative remedies by permitting "reasonable administrative costs" to be recovered, in addition to "reasonable litigation costs." "Reasonable administrative costs" is defined to include the same types of costs recoverable from litigation, as well as "any administrative fees or similar charges imposed by the Internal Revenue Service." But the 1988 amendments had the opposite effect of what Congress had intended. The reason was that only those costs and fees incurred after the statutory notice of deficiency was issued, or the Appeals Office had notified the taxpayer of its decision (whichever occurred first) could be recovered under the 1988 rules. In practice, receipt of the notice of deficiency is often the way the taxpayer learns of the Appeals Office decision.

This meant that none of the costs and fees incurred during audit, preparation of the protest, or Appeals conferences could be recovered. In other words, even if the court concluded that the Government's position was unreasonable ("not substantially justified," in the language of the current standard), none of the fees or costs incurred by the taxpayer during the administrative process prior to the issuance of the statutory notice of deficiency could be recovered.

Congress rectified this problem in its 1998 amendments. Effective for fees and costs incurred 180 days after enactment (July 22, 1998), taxpayers may now recover fees and costs incurred after receipt of the "30–day letter."

E. Exhaustion of Administrative Remedies

A taxpayer cannot qualify for recovery of costs under section 7430 unless he has exhausted administrative remedies. I.R.C. § 7430(b)(1). In practice this means that, if the IRS offers the taxpayer an Appeals Office conference after an audit, and if that conference is skipped by the taxpayer, then neither administrative costs nor litigation costs can be recovered. If the taxpayer is not aware that his return is being examined, or if no Appeals Office conference is offered by the Service, then recovery under section 7430 is possible because the administrative remedies were not available to the taxpayer.

A more difficult question is how cooperative and helpful the taxpayer must be at the Appeals Office conference to qualify under section 7430. Regulations indicate that the taxpayer must "participate" in the conference by, among other things, disclosing "all relevant information regarding the party's tax matters to the extent such information and its relevance were known or should have been known" when the conference occurred. Reg. § 301.7430–1(b)(2). As discussed in Chapter 6, an Appeals Office conference is usually offered after the taxpayer has filed his Tax Court petition. Thus, even if the taxpayer has already "participated" in an Appeals

Office conference, he must participate again after his Tax Court petition is filed. In *Rogers v. Commissioner* (Tax Ct. Memo.1987), the Tax Court recognized that the degree of participation required of the taxpayer after suit has been filed should be less than that required before litigation, because of the obvious potential for the IRS to conduct open-ended discovery through the conference "participation" requirement.

If the disclosure rules seem to require significant taxpayer cooperation in what could be a quite dubious IRS position, consider another section of the Regulations that formerly provided that a taxpayer who refused to extend the statute of limitations, and thus precluded pre-petition review by the Appeals Office, would not be considered to have exhausted his administrative remedies. Reg. § 301.7430–1(f)(2). In *Minahan v. Commissioner, supra*, the Tax Court held this portion of the Regulations invalid and ruled that a refusal to extend the statute of limitations does not necessarily amount to a failure to exhaust administrative remedies. Congress agreed with the Tax Court in the Taxpayer Bill of Rights 2 (1996) and amended section 7430 to provide that failure to extend the statute of limitations is not relevant to determining whether administrative remedies have been exhausted. Such a refusal, however, when combined with other delaying or uncooperative conduct, could certainly be a factor that the court could consider in determining whether the taxpayer has exhausted his administrative remedies.

CHAPTER 16

CRIMINAL INVESTIGATIONS

Thus far, discussion has focused almost exclusively on civil liabilities under the Code. This chapter and those that follow focus on criminal investigations and prosecutions for tax offenses, but in reality, the distinction between civil fraud and criminal tax evasion may be murky.

§ 16.1 Tax "Avoidance" versus Tax "Evasion"

Few people relish either the task of preparing tax returns or paying taxes; fewer still forego legal and known opportunities to minimize their tax liabilities. In the words of Judge Learned Hand: "[N]obody owes any public duty to pay more than the law demands: taxes are enforced exactions, not voluntary contributions. To demand more in the name of morals is mere cant." Commissioner v. Newman (2d Cir.1947) (Hand, J., dissenting).

Tax avoidance is perfectly legal; tax evasion (or tax fraud) is not. The difference between legal avoidance and illegal evasion is often unclear, however, and numerous sections of the Code ignore the distinction by referring to transactions motivated by a desire to "evade or avoid" taxes. *See, e.g.,* §§ 269A, 6662(d)(2)(C)(ii). Cynics would say that only in hindsight can the real distinction be drawn: that is, a position ultimately upheld as legal is avoidance, while a scheme held to be illegal is evasion. In truth, however, there are identifiable (and therefore predictable) differences between avoidance and evasion, all of which hinge on the taxpayer's state of mind. A taxpayer who takes a position that he honestly believes to be legal has not engaged in tax fraud or evasion, even if that position is ultimately found to be prohibited under the Code. On the other hand, a taxpayer who takes a position on his return that he knows or believes to be contrary to the law has gone beyond mere avoidance and into the realm of evasion.

In practice, the tax laws are so complex, and their application to specific facts depends on so many variables, that the line between legal avoidance and unlawful evasion of taxes is often difficult to draw. Even when the law is perfectly clear, the taxpayer may not understand the law or how it applies to the situation at hand. In such circumstances, imprisonment would clearly be inappropriate, but some civil penalty may be justified to foster more diligent taxpayer behavior. Similarly, when the legal issue involved is exceedingly complex or completely novel, criminal sanctions might be prohibited by the Due Process Clause of the 5th Amendment. On the other hand, because the tax laws *are* complex and technical and *are* frequently amended, novel and complicated issues frequently arise. The threat of civil or criminal sanction should discourage taxpayers from taking advantage of the complexity of the law with overly "aggressive" positions.

Chapters 10, 18 and 19 discuss the civil and criminal penalties under the Code and the available defenses. Chapter 3 discussed the standards governing tax advisors and those who represent taxpayers before the IRS, and the possible sanctions for noncompliance.

§ 16.2 Selecting Cases for Criminal Investigation

Although tax prosecutions initially involved notorious gangsters such as Al Capone, today every taxpayer is a potential target of a criminal investigation. The threat of possible criminal sanctions is a potent deterrent for many citizens who diligently attempt to comply with the federal tax laws. If the Government were to "show its hand" and disclose exactly how it decides to pursue a criminal case, the deterrent effect of the criminal penalties might be jeopardized. For this reason, there is far less public information concerning the criminal investigation function than there is concerning civil audit and penalty procedures. Nonetheless, it is clear that the principal sources of criminal investigations are information developed by the Criminal Investigation Division ("CID," also known as the "Criminal Investigation Unit" or "CIU") itself, other IRS employees (such as revenue agents auditing returns), and tips from citizens.

As a starting point, it is fair to say that every civil examination or audit is a potential criminal investi-

gation, and every criminal investigation is a potential criminal prosecution. Many (if not most) criminal investigations result from routine audits during
which the revenue agent discovers some information that triggers a suspicion of fraud. The Internal
Revenue Manual outlines the steps a revenue agent
must take when she suspects fraud. In the past, the
Manual required the agent to suspend civil activities and refer the case to the CID, while preserving
and perfecting indications of fraud by promptly
gathering evidence that the taxpayer might destroy
or alter if made aware that the IRS suspected fraud.
Recently, however, the Service has announced that
it will no longer suspend a civil audit when a case
has been referred to the CID. Note that if a revenue
agent suspects fraud, the taxpayer is not given a
Miranda-type warning that the agent is functioning
as a criminal investigator at this point, and that
anything the taxpayer says can be used to prosecute
him. After referring the case to the CID, the revenue agent may work with the CID in the investigation.

In addition to referrals from the auditing agents,
the CID also develops its own cases and acts on tips
from informants seeking bounties. The CID investi-
gates individuals and industries based on projects
designed to target areas of significant noncompliance. For example, illegal drug and racketeering
activities are notoriously high in noncompliance
with the tax laws, and the CID targets such industries (and the people involved in them) for investigation. Special agents of the CID also participate in

Justice Department Strike Force programs aimed at racketeering and money laundering. Some CID projects are nationwide, while others are confined to a particular region or district. A region or district might target, for instance, doctors or lawyers or carpenters. In a sense, becoming a target of such an investigation can be the ultimate bad luck for the taxpayer involved, because the IRS may have decided to make an example of those who fall within a certain category (e.g., those who regularly engage in cash transactions) and the CID employees might vigorously pursue cases that otherwise might have been handled purely on a civil penalty basis.

People seeking revenge or bounty are another important source of information leading to criminal investigations. Ex-spouses and ex-employees with detailed knowledge of the taxpayer's actions are a great source of leads. Sometimes these tips are sent anonymously, but frequently the informant will hope to reap a reward or bounty. Section 7623 authorizes the Commissioner to pay to an informant a reward for tax collected as a result of the informant's tip. In practice, however, only a small percentage of informants actually receive a reward, and the rewards are usually minimal. The maximum reward is 10% of the amount of tax, penalties and fines paid to the Government as a result of the tip. No reward is made unless two conditions are met: the informant must provide specific and responsible information that caused the investigation and resulted in recovery, and the information must lead to the collection of taxes that would not ordinarily have been collected.

The reward program has generated some controversy because in the past informants with a grudge would take revenge by reporting an ex-employer or former spouse to the IRS. Even if the Service ultimately collected nothing as a result of the tip, the taxpayer could spend a great deal of time and money fighting the IRS. Also, the amount of money that the Service has collected as a result of the program is only a small percentage of the overall collections. The all-time high year for the IRS was 2000, when the IRS collected $266 million. Further, very few informants actually collect a reward. In 2003, for example, 4,765 people sought rewards, but only 190 collected them. The amount of the reward depends upon the value of the information. If the information provided is the originating cause of the investigation and a direct factor in the recovery, the informant can receive 15 percent of the taxes and penalties (but not interest) recovered up to $10 million. If the information was not specific but resulted in an investigation and determination of tax liability, the informant could receive 10 percent of the amount recovered. If the informant supplied general information (e.g., a name) that led to an investigation but otherwise had no direct relationship to the determination of the tax liability, the informant can receive 1 percent of the amount recovered.

Fraud investigations are sparked in numerous other ways, including newspaper articles, informa-

tion from state taxing authorities, and close obser-
vation of individuals known or suspected to be
engaged in illegal activities. In identifying its law
enforcement criteria, the Service looks to (1) high
profiles, (2) egregious allegations, (3) deterrent effects, and (4) conformance with the business plan
issued annually by the Chief of the CIU. The much-
publicized prosecution and conviction of hotel mag-
nate Leona Helmsley in 1989 is a good example of
the Government's efforts to enhance compliance by
prosecuting high-profile individuals. United States
v. Helmsley (2d Cir. 1991).

§ 16.3   Steps and Personnel Involved in the Investigation

The taxpayer usually first learns that he is under
investigation when special agents from the CID
appear at his home or place of business, sometimes
early in the morning or late at night. The special
agents should identify themselves and warn the
taxpayer that they are conducting a criminal investigation, that the taxpayer has the right not to
cooperate with the agent and to retain counsel, and
that anything the taxpayer says may be used
against him. These partial *Miranda* warnings are
required by IRS procedures contained in the Internal Revenue Manual, despite the fact that the taxpayer is not in custody and therefore is not entitled
to the regular *Miranda* warning. IRM 9.4.5.11.3.1.1
(Feb. 1, 2005). Specifically, according to the Manual,
after identifying herself and producing identification, the special agent should state: "As a special

agent, one of my functions is to investigate the possibility of criminal violations of the Internal Revenue laws, and related offenses.'' The special agent should then give the following partial *Miranda* warning:

In connection with my investigation of your tax liability (or other matter) I would like to ask you some questions. However, first I advise you that under the Fifth Amendment to the Constitution of the United States I cannot compel you to answer any questions or to submit any information if such answers or such information might tend to incriminate you in any way. I also advise you that anything which you say and any documents which you submit may be used against you in any criminal proceeding which may be undertaken. I advise you further that you may, if you wish, seek the assistance of an attorney before responding.

Full *Miranda* warnings (including the right to free legal representation) must be given if the taxpayer is in custody or otherwise deprived of his freedom. Mathis v. United States (S.Ct.1968). The taxpayer in *Mathis* was in prison serving a state sentence when he was interviewed by IRS agents. The Court held that the failure to give the *Miranda* warnings rendered the statements and documents obtained from the taxpayer inadmissible because he was in custody at the time of the interrogations. On the other hand, the mere presence of IRS special agents in one's home (or a home where the taxpayer sometimes stays) does not render the situation "custodial," and special agents need not give full *Miranda* warnings before interviewing the taxpayer. Beckwith v. United States (S.Ct.1976). According to *Miranda*, "a 'custodial interrogation' occurs whenever law enforcement officers question a person after taking that person into custody or otherwise significantly deprive a person of freedom of action." Miranda v. Arizona (S.Ct.1966). General questioning on the scene concerning the facts and circumstances surrounding a crime or other general questioning of citizens during the fact-finding process do not trigger *Miranda* warnings. *Id.* at 477–78, 86 S.Ct. at 1629–30.

Failure to give the partial *Miranda* warnings that are required by the Internal Revenue Manual but not required constitutionally in a non-custodial situation has been held not to render inadmissible statements made by the taxpayer. Thus, statements made by a taxpayer to a special agent who did not give the partial *Miranda* warnings were admissible. United States v. Kontny (7th Cir.2001); United States v. Irvine (1st Cir.1983). The *Irvine* court based its holding on *Beckwith*, *supra*, and *United States v. Caceres* (S.Ct.1979) in which the Court held that the IRS need not follow its own procedural requirements when such requirements are not mandated by statute or the Constitution.

As a matter of strategy, the taxpayer should say nothing to the special agents and should immediately contact his lawyer. Frequently, however, taxpayers will talk to the agents and thus seriously aggravate an already bad situation. Being evasive will heighten the already strong suspicion of fraud, and telling lies or attempting to mislead the agent will constitute another federal crime. There are usually two agents present so that there will be more than one witness to any statements the taxpayer makes.

Initially, the taxpayer should ask the agents to identify themselves. If one is a revenue agent and the other a special agent, then the investigation is being conducted jointly by the CID and the auditing branch of the IRS. In joint investigations, the criminal aspect predominates and the special agent is primarily responsible for conducting the investigation.

The investigative techniques used will depend on the type of suspected crime involved. For instance, a case involving a failure to file a return under section 7203 is usually an uncomplicated investigation, since the Government need only establish that the taxpayer had sufficient income to be required to file and that he willfully failed to do so. Circumstantial evidence tending to prove willfulness (such as false W–4 withholding certificates or failure to file for three years) can often be quickly obtained. On the other hand, investigations into suspected evasion can be quite complex, since the Government will have to prove that income was underreported or deductions overstated. See Chapter 18 for a discussion of methods of proof of evasion.

The special agent will attempt to interview the taxpayer and every other person who can provide information to aid in establishing the Government's case. A witness who makes a statement to the agent or signs an affidavit prepared by the agent is entitled to a transcript of the interview or a copy of the affidavit. The special agent will also want to inspect the taxpayer's books and records, as well as the records of those who had business dealings with the taxpayer, and records held by banks, Government agencies and others. The power of the IRS to compel production of such records is discussed in Chapter 17.

When the special agent completes her investigation, she must file a report detailing the evidence gathered and either recommending prosecution or recommending against it. Prosecution should be recommended only if there is sufficient evidence to establish both guilt beyond a reasonable doubt and a reasonable probability of conviction. IRM, § 9.5.8 (Aug. 10, 2004). The report is reviewed by the agent's supervisor and the Area Director, and if they agree with the recommendation to prosecute, the report will be forwarded to the Chief or Deputy Chief of the Criminal Investigation Division. If the Chief (or Deputy Chief), assisted by dedicated attorneys from the Chief Counsel's Office concur, the report will be reviewed by the Criminal Section of the Justice Department Tax Division when the case is sent to it with the recommendation to prosecute.

§ 16.4 The Decision to Prosecute

Because unsuccessful tax prosecutions are believed to undermine our voluntary compliance system, and because of budgetary limitations, those involved at all levels in making the decision to prosecute focus primarily on the probability of success in light of the evidence. The CID's prosecution recommendation is reviewed by attorneys of the Chief Counsel's Office, by attorneys in the Criminal Section of the Justice Department Tax Division, and by the U.S. Attorney, any of whom can decline prosecution.

While there are no precise rules for predicting whether any given case will result in a recommendation by the IRS to prosecute, the following factors appear to influence the decision.

1. Voluntary Disclosure. Although the Service has long since abandoned its formal policy (in effect between 1945 and 1952) of not prosecuting taxpayers who voluntarily disclose their transgressions, an informal policy against prosecution still exists. The Internal Revenue Manual states that the IRS will consider a voluntary disclosure, "along with all other factors in the investigation in determining whether criminal prosecution will be recommended." IRM 9.5.3.3.1.2.1. To qualify, a taxpayer must make his disclosure prior to an IRS investigation and prior to the occurrence of an event that would ordinarily alert the IRS to the fraud. Prosecuting those who make such voluntary disclosures is recognized to be counterproductive, both because juries tend to find that such individuals did not act "willfully," and thus committed no crime, and because prosecution sends the message to others not to come forward but to conceal their crimes. Disclosure after the investigation has begun is not considered voluntary, and the IRS will pursue criminal

and civil sanctions. *See, e.g.*, Badaracco v. Commissioner (S.Ct.1984) (taxpayers who filed correct amended returns after grand jury subpoenaed their records were convicted for filing false returns; Supreme Court upheld imposition of civil fraud penalty) (see discussion in § 7.2.D, *supra*).

2.   Amount of Tax Involved. Unless the taxpayer is a high-profile individual, such as an entertainer or politician, or unless the taxpayer's conduct is outrageous (thus making conviction more likely), prosecution generally will not be recommended unless the tax involved is substantial. In practice, this appears to mean additional tax due of at least $2,500 in most cases.

3.   Health of the Taxpayer. Although a serious mental or physical disease or impairment will not necessarily preclude prosecution, it is one of the factors to be considered in deciding whether to prosecute.

4.   Evidence of Willfulness. Because all tax crimes require the Government to prove willfulness, the presence or absence of badges of fraud will influence the decision whether to prosecute. Evidence that the taxpayer has lied to investigators or destroyed or falsified records will bolster the chances of prosecution.

§ 16.5   Conferences and Justice Department Policies

Representatives of taxpayers under criminal investigation usually have a number of opportunities for conferences. If requested, the representative usually may obtain a conference with the Special Agent in charge and with the CID Regional Director of Field Operations, an attorney from the Chief Counsel's Office, as well as with the Justice Department Tax Division, and the U.S. Attorney if prosecution is recommended. If the case was investigated by a federal grand jury (*see* § 17.2, *infra*) rather than the IRS, the only conference opportunities are with the Justice Department and the U.S. Attorney.

While it is the policy of the IRS that no information will be disclosed to the taxpayer that might reveal the identity of confidential informants, endanger prospective witnesses, or be detrimental to either the investigation or a subsequent prosecution, nevertheless, conferences can be a valuable source of information both for the taxpayer's representative and for the Government. The representative should focus on potential trial problems for the Government, because the standard by which prosecution decisions are made is the probability of success in light of all the evidence. Thus, the representative should emphasize any such problems (for example, severe mental or physical illness, or misconduct by investigating agents) at the earliest possible time.

It is crucial that the taxpayer's representative request a conference, particularly when the case is referred to the Justice Department for prosecution. When the case is received by the Justice Department, it will be classified as either "complex" (generally because it involves an indirect method of proof of income or complex legal issues) or "noncomplex." For cases classified as "noncomplex," if there is no conference request on file the Justice Department will simply forward the case to the U.S. Attorney for prosecution, and no conference with the Justice Department will be permitted. "Noncomplex" cases in which there is a request for a conference on file will be reclassified as "complex" and the conference request will be granted. Therefore, to preserve the right to a conference, the representative should request a conference with the Justice Department promptly upon receipt of notice that the case is being referred to the Justice Department.

Conferences with Justice Department attorneys are held at the Tax Division of the Justice Department in Washington, D.C. Normally, neither the taxpayer nor IRS officials attend. The taxpayer's representative may make oral and written presentations. Many view the Justice Department conference as the first realistic opportunity for serious consideration of the merits of the Government's case, because at the IRS level, it is widely perceived that IRS employees often have already decided in favor of prosecution and are more interested in obtaining additional information to support that decision than in further considering the merits.

The Tax Division of the Justice Department has written policies concerning conferences and factors to consider in deciding whether to prosecute. In 1986, the Tax Division reversed its prior position that vicarious admissions made by attorneys for the taxpayer at the conference would be used against the taxpayer. Vicarious admissions of an attorney now are not used against the taxpayer, except where the admission provides the authentication of a written instrument. If the admission provides a lead against the taxpayer, however, the lead will be investigated.

Another important policy change made in 1986 is that plea negotiations may now occur at the Justice Department conference, except in cases being investigated by a grand jury. The 1986 changes also provide for the possibility of more than one conference and for the potential appearance of the taxpayer or a witness at the conference. According to the official Tax Division Directive issued in 1986, "[w]hile it is the function of the Tax Division to carefully review the facts, circumstances, and law of each criminal tax case as expeditiously as possible, the taxpayer should be given a reasonable opportunity to present his/her case at a conference before the Tax Division." Tax Div. Directive 86–58, May 14, 1986.

The factors considered significant by the Tax Division of the Justice Department do not always coincide with the factors considered significant by CID and the Chief Counsel. For example, the Justice Department generally will not decline prosecution on the basis of the taxpayer's poor health. Tax Division attorneys are directed to recommend prosecution if there is a "reasonable probability of conviction." U.S. Attorneys' Manual § 6–2.213. The Government's success rate in prosecuting tax crimes is very high and recently, the Government has increased its efforts "to identify, investigate and punish tax cheats." IR 2004–48, April 6, 2004. For instance, the number of cases referred by the Justice Department's Tax Division to U.S. Attorneys for criminal tax prosecution in 2003 represented an increase of 35 percent over the year 2000.

If the Tax Division recommends prosecution, the case will be forwarded to the U.S. Attorney. Again, the taxpayer's representative should make a written request for a conference. The conference will be held at the U.S. Attorney's office and will be conducted by an assistant U.S. Attorney. Attorneys from the Tax Division usually do not attend, although they will assist the U.S. Attorney in the prosecution. Plea negotiations may take place at the conference.

§ 16.6   Plea Agreements

A.   *Expedited Plea Procedures*

The IRS and the Tax Division of the Justice Department instituted an expedited plea procedure in 1986. If certain criteria are met, the case will be referred simultaneously by the CID and the Chief Counsel's Office to the Tax Division for plea negotiations with the taxpayer's attorney. The benefit to the taxpayer of this expedited procedure is the avoidance of a lengthy CID investigation and a possibility of a lesser sentence or fine than he would receive at trial. To qualify for this "quicky plea" procedure, the plea agreement must:

a.   involve legal source income (drug dealers will not qualify, for example)

b.   establish culpability for the violations charged

c.   include the most significant violation

d.   consider the totality of the fraud committed by the taxpayer

e.   not reduce tax return felony counts to misdemeanors

[IRM 9.6.2.2.1.1., July 1, 2004]

Consideration of this procedure should begin at the early stages of the investigation, since the benefit to the taxpayer will diminish as the investigation proceeds. A factor to consider in deciding whether to use this procedure is the effect it will have on the taxpayer's civil liability. In exchange for access to the expedited procedure, the CID special agent will normally demand that the taxpayer sign an affidavit admitting facts that may cover several years. Thus, even though the criminal case might be concluded on the basis of one major count covering only one year (see discussion at § 16.6.B., *infra*), the taxpayer's admissions could ensure substantial civil penalties. In this regard, consideration should be given to limiting the admissions and negotiating a plea to a charge that will not collaterally estop the taxpayer from denying fraud, if possible. See § 10.3.E., *supra*, for a discussion of the collateral estoppel effects of criminal convictions.

B.   *Major Count Policy*

If there are multiple crimes alleged, the Tax Division may accept a guilty plea to the most serious count and dismiss the remaining counts. For example, if there is a count of evasion (§ 7201) and several false statement (§ 7206) counts, the Tax Division may accept a guilty plea to the evasion count and drop the false statement counts. Doing so does not prejudice the Government, since the taxpayer will be collaterally estopped to challenge the civil fraud penalty (if he pleads guilty to an evasion count) and a stiff criminal penalty will follow from the major count.

C. *Nolo Contendere Pleas*

The Tax Division will not accept a *nolo contendere* plea except in extraordinary circumstances. The reason is the collateral estoppel effect of the plea. A taxpayer who pleads *nolo contendere* to a felony evasion charge is not collaterally estopped to challenge the civil penalty for fraud.

CHAPTER 17

IRS INVESTIGATORY POWERS AND TECHNIQUES

To equip the IRS to carry out its mission of enforcing the tax laws, Congress has given it enormous investigatory powers, chief of which is the summons power contained in section 7602 and discussed at length in this chapter. Of increasing importance in the recent past are two other investigatory techniques, undercover operations and grand jury investigations, both of which are being used extensively. For obvious reasons, there is little public information concerning the types and scope of IRS undercover investigations. The Internal Revenue Manual, however, describes the basic procedures governing undercover operations. IRM 9.4.8. Moreover, case law reveals that IRS agents have posed as clients of return preparers and tax shelter promoters who are suspected of fraud, as well as prospective buyers of businesses. These guises are probably only a fraction of the "covers" actually utilized. Grand jury investigations, and the reasons why they are increasingly utilized in tax cases, are discussed in § 17.2, *infra*. Search warrants and the privileges and protections of persons under investigation are discussed in § 17.3, *infra*.

§ 17.1   The IRS Summons Power

A.   Purposes

The broad investigatory powers of the Service are defined and described in sections 7601 through 7610 of the Code. The principal provision is section 7602, which permits the IRS to issue a summons for any statutorily authorized purpose to compel production of books and records, take testimony under oath, and summon a taxpayer or third party to appear and produce books and records and testify under oath. Section 7602(a) authorizes the Service to issue a summons for any of five listed purposes:

1.   to ascertain the correctness of any return;

2.   to make a return where none has been made;

3.   to determine the liability of any person for any internal revenue tax;

4.   to determine the liability of any transferee or fiduciary; and

5.   to collect any internal revenue tax liability.

In 1982, Congress added section 7602(b) to eliminate the delay and uncertainty caused by objections to summonses on the basis that they were being used improperly for a "criminal purpose." This provision authorizes the IRS to issue a summons for the purpose of "inquiring into any offense connected with the administration or enforcement of the internal revenue laws." However, section 7602(c), also added in 1982, prohibits the issuance of a summons after the IRS has referred the case to the Justice Department with a recommendation of prosecution or grand jury investigation. In addition, no summons may be issued if the Justice Department has requested disclosure of a return or return information under section 6103(h)(2). (Section 6103 is discussed in § 4.2, *supra*). Once the Justice Department referral has been terminated, the power to issue summonses is restored. The Justice Department terminates a referral by declining to prosecute or by discontinuing a grand jury investigation, as well as by the final disposition of any actual criminal prosecution. I.R.C. § 7602(c)(2)(B). Thus, the IRS is now expressly authorized to issue summonses in criminal investigations, as long as no Justice Department referral is "in effect."

B. *Service of Summons, Time and Place of Examination*

Authority to issue summonses has been delegated to IRS employees engaged in the examination of returns, collection or investigation. Thus, special agents, revenue agents and revenue officers all have authority to issue a summons.

Section 7603 governs the manner of service of the summons. It requires that an attested copy of the summons be handed to the witness or left at her "last and usual place of abode." Summons on a corporation may be served on an officer, director or person authorized to accept service. A summons directed at a specific officer or director may be served either at the corporate offices or wherever the person can be found. Except for so-called "John Doe" summonses, discussed below, the summons must identify the taxpayer whose tax liability is the cause for issuing the summons.

The time and place of examination pursuant to the summons is governed by section 7605(a), which provides that the time and place must be "reasonable under all the circumstances" and that the date fixed be not less than 10 days from the date the summons is served. The purpose of this 10–day period is to afford the witness sufficient time to gather the required information and records.

C. *Summoned Persons' Rights*

A person who has been summoned is entitled to witness fees and mileage. I.R.C. § 7610(a)(1). In addition, if a summons for books and records is issued to anyone other than the taxpayer, or an officer, agent, attorney or accountant of the taxpayer, that person is entitled to reimbursement for costs reasonably incurred in locating, reproducing and transporting the documents. I.R.C. § 7610(a)(2).

A summoned person is entitled to be accompanied by and represented by counsel or other representative with a power of attorney. She also may consult with her accountant during any phase of the interview in which technical matters are discussed. Section 7521, added to the Code by the Omnibus Taxpayer Bill of Rights Act of 1988 (TBOR1), defines taxpayers' rights in interviews with the IRS not involving criminal investigations. It requires that in any interview (except an interview pursuant to a summons), if the person being interviewed clearly states that she wishes to be represented by counsel, the interview must be suspended immediately. This is true even if the person has already answered some questions.

Another change made by the TBOR1 was to codify the right of persons interviewed to record the interview or be furnished a transcript of the interview if the IRS records it. If the summoned person wishes to record the interview, she must notify the IRS in advance and furnish her own recording equipment. If the IRS intends to record the interview, it must so inform the witness. If requested by the witness, the IRS must furnish (at the witness's expense) a transcript of the recorded interview. I.R.C. § 7521(a).

D.   *Compliance*

The summoned person complies with the summons by appearing at the designated time and place with any books or records that may have been requested, and by giving oral testimony. The IRS may conduct the interview under oath, often in a "question and answer" format, or it may conduct an informal interview. A witness cannot be compelled to create or prepare any new document or sign a written statement in lieu of giving oral testimony. United States v. Davey (2d Cir.1976); United States v. Levy (5th Cir.1976).

If a summoned person believes in good faith that she has valid objections to compliance with the summons, she may decline to comply. The summoned person should make her objections known to the IRS hearing officer who summoned her. If the hearing officer disagrees with the stated objections, he may not impose sanctions against the witness. Instead, a summons enforcement action under section 7402(b) must be brought. If the court orders the summoned person to comply with the summons, and the person refuses, she is subject to contempt proceedings. Prior to this point, though, no sanctions may be imposed upon her. Reisman v. Caplin (S.Ct.1964). Objections raised for the first time at a contempt proceeding for defying a court order to comply are not timely, and contempt sanctions are appropriate. United States v. Rylander (S.Ct.1983).

It should be obvious that a summoned person cannot legally avoid producing summoned books and records simply by destroying them or turning them over to another person. Destruction of the records could well be a criminal act, and releasing them to a third party could subject the summoned person to a contempt citation. *See* United States v. Schoeberlein (D.Md.1971).

In a summons enforcement action, may the U.S. district court judge order compliance with the summons, but also restrict the Government's use or dissemination of the summoned materials? While the answer remains uncertain, it appears that the district court may not restrict the enforcement of the summons. In *United States v. Barrett* (5th Cir. 1988), the Fifth Circuit held that "in a summons enforcement proceeding, the district court's only task is to determine whether the summons should or should not be enforced." In contrast, the Ninth

Circuit upheld, and the Supreme Court affirmed (by a 4 to 4 vote) a district judge's restriction that specified: "The documents delivered hereunder shall not be delivered to any other government agency by the IRS unless criminal tax prosecution is sought or an Order of Court is obtained." United States v. Zolin (S.Ct.1989) (involving documents and tapes of L. Ron Hubbard and the Church of Scientology). The Third and Eighth Circuits also have adhered to the view that a district court can issue a restricted summons. Subsequently, however, the Ninth Circuit changed its view and adopted the reasoning of the Fifth Circuit. *See* United States v. Jose (9th Cir.1997).

E. Objections

Relevancy. Section 7602(a) authorizes the IRS to issue a summons for any information that "may be relevant or material" to an audit or investigation. This statutory language is very broad, and the courts have interpreted it liberally to allow a summons seeking any information that "might throw light on" the taxpayer's tax liability.

Unnecessary examinations and second inspections. Section 7605(b) states that "[n]o taxpayer shall be subjected to unnecessary examination or investigation, and only one inspection of a taxpayer's books of account" is normally allowed. Second (and subsequent) inspections are not permitted "unless the taxpayer requests otherwise or unless the Secretary, after investigation, notifies the taxpayer in writing that an additional inspection is necessary." This section offers very little protection because the scope of the authority under section 7602 is so broad. It is difficult to imagine how a taxpayer could successfully challenge an audit or investigation as "unnecessary." In addition, the Supreme Court has interpreted the term "unnecessary" and the no-second-inspection rule to permit additional inspections after the statute of limitations has expired on the year in question even if the Government does not have probable cause to suspect fraud. United States v. Powell (S.Ct.1964). According to the *Powell* Court, the purpose of the statutory ban on "unnecessary" inspections "was no more than to emphasize the responsibility of agents to exercise prudent judgment in wielding the extensive powers granted to them by the Internal Revenue Code." The Supreme Court in *Powell* indicated that a court should refuse to enforce a summons only if it was issued for an improper purpose.

Improper purpose and bad faith. To succeed in challenging a summons under the *Powell* improper purpose test, the taxpayer or other summoned person must establish that the summons was issued "to harass the taxpayer or to put pressure on him to settle a collateral dispute, or for any other purpose reflecting on the good faith of the particular investigation." Thus, a summons issued primarily out of spite or for harassment should not be enforced.

Prior to the 1982 amendment to section 7602 authorizing issuance of a summons in a criminal investigation, the IRS could issue a summons only for the purpose of determining potential civil tax liability. There was a great deal of litigation prior to the 1982 amendment concerning whether a summons was issued for the "improper purpose" of furthering a criminal investigation. Now that section 7602 explicitly authorizes issuance of summonses for criminal investigation prior to referral of the case to the Justice Department, a possible challenge to a summons under this section would be that the IRS intentionally delayed referring the case to the Justice Department in order to use the summons for expanded criminal discovery. In a case decided prior to the 1982 expansion of section 7602 to include criminal investigations, the Supreme Court stated that for the IRS to so delay a referral to the Justice Department "when there is an institutional commitment to make the referral" would amount to bad faith. United States v. LaSalle National Bank (S.Ct.1978).

It is not clear whether the 1982 amendments made the "institutional commitment" of the IRS to refer the case to the Justice Department irrelevant, but it is possible that Congress' intent to create a "bright line" test (referral has occurred) will render the "institutional commitment" argument moot. The better result would seem to be that such a delay is evidence of institutional bad faith, and hence any summons issued after a decision to refer the case should not be enforced. In holding that the 1982 amendments did not eliminate the improper purpose—bad faith objection, one court stated:

We do not doubt that portions of the *Powell* and *LaSalle* discussions of bad faith retain vitality and that where the taxpayer can prove that the summons is issued solely to harass him, or to force him to settle a collateral dispute, *Powell,* * * * or that the IRS is acting solely as an information-gathering agency for other departments, such as the Department of Justice, *LaSalle,* * * * or the FBI, the summons will be unenforceable because of the IRS's bad faith. [Pickel v. United States, 746 F.2d 176, 185 (3d Cir.1984).]

Information already in possession of IRS. Another valid objection to an IRS summons identified by the Supreme Court in *Powell* is that the information is already in the possession of the IRS. Courts have interpreted this to mean that the IRS must be in actual physical possession of the information. Simply showing that the IRS had access to the information in an inspection of records pursuant to a previous summons will not defeat the subsequent summons on this basis. Furthermore, some courts have enforced summonses for information that probably was in the possession of the IRS, but where it would be unduly burdensome for the IRS to locate, provided the burden on the summoned party to produce the records is not great.

F. *Summons Enforcement Proceedings*

The IRS is not authorized to punish someone who resists a summons, nor is it empowered to compel compliance. Instead, it must either institute a summons enforcement proceeding under Code section 7402(b) or seek a court order to have the person arrested and held for a contempt and enforcement hearing under section 7604(b). Another option is to refer the case to the Justice Department for prosecution under section 7210, which makes it a misdemeanor to neglect to appear or produce documents pursuant to a summons. This option, however, is rarely exercised.

The initial burden of proof in a summons enforcement proceeding is on the Government. It must establish a prima facie case for enforcement by establishing that it has complied with the four criteria set out in *United States v. Powell*:

1.   the examination that the summons relates to is being conducted for a legitimate purpose;

2.   the summons seeks information that may be relevant to that purpose;

3.   the IRS is not already in possession of the information; and

4.   the administrative steps spelled out in the Code have been followed.

If the Government establishes compliance with these standards, the burden shifts to the summoned person to rebut the showing by proof of an improper purpose or bad faith.

It is crucial that a person wishing to resist a summons appear at the appointed time and place and make his objections known to the hearing officer. Failure to do so could result in the person's arrest and detention under section 7604(b). In addition, a court may refuse to entertain any objections that were not previously stated to the hearing officer.

If the hearing officer agrees that the objections are sound, she can simply take no action to attempt to enforce the summons. If the hearing officer wishes to pursue the matter, she can refer it to the Division Area Counsel for enforcement action. The Area Counsel then must decide whether to initiate the enforcement action. The Internal Revenue Manual describes the review procedures that the Area Counsel should follow in determining whether a summons enforcement action is warranted. IRM 25.5.10.

Jurisdiction to enforce a summons is conferred on the United States district court located where the summoned person "resides or is found." I.R.C. § 7604(a). The Division Counsel files an *ex parte* petition with the federal district court, together with an affidavit of the IRS employee who issued the summons stating that the IRS has satisfied each of the four *Powell* criteria. On the basis of this *ex parte* showing, the court will order the summoned person to show cause why the summons should not be enforced.

Because the court will order enforcement unless the summoned person can establish facts that are usually known only by the IRS, such as improper purpose, bad faith or that one of the four *Powell* standards is not in fact satisfied, the availability of pre-hearing discovery or an evidentiary hearing is important. Since the 1982 amendments adding authority to issue summonses in criminal investigations and creating a "bright line" test permitting summonses any time prior to a Justice Department referral, courts have rejected earlier case law permitting pre-hearing discovery. An evidentiary hearing is apparently still possible, if the summoned person can make a substantial preliminary showing of bad faith. *See* United States v. Millman (2d Cir.1985).

A district court order enforcing a summons is final and appealable, and becomes enforceable (unless stayed) 10 days after its entry. If the district court refuses to grant a stay, the summoned party may apply to the federal court of appeals for a stay and review of the order. If a stay is not granted, the witness must comply with the summons or be held in contempt of court. As mentioned earlier, the court will not entertain any objections in the contempt proceeding that were not raised earlier.

G. *Third–Party Recordkeeper Summonses*

Nothing in section 7602 limits the IRS to issuing summonses only to the taxpayer under audit or investigation. If the IRS issues a summons to your neighbor or your bank concerning your tax liability, are you entitled to notice of the summons? What if the IRS simply telephones your neighbor or co-worker? Prior to enactment of the 1998 Taxpayer Bill of Rights 3, the answer depended on whether the third party was a "third-party recordkeeper" within the meaning of section 7609. If he is a "third-party recordkeeper," and if the summons requires the production of business records, then the taxpayer whose liability is the subject of the summons must be given notice of the summons and the right to contest its enforcement, under section 7609. The 1998 amendment did not change this rule, but it does change the rule regarding IRS contacts of third parties who are not "third-party recordkeepers." Under pre–1998 law, if the third party was not a "third-party recordkeeper," the taxpayer was not entitled to notice of the IRS summons or other contact. For contacts made more than six months after July 22, 1998, section 7602 requires the IRS to notify the taxpayer before contacting third parties. This notice is not required in criminal cases or jeopardy collection situations.

"Third-party recordkeeper" is defined in section 7609(a)(3) to include:

1. a bank, savings and loan institution, or similar institution;

2. a consumer reporting agency as defined under § 603 of the Fair Credit Reporting Act;

3. anyone extending credit through the use of credit cards or similar devices (interpreted in Regulations to mean only those who issue credit cards, and not those who honor the credit cards);

4. brokers (as defined in § 3(a)(4) of the Securities Exchange Act of 1934);

5. attorneys who represent the taxpayer;

6. accountants; and

7. barter exchanges (see § 6045(c)).

Even though the party summoned may be a "third-party recordkeeper" under one of the above categories, this does not ensure that the taxpayer under investigation will be entitled to notice of the summons and an opportunity to contest it. These rights depend on the type of information sought in the summons. The statute limits the right to notice and intervention to situations in which the "summons requires the production of any portion of records made or kept of the business transactions or affairs of any person (other than the person summoned)." I.R.C. § 7609(a)(1)(B). What does this mean? The answer is uncertain, although some courts have interpreted the language to mean that records of a third party that are not kept as part of its function as a "third-party recordkeeper" status can be summoned without notice to the taxpayer or a right to contest. For example, a bank employee who is being investigated apparently is not entitled to notice of a summons served on his employer, the bank (which is clearly within the definition of "third-party recordkeeper"), if the summons seeks information concerning the employee's employment records (as opposed to his banking transactions). Reg. § 301.7609–2(b) supports this approach.

Section 7609 contains a number of exclusions from the normal right to notice and intervention rules. The statutory exclusions include:

1.   The person summoned is not a "third-party recordkeeper" either in general or with respect to the taxpayer whose liability is under investigation.

2.   The summons is served on the taxpayer itself or one of its officers or employees. (In other words, banks and other third-party recordkeepers are not privileged; they may be investigated without notice and right to contest, the same as any other taxpayer.)

3.   The summons was issued merely to determine whether records were kept concerning any transactions with the taxpayer under investigation.

4.   The summons seeks merely to identify the person who has a numbered account with a financial institution.

5.   The summons is issued for collection purposes.

The right of a taxpayer to be notified of a third-party summons and to contest its enforcement is thus limited by statute. Although the person to whom the summons is issued may be a "third-party recordkeeper" for other purposes, he may not fit the definition with respect to the particular taxpayer under audit or investigation.

Although a taxpayer has no statutory right to contest a summons issued to a third party who is not a third-party recordkeeper, a court may permit the taxpayer to intervene if the taxpayer has a "significantly protectable interest," such as a claim of privilege or IRS abuse of process. Donaldson v.

United States (S.Ct.1971). Such permissive intervention is rarely allowed, however.

H. "John Doe" Summonses

Generally, the summons must identify the taxpayer whose tax liability is the subject of the summons. In some circumstances, however, the Code permits the IRS to issue a summons to determine the identity of the taxpayer. That is the purpose of the so-called "John Doe" summons.

Section 7609(f) provides the rules governing "John Doe" summonses. It requires an *ex parte* hearing prior to the service of such a summons in which the IRS must show that:

1. the summons relates to an ascertainable group or class of taxpayers (such as buyers of a particular tax shelter offering);

2. there is a reasonable basis for believing these persons may have failed to comply with the tax laws; and

3. the information sought by the summons is not readily available from other sources.

If the IRS fails to establish that these criteria are satisfied, the court should refuse to enforce the summons.

I. Special Rules for Churches

Widespread use of alleged "churches" as tax shelter devices prompted Congress to enact special legislation governing the sensitive problem of IRS summons authority for church records. For investigations after January 1, 1985, Code section 7611 provides special rules for any "church tax inquiry" (an investigation to determine whether the alleged church in fact qualifies for tax-exempt status) and for audits of churches. In general, section 7611 requires approval of a high-level Treasury official for any "church tax inquiry" and the IRS must furnish prior written notice to the church before any inquiry or audit explaining in detail the nature and purpose of the inquiry and the church's rights.

§ 17.2   Grand Jury Investigations

In-depth discussion of the federal grand jury system is beyond the scope of this book. Some discussion is warranted, however, because the broad investigatory powers of federal grand juries are used with increasing frequency in tax investigations.

A.   Functions of the Grand Jury

Federal grand juries have broad investigatory powers, limited only by the fact that their purpose is to issue indictments if they determine that probable cause exists to believe that a person has committed a crime. So long as their investigation is in furtherance of this purpose, their investigatory powers are enormous. For example, they may inquire into a possible criminal violation even though no particular crime and no particular defendant have been identified. However, they must investigate the possible commission of federal crimes; grand juries may not be used to gather evidence for use in a civil proceeding. United States v. Sells Engineering, Inc. (S.Ct.1983).

Federal grand juries are composed of 16 to 23 individuals, and indictments require the affirmative vote of at least 12 members. Government prosecutors (Assistant United States Attorneys) effectively control the grand jury by deciding when it will convene, who will be subpoenaed to testify, etc. The Federal Rules of Evidence do not apply to grand jury proceedings, and the grand jurors may consider evidence not admissible at trial. The Government is not required to disclose exculpatory evidence in a grand jury proceeding because the grand jury is only an accusatory body. It does not determine guilt or innocence. *See* United States v. Williams (S.Ct. 1992).

The Fifth Amendment prohibits prosecution of a felony charge without an indictment, unless the indictment is waived. Thus, a federal grand jury will be involved at some point in almost every criminal tax investigation. The grand jury can become involved either after the Justice Department has reviewed the case and concluded that prosecution is warranted without further investigation, or the Justice Department can turn the case over to the grand jury for further investigation. According to the Internal Revenue Manual, grand jury investigations are normally requested (1) in the interest of efficiency, when it is apparent that "the administrative process cannot develop the relevant facts within a reasonable period of time" and (2) when "an investigation has proceeded as far as the administrative process allows, but prosecution potential would be strengthened by the grand jury process." IRM 9.5.2.2. In addition, investigations of non-tax crimes can expand to include tax investigations if evidence of tax crime is discovered.

B.   Subpoena Power

The grand jury equivalent of the IRS summons is the subpoena. Unlike the IRS summons, which is governed by elaborate statutory rules, the subpoena is a creature of Federal Rule of Criminal Procedure 17. The target of an investigation is not entitled to notice that another party has been subpoenaed to supply information concerning the target. The person subpoenaed is not entitled to have his lawyer present during the grand jury proceedings.

Challenges to the subpoena can be lodged only by the person subpoenaed and must be based on that person's own rights, not on the rights or privileges of the target of the investigation. Such challenges, in the form of motions to quash or modify the subpoena, will succeed only in extraordinary circumstances. If the motion to quash is denied, the witness must comply with the subpoena or risk civil or criminal contempt charges.

C.   Comparison of IRS Summons and Grand Jury Subpoena

Although the taxpayer is not entitled to notice of a grand jury subpoena issued to a third party, he is generally entitled to notice of an IRS summons issued to a third-party recordkeeper. Outside of this distinction, most of the principal differences between an IRS summons and a grand jury subpoena relate to enforcement. The consequences of failing to comply with a grand jury subpoena can be imposed much more quickly than those for failure to comply with an IRS summons, because the IRS lacks the authority to compel compliance or punish a witness for noncompliance. Instead, it must petition a court for enforcement and possible punishment of a recalcitrant witness.

Recall that a summoned person can state her reasons for not complying with a summons and force the IRS to initiate a summons enforcement proceeding in a United States district court. At the summons enforcement hearing, the IRS bears the initial burden of establishing its compliance with the four *Powell* standards for enforceability of the summons. The burden then shifts to the summoned party to show that enforcement is inappropriate. If the IRS prevails at the hearing, the person must comply or risk being held in contempt.

Grand jury subpoenas, on the other hand, are themselves orders of the federal court, and the witness must comply or be held in contempt. No separate judicial proceeding is necessary to make failure to comply with the subpoena punishable by sanctions for contempt. Motions to quash subpoenas must be initiated by the witness, who bears the burden of establishing the impropriety of the summons. A witness can quickly find herself in custody for failing to comply with a grand jury subpoena.

D. Secrecy of Grand Jury Proceedings

All those entitled to be present during grand jury proceedings, except witnesses, must keep secret all "matters occurring before the grand jury." Federal Rule of Criminal Procedure 6(e)(2). There are many reasons for this blanket rule of secrecy, including potential damage to unindicted targets and potential abuse of the grand jury's criminal investigatory powers to pursue a civil action. Given the IRS's mission of enforcing the tax laws and collecting the revenue, the potential for abuse of the grand jury system to aid the IRS in its civil functions is obvious.

There are some narrow exceptions to the general rule of secrecy. For example, disclosure may be made when ordered by a court "preliminary to or in connection with a judicial proceeding" under Federal Rule of Criminal Procedure 6(e)(3)(C)(i). Does this exception permit disclosure of grand jury information to the IRS for its use in a civil tax audit? In 1983 the Supreme Court held that such disclosure to the IRS is not permissible, because the principal purpose of an IRS audit is not to prepare for litigation, but to determine the correct amount of the taxpayer's tax liability. United States v. Baggot (S.Ct.1983).

Another exception permits disclosure of grand jury materials to an attorney for the Government for use in the performance of the attorney's duty. Federal Rule of Criminal Procedure 6(e)(3)(A)(1). The Supreme Court has held that this exception does not authorize disclosure to attorneys in the Justice Department Civil Division, but only to federal prosecutors involved in the criminal investigation. Government attorneys not directly involved in the criminal investigation must petition a court for access to the grand jury materials and demonstrate a "particularized need" for the information. United States v. Sells Engineering, Inc. (S.Ct.1983).

Sweeping as the investigatory powers of the IRS and grand juries are, taxpayers and witnesses can lawfully refuse to testify or produce documents and records under some circumstances. The primary lawful grounds for such a refusal are the Fifth Amendment privilege against self-incrimination (see § 17.3.B., *infra*), the attorney-client privilege (see 3.5.B., *supra*) and the attorney work product doctrine (see § 3.5.C., *supra*).

§ 17.3 Privileges and Protections

A. *Fourth Amendment*

In circumstances in which the IRS believes that neither the summons nor the grand jury subpoena will ensure production of the records it seeks, it can obtain a search warrant authorizing it to search a taxpayer's premises and seize the records. The Fourth Amendment to the U.S. Constitution provides

> The right of the people to be secure in their persons, houses, papers, and effects, against unreasonable searches and seizures, shall not be violated, and no Warrants shall issue, but upon

probable cause, supported by Oath or affirmation, and particularly describing the place to be searched, and the persons or things to be seized.

Rule 41 of the Federal Rules of Criminal Procedure governs the procedures to be followed to insure that the Fourth Amendment is not violated. Rule 41 requires generally that the request for the warrant specify sufficient grounds to establish probable cause to believe that a crime has been committed and that evidence of the crime is on the premises. An unreasonably broad or general search warrant can violate the Fourth Amendment. Coolidge v. New Hampshire (S.Ct.1971). Thus, the warrant must describe with particularity the objects of the search. *See* Vonderahe v. Howland (9th Cir.1974). Seizure of a taxpayer's records pursuant to a valid search warrant does not violate the Fifth Amendment protection against compelled self-incriminating testimony. Andresen v. Maryland (S.Ct.1976).

B. *Fifth Amendment*

(1) Self–Incrimination

The Fifth Amendment provides that no person "shall be compelled in any criminal case to be a witness against himself." The privilege may be asserted not only during a criminal trial, but also in any administrative, investigatory, or civil proceeding. The Supreme Court has held that the privilege may be validly asserted if there is governmental compulsion, explicit or implicit testimony, and self-incrimination. Fisher v. United States (S.Ct.1976). Can filing a federal tax return fit those categories?

The U.S. Supreme Court decided in 1927 that the privilege against self-incrimination does not excuse the failure to file a return. United States v. Sullivan (S.Ct.1927). Thus, a taxpayer who refuses to file may be prosecuted for the willful failure to file a return and/or the Service could prepare the return administratively under section 6020(b)(1). On the other hand, if the taxpayer files a return that contains incriminating information, the Government may use the information against the taxpayer. *See* Garner v. United States (S.Ct.1976).

The Supreme Court has indicated that the Fifth Amendment privilege may be validly asserted on a tax return if asserted against specific disclosures, (see *Sullivan*, above) and if enough information is provided that the form constitutes a return. For example, in *United States v. Neff* (9th Cir.1980), the taxpayer responded to more than 25 questions with the words "Object: Self–Incrimination." The Government argued that the form that Neff filed did not constitute a valid tax return and the Ninth Circuit agreed. Also, the Fifth Amendment may not be asserted to avoid incrimination for a past violation of the income tax laws. *See* United States v. Carlson (9th Cir.1980) (cannot avoid prosecution under § 7203 for failure to file a return by hiding behind the Fifth Amendment).

The Fifth Amendment privilege against self-incrimination also applies to compelled production of documents. Both an IRS summons issued pursuant to section 7602 and a grand jury subpoena constitute governmental compulsion, and the privilege may thus be claimed if the other two elements under *Fisher* exist. The most difficult question concerns the compelled production of documents: under what circumstances may a person refuse to produce incriminating documents? If the act of producing those documents is testimonial in nature, then the Fifth Amendment should provide some protection.

In 1886, the Supreme Court ruled that the Fifth Amendment protected a person from being compelled to produce "private papers" whose contents might incriminate him. Boyd v. United States (S.Ct. 1886). Although the Court has not overruled *Boyd*, it has completely rejected its holding and analysis. Now the contents of records are not protected, but the act of producing those records can be testimonial and thus protected.

When a person served with an IRS summons or a grand jury subpoena *duces tecum* produces the records sought, that person implicitly acknowledges (and thus implicitly testifies) that the documents exist, that he possesses them, and that they are authentic. United States v. Doe (S.Ct.1984); Fisher v. United States (S.Ct.1976). When the act of producing documents is testimonial, and the documents pertain to sole proprietorship records or personal records, then the person producing the documents is entitled to immunity from prosecution based on the act of producing the documents. *Doe, supra*. The limited immunity is granted pursuant to 18 U.S.C. §§ 6002–6004, and the Government is prohibited from using the "testimony" of producing the records directly or derivatively against the person. United States v. Hubbell (S.Ct. 2000).

On the other hand, "collective entities," such as partnerships and corporations, have no Fifth Amendment privilege. A divided (5 to 4) Supreme Court has held that when a summons or subpoena requires the production of records of the entity, the agent who must produce the records cannot validly invoke the Fifth Amendment privilege, even though by producing the records he might incriminate himself personally. Braswell v. United States (S.Ct. 1988). In a footnote, the Court left open the possibility that the agent could establish a valid Fifth Amendment claim "by showing for example that he is the sole employee and officer of the corporation, [and] that the jury would inevitably conclude that he produced the records." *Id.* at 118 n.11.

(2) Double Jeopardy

The Fifth Amendment also states: "nor shall any person be subject for the same offence to be twice put in jeopardy of life or limb." This phrase generally is interpreted to mean that a person may not be tried twice or punished twice for the same offense. There are a number of exceptions to this interpretation, however. For instance, if a defendant successfully appeals a conviction on grounds of procedural faults, he is subject to retrial. Also, the state and federal governments are considered separate sovereigns, so a defendant may be prosecuted for a crime in state court and then re-prosecuted for the same crime in federal court, or vice versa.

Sometimes, the same conduct may violate more than one statute, and if so, the Double Jeopardy provision may not apply to bar double punishment. The U.S. Supreme Court has postulated a test to determine whether double jeopardy applies in this situation. Under this test, if "each provision requires proof of an additional fact which the other does not," the conduct will constitute separate offenses and the Double Jeopardy Clause will not apply. Blockburger v. United States (S.Ct.1932). But if the evidence needed to convict the defendant is the same for both prosecutions, the Double Jeopardy Clause applies to prevent any subsequent trial attributable to that conduct. For example, evasion requires an affirmative act, a deficiency, and willful intent (see § 18.1.A) and false statements requires a materially false statement under penalties of perjury and willfulness (see § 18.1.C). If the affirmative act needed to establish evasion is a false statement, and the same act would be needed to convict the defendant of both offenses, the defendant could be convicted of either evasion or false statements, but not both, unless there is independent evidence that establishes the act in either case.

The Fifth Amendment's self-incrimination and double jeopardy clauses apply only to criminal cases. Thus, a conviction of a tax offense does not insulate the defendant from the imposition of a civil penalty. *See, e.g.*, Louis v. Commissioner (9th Cir.1999) (defendant convicted of tax fraud was also subject to civil fraud penalty). The United States Supreme Court has held, however, that under certain rare circumstances, a civil penalty may be considered punitive. If so, the penalty would fall within the Double Jeopardy Clause. *See* United States v. Halper (S.Ct.1989). According to the Court, this occurs when the penalty is overwhelmingly disproportionate to the damage caused. *Id.*

CHAPTER 18

FEDERAL TAX CRIMES

The Internal Revenue Code contains numerous criminal provisions, and a wide (and ever-growing) number of Title 18 and other general federal criminal statutes that are employed in tax and tax-related prosecutions. This chapter discusses the principal criminal provisions of the Internal Revenue Code and the general federal criminal provisions under Title 18 that are most frequently employed in tax prosecutions. This chapter also discusses the penalties for convictions of tax crimes and the methods of proving the crimes. Chapter 19 discusses the various defenses to these crimes.

§ 18.1 Criminal Provisions of the Internal Revenue Code

A. Section 7201—Attempted Evasion

The tax evasion statute, section 7201, is the "capstone of a system of sanctions which singly or in combination were calculated to induce prompt and forthright fulfillment of every duty under the income tax law and to provide a penalty suitable to every degree of delinquency." Spies v. United States (S.Ct.1943). The evasion statute (also called criminal fraud) provides the harshest punishment, and requires a greater quantum of proof by the Government, than any other tax crime.

Section 7201 makes it a felony to willfully attempt to evade or defeat any tax or the payment of any tax. The exact statutory language is as follows:

> Any person who willfully attempts in any manner to evade or defeat any tax imposed by this title or the payment thereof shall, in addition to other penalties provided by law, be guilty of a felony and, upon conviction thereof, shall be fined not more than $100,000 ($500,000 in the case of a corporation) or imprisoned not more than 5 years, or both, together with the costs of prosecution.

The Criminal Fines Enforcement Act of 1984, codified at 18 U.S.C. § 3623, substantially increased the maximum fines for most federal criminal offenses. These maximum fines apply to crimes committed after November 1, 1987, and are described in more detail in section 18.5, *infra*. For felonies, such as section 7201, the maximum fine for an individual is $250,000, and the maximum fine for corporations is $500,000; for misdemeanors, the maximum fine for both individuals and corporations is $100,000.

"Persons" who are potentially liable under section 7201 include individuals, partners, corporate officers and employees, and corporations, and conviction is possible even if the tax evaded is not the defendant's tax. In other words, a person can be convicted under this provision for attempting to evade someone else's tax.

Section 7201 defines two distinct crimes: the attempt to defeat or evade a tax (for example, by underreporting income on a return), and the attempt to defeat or evade the payment of any tax (for example, by concealing assets after an assessment and during the collection process). The former is far more frequently prosecuted than the latter, and its elements and requirements are the sole focus of the balance of this discussion.

To obtain a conviction under section 7201, the Government must establish beyond a reasonable doubt:

1.   An affirmative act of evasion or attempted evasion;

2.   An additional tax due and owing; and

3.   Willfulness.

In the landmark tax evasion case, *Spies v. United States, supra,* the Supreme Court distinguished the felony of tax evasion from the tax misdemeanors by focusing on the word "attempt." The Court concluded that "in employing the terminology of attempt to embrace the gravest of offenses against the revenues Congress intended some willful commission in addition to the willful omissions that make up the list of misdemeanors." Thus, a willful failure to file a return, a misdemeanor under section 7203, is not sufficient for section 7201 evasion unless accompanied by some affirmative conduct evidencing an attempt to evade. However, a taxpayer who files false W–4 withholding certificates claiming exempt status (thereby causing his employer to withhold no federal taxes), and who fails to file a return, can be convicted of felony evasion; the affirmative and willful act of filing the false withholding certificates satisfies the affirmative act requirement of *Spies*. *See, e.g.*, United States v. House (W.D.Mich. 1985). The Supreme Court has held that filing a false tax return is itself a sufficient affirmative act to support conviction under section 7201. Sansone v. United States (S.Ct.1965).

Unless there is a deficiency in tax, a conviction under section 7201 cannot be sustained. The government need not prove the exact amount of the deficiency, however. Some courts have indicated that the deficiency must be "substantial," but this element is not based on either the statute or the principal Supreme Court decisions construing it. The "substantiality" of a deficiency, according to one court, "is not measured in terms of gross or net income nor by any particular percentage of the tax shown to be due and payable. All the attendant circumstances must be taken into consideration." United States v. Nunan (2d Cir.1956). For example, a taxpayer who refuses to cooperate during an audit, and whose suspicious behavior prompts a criminal investigation, could be prosecuted and convicted under section 7201 for omitting a relatively small amount of income (or overstating deductions by a similar amount). Similarly, a "high-profile" individual, such as a politician or entertainer, might be prosecuted and convicted under the felony evasion statute for relatively minor transgressions, if committed willfully and accompanied by the requisite affirmative act to evade. In these circumstances, the deterrent effect of "making an example" of the individual can outweigh the general reluctance to prosecute for relatively small deficiencies.

(1) Willfulness

Conviction of any of the principal tax crimes, whether felonies or misdemeanors, requires that the Government prove beyond a reasonable doubt that the defendant acted "willfully." The Supreme Court has observed that Congress included this element in the tax crimes to ensure that a person would not "become a criminal by his mere failure to measure up to the prescribed standard of conduct." United States v. Murdock (S.Ct.1933). Precisely what is meant by the term, and whether it might mean different things in different contexts, has been a continuing puzzle for the courts.

Because it involves the defendant's state of mind, willfulness must ordinarily be proven by circumstantial evidence. Its existence is a question of fact for the jury. Typically, those with actual information about the alleged crime will not confess or assist in the prosecution, thus necessitating the use of circumstantial evidence. In this respect, the 1989 prosecution and conviction of Leona Helmsley, aided largely by testimony of former employees, is somewhat unique.

The complexity of the tax laws, and the human tendency to make errors, require that our society impose some sort of buffer between taxpayers and the threat of a prison sentence. The buffer provided by Congress is the willfulness requirement, which shields from conviction those who make innocent or even negligent errors, or who genuinely misunderstand the law.

The Supreme Court's first attempt to define willfulness came in its 1933 decision in *Murdock*, *supra*. The Court first observed that the term "denotes an act which is intentional, or knowing, or voluntary, as distinguished from accidental." In language that would bedevil the courts for years thereafter, the *Murdock* Court further stated that "willfully" usually means "an act done with a bad purpose; without justifiable excuse; stubbornly, obstinately, perversely * * * or with bad faith or evil intent." Ten years later, the Court in *Spies v. United States* (S.Ct.1943) stated that the term willfulness connotes "evil motive and want of justification." Thirty years after *Spies*, in 1973, the Supreme Court was still referring to the willfulness requirement in terms of bad purpose or evil motive. In *United States v. Bishop* (S.Ct.1973), the Court stated that it "shall continue to require, in both tax felonies and tax misdemeanors that must be done 'willfully,' the bad purpose or evil motive described in *Murdock*."

Finally, in 1976, the Supreme Court ended the confusion caused by these early and continuing references to bad purpose and evil motive. Simply put, the issue was whether proof of a specific intent to violate the law was sufficient, or whether the jury was required to find that the taxpayer acted with bad purpose or evil motive. In *United States v. Pomponio* (S.Ct.1976), a *per curiam* decision, the

Court seemed surprised that lower courts were requiring a finding of bad purpose or evil motive. The Court stated that the lower courts "incorrectly assumed that the reference to an 'evil motive' in *United States v. Bishop* and earlier cases meant something more than the specific intent to violate the law * * *." The Court then stated the meaning of the term in language that remains the standard definition: willfulness "simply means a voluntary, intentional violation of a known legal duty."

Although courts and commentators still refer to the evil motive or bad purpose requirement, it is important to recognize that these terms are illustrative and do not impose any additional proof requirement. Thus, a jury finding that a defendant acted with an evil motive is tantamount to the ultimate finding of willfulness; on the other hand, a jury can find that a defendant acted willfully without finding that he acted with a bad purpose or evil motive. In other words, although a voluntary and intentional violation of a known legal duty may reflect a bad purpose or evil motive, the Government need not prove, and the jury need not find, both the specific intent to violate the law and evil motive or bad purpose.

As *Bishop, supra*, makes clear, the term willfulness means the same thing in tax felonies as it does in tax misdemeanors. There is no lesser standard of intent for the willful failure to file misdemeanor than for the felony of attempted tax evasion: both require a voluntary, intentional violation of a known legal duty. Carelessness or mistake is insufficient in both the felony and the misdemeanor contexts.

In 1991, the U.S. Supreme Court again addressed the issue of willfulness in the criminal tax context in the case of *Cheek v. United States* (S.Ct.1991). John Cheek was an airline pilot who failed to file tax returns for several years and was charged with a variety of tax offenses. Cheek testified that he had attended seminars conducted by lawyers and other professionals in which he had been told that the federal tax system was unconstitutional. Cheek testified that he had been indoctrinated by these seminars and that he had honestly and reasonably believed that the tax laws were being unconstitutionally enforced and that his actions were legal. Thus, he argued that he lacked the willfulness required to be convicted of the offenses with which he was charged. When the jury requested further clarification of the term "willfully," the judge instructed that "beliefs that the tax laws are unconstitutional and that wages are not income [are not] objectively reasonable." The jury then returned a verdict of guilty and Cheek appealed. The Supreme Court held that willfulness is determined under a subjective standard and that the Government must establish that the law imposed a duty upon the defendant, that the defendant knew of this duty, and that he voluntarily and intentionally violated that duty. By instructing the jury on the unreasonableness of Cheek's beliefs, the judge effectively deprived Cheek of his defense. The Court opined that a defendant's views about the constitutionality of the tax laws "are irrelevant to the issue of willfulness and need not be heard by the jury."

Given the subjective nature of willfulness, how does the Government prove that the defendant acted willfully? Proof of willfulness generally is accomplished through circumstantial evidence of what are known as "badges of fraud"—conduct from which the jury can infer willfulness. The badges of fraud identified by the Supreme Court in *Spies* as satisfying the affirmative act requirement of section 7201 evasion also will present a jury question on the issue of willfulness. The *Spies* Court listed the following badges of fraud: "keeping a double set of books, making false entries or alterations, or false invoices or documents, destruction of books or records, concealment of assets or covering up sources of income, handling of one's affairs to avoid making the records usual in transactions of the kind, and any conduct, the likely effect of which would be to mislead or conceal."

The Internal Revenue Manual contains a lengthy listing of conduct that the Service considers to be badges of fraud. IRM § 20.1.5.12.1. Additional examples of the type of conduct that will satisfy the affirmative act element include lying to IRS agents, consistently overstating deductions, holding property in nominee names, diverting corporate funds to pay an officer's personal expenses, and concealing bank accounts. A taxpayer whose conduct amounts to one or more badges of fraud will not only have satisfied the affirmative act element of evasion, but also will have minimized his chances of defeating the element of willfulness, since the badges of fraud are circumstantial evidence supporting willfulness.

Over the years, other types of conduct have proved significant in establishing an inference of willfulness. Perhaps chief among them is a pattern of underreporting income, or overstating deductions, or failing to file returns. Such a pattern of conduct will permit an inference of willfulness sufficient to create a jury question. If such a pattern is coupled with one or more affirmative acts of falsification or concealment, the Government's case is strengthened even further.

(2) Methods of Proof of Unreported Income

Aside from the willfulness element, the most difficult trial problem for the Government can be proving that the defendant actually had more income than reported on his return. An essential ingredient of a prosecution for attempted evasion under section 7201 is proof of a tax deficiency. If the Government cannot establish the existence of a deficiency, then a conviction will not be sustained. Although proof of a deficiency is not an element of the other tax offenses, many of the tax crimes do require the Government to prove that a return or statement was materially false. Thus, to convict under these sections (section 7206(1) and 7207, for example) the Government often must establish that the defendant underreported income on his return and that the return was materially false.

A deficiency also can be caused by overstating deductions, but most tax evasion prosecutions are based on understating income. Although the Government need not prove the exact amount of a defendant's income, it must establish beyond a reasonable doubt that the defendant had greater income than he reported. There are two basic methods of proving unreported income: the direct or "specific items" method, and the indirect method, which includes the net worth method, the bank deposits method, and other (often hybrid) approaches.

Direct Proof Via the "Specific Items" Method. Under the specific items method, the Government bases its case on specific, identified transactions, such as the receipt of interest, dividends or constructive dividends, wages or bribes. Where proof of the transaction exists, such as a W–2 Form reflecting wages paid to an employee, the only realistic defense is that the item in question is not in fact income. For example, a specific items prosecution based on a theory of constructive dividends (often involving use by a shareholder of a corporation's property) could be defended by challenging the characterization of the transaction as resulting in income or by proving that the corporation had no earnings and profits and thus the distribution to the shareholder was not taxable as a dividend under Code section 316.

Indirect Methods of Proof. Far more difficult questions are presented by the Government's use of indirect methods to prove unreported income. In such cases, the taxpayer's apparent spending beyond his means or a sudden increase in net worth can result from many factors, such as the accumulation over time of a "cash hoard" that the taxpayer is now spending, or the receipt of a loan or inheritance, none of which involve taxable income. In indirect proof cases, the Government has the problematic task of proving that the defendant had taxable income that was not reported, and it must do so despite the absence of any identifiable records that would permit it to use the specific items method.

1. Net Worth Method. The net worth (or net worth plus expenditures) method, which compares a taxpayer's net worth at the beginning of the year to the net worth at the end of the period to establish unreported income, was condoned by the Supreme Court in 1943, and its widespread use thereafter prompted the Court to reconsider the propriety of the method in *Holland v. United States* (S.Ct.1954). While recognizing that the use of the net worth method "involved something more than the ordinary use of circumstantial evidence in the usual criminal case," the Court upheld the legality of the method. The *Holland* Court discussed the numerous "pitfalls" of the method, including determining whether the taxpayer had any nontaxable income for the period (that is, whether he had accumulated a cash hoard through thrift or had received a gift or a loan), for which he might not be able to reconstruct the exact timing and source of the income. In such cases, the mere unexplained "bulge" in income could cause a jury to convict based on the assump-

tion that the increase represented taxable income for the year.

An "essential condition" to the successful use of the net worth method is the establishment with "reasonable certainty" of an opening net worth for the year. *Holland*. This is accomplished by identifying and valuing all the taxpayer's assets as of the beginning of the year in question. To disprove the existence of a cash hoard on hand at the beginning of the year, the Government can introduce credit records, testimony of the taxpayer or third parties, or prior years' tax returns. The beginning net worth is then compared to the net worth at the end of the year, with adjustments for living expenses and provable nontaxable receipts, to establish the taxpayer's income.

After establishing a discrepancy between the taxpayer's increase in net worth and his reported income, the Government must introduce evidence supporting the inference that the income is taxable. It can do so by establishing a "likely source" for the income or by negating all possible nontaxable sources of income. United States v. Massei (S.Ct. 1958). If the taxpayer offers explanations of the source of the income, the Government must investigate the "leads," provided they are reasonable, but if no such leads are offered, the Government's burden is met by showing that it engaged in a diligent investigation with no nontaxable sources of income discovered.

2. Bank Deposits Method. The bank deposits method of proving unreported income simply compares the total deposits in the taxpayer's bank accounts to the reported income for the period, after subtracting "non-income" deposits, such as loans. The excess of income as shown by this computation over the amount of income reported for the year is the unreported income. As in the net worth method, there must be some evidence to support the inference that the unreported income is taxable.

3. Cash Expenditures Method. The cash expenditures method is employed to convict persons whose expenditures exceed their apparent means, but for whom no records exist to trace the income to bank deposits or net worth increases reflected in identifiable assets. In other words, this method would be the likely method to convict a gambler or drug dealer whose conspicuous consumption is disproportionate to the amount of taxable income reported on his returns. The unreported income is the excess of expenditures for the period over the reported income, nontaxable items (such as loans), and cash on hand. As with the other indirect proof methods, there must be some evidence to support the inference that the unreported income is taxable.

4. Combination of Methods. Additional methods to prove unreported income, such as the percentage mark-up method, are sometimes employed in connection with one or more of the methods discussed above. In addition, one case can involve the use of

several of the methods, such as bank deposits and cash expenditures.

B. Section 7203—Willful Failure to File or Pay

It is a misdemeanor to willfully fail to file any return, or keep any records, or supply any information required by the Code. Failure to comply with the cash transaction reporting requirements of section 6050I, however, is punishable as a felony under section 7203. See § 18.3.B., *infra*, for a discussion of section 6050I.

Section 7203 also makes it a misdemeanor to willfully fail to pay any tax due. The elements of a section 7203 crime are as follows:

1. Failure to make a return, pay a tax, keep records or supply information;

2. By a person under a legal duty to do so;

3. At the time required by law; and

4. Willfulness.

As is true of felony evasion, a section 7203 offense can be committed by a person other than the taxpayer. Thus, a corporate officer responsible for filing corporate returns, or a tax lawyer who advises against the filing of a return, can be convicted under section 7203.

The first element, the failure to file, is easily established by the Government's testimony that a search was made and no return was found. Especially during the past two decades, the Government has used this section to prosecute tax protestors who either filed no returns, or filed returns lacking sufficient information from which to compute the tax. *See* United States v. Kimball (9th Cir.1991). As discussed in Chapters 5 and 10, the filing of purported "returns" that lack sufficient information to permit determination of the tax due does not constitute the filing of a "return," and the protestor can be prosecuted under section 7203 and assessed civil penalties for delinquent filing. *See, e.g.*, United States v. Daly (8th Cir.1973) (section 7203 conviction upheld against person whose "return" contained only demographic information and documents questioning the constitutionality of the tax laws). Similarly, a return that simply identifies the taxpayer and makes a blanket "Fifth Amendment" claim is neither a "return" nor a valid assertion of the Fifth Amendment protection against self-incrimination. *See, e.g.*, United States v. Vance (11th Cir.1984); United States v. Carlson (9th Cir.1980). To avoid the "no return" problem and at the same time validly invoke the Fifth Amendment, the claim must be made only as to specified types of questions, such as the source of the taxpayer's income, and the return must be otherwise correct and complete. *See, e.g.*, United States v. Edwards (11th Cir.1985).

As in any tax prosecution, the principal consideration usually is willfulness, which obviously can be difficult to establish in the context of a failure to take action. In the tax protestor cases, this element is more easily proved because the protestor's course of conduct will evidence an intent to avoid fulfilling a known legal duty.

C. Section 7206(1)—False Statements

It is a felony under section 7206(1) for any person willfully to make and subscribe "any return, statement, or other document, which contains or is verified by a written declaration that it is made under penalties of perjury, and which he does not believe to be true and correct as to every material matter." The elements of section 7206(1) are:

1. Willful subscription of a return, statement or other document;

2. Under penalties of perjury (federal income tax returns are signed under penalties of perjury);

3. That the subscriber did not believe to be true in every material respect.

Note that violation of this section, like the evasion statute, is a felony. Unlike section 7201, however, the maximum prison term is 3 years (rather than 5), and it does not require proof of a tax deficiency (or additional tax owing). The crime is complete when the taxpayer signs and delivers any return or other document under penalties of perjury knowing that it is false as to any material matter.

The issue of whether "materiality" is a question of law for the judge to decide or a question of fact for the jury is not entirely clear. In *United States v. Gaudin* (S.Ct.1995), the Supreme Court held that a defendant has a constitutional right to have the issue submitted to the jury when materiality is an element of the offense. Subsequently, however, the Court held that the failure to instruct the jury on the materiality of false statements was harmless error because the defendant had omitted "substantial" amounts of income. Neder v. United States (S.Ct.1999). The Court indicated that, by definition, the omission of a substantial amount of income is material. *Id.*, at 16.

In the wake of *Gaudin*, the lower courts have rendered conflicting decisions. The First and Fifth Circuits have held that materiality is an issue of fact for the jury, while the Second Circuit has held that the falsity of deductions is a question for the jury, but the materiality of the false deductions is a question of law for the court to decide. The Ninth Circuit has adopted a hybrid approach, holding that materiality is a question for the jury but where the jury is not instructed on materiality and the defense does not make a timely objection, the decision should be reviewed on appeal for plain error. United States v. Uchimura (9th Cir.1997).

Falsely identifying one's source of income is material, even though the correct amount of income was reported. Similarly, reporting the income of one spouse as having been earned in part by the other spouse, to enable the non-earner spouse to establish credit, has been held to be "material" under section 7206(1) and sufficient to sustain a conviction, even though there was only a nominal deficiency ($48) and the taxpayer had no intent to evade or to understate the tax liability. United States v. Greenberg (2d Cir.1984). The Second Circuit in *Greenberg* reasoned that any false statement that could hinder the IRS in its mission of administering and enforcing the tax laws is material. Not surprisingly, an omission of a material fact makes the statement false and subjects the subscriber to the section 7206(1) penalty.

A return preparer who knowingly makes a false statement on a return can be convicted under section 7206(1), as well as under section 7206(2). United States v. Shortt Accountancy Corp. (9th Cir. 1986). A number of interesting aspects of *Shortt* deserve mention. The case involved an accounting firm that backdated investment documents to give its clients artificial losses for years in which they were not actual owners of the investments. The employee who actually subscribed the returns for the firm had no knowledge of the backdating, but the firm's chief operating officer was involved in the backdating scheme. The corporate defendant (the accounting firm) was convicted of seven counts of violating section 7206(1). On appeal, the firm contended that it could not be guilty because the employee who actually signed the returns lacked knowledge of the illegality and thus could not have acted willfully. Therefore, the defendant contended, actual knowledge of and participation in the scheme by another employee was irrelevant. In addition, the firm argued that only a taxpayer can "make" a return within the meaning of section 7206(1).

The Ninth Circuit rejected both arguments. First, it stated that if the no-knowledge-by-the-signing-employee argument were accepted, "any tax return preparer could escape prosecution for perjury by arranging for an innocent employee" to sign the false return. Next, the court held that the perjury involved in subscribing a false return is chargeable against a return preparer under either section 7206(1) or the aiding and abetting statute, section 7206(2). The fact that only a taxpayer, and not his advisor, is under a statutory duty to "make" a return is irrelevant.

D. *Section 7206(2)—Aiding and Assisting*

Section 7206(2), the aiding and assisting provision, is a very broad statute that provides:

Any person who—

Willfully aids or assists in, or procures, counsels, or advises the preparation or presentation under, or in connection with any matter arising under, the internal revenue laws, of a return, affidavit, claim, or other document, which is fraudulent or is false as to any material matter, whether or not such falsity or fraud is with the knowledge or consent of the person authorized or required to present such return, affidavit, claim or document; * * *

shall be guilty of a felony * * *.

This provision carries the same maximum 3–year prison term as section 7206(1). It is this provision that is most frequently used to prosecute tax practitioners. Its elements are:

1. Willfulness;

2.　Aiding or assisting, or counseling with respect to, the preparation of any document in connection with any matter arising under the internal revenue laws; and

3.　Falsity of the document with respect to any material matter.

"Materiality" has the same meaning as in section 7206(1). Like section 7206(1), this provision does not require proof that a tax deficiency exists or that the defendant intended to evade tax. The crime is complete when the defendant assists in preparing a false document. A conviction will be sustained even if the taxpayer had no knowledge of the falsity; the taxpayer's knowledge or intent is irrelevant.

Prosecutions under section 7206(2) have involved such actions as backdating documents and using inflated appraisals to increase a taxpayer's write-offs. Tax shelter promoters, in addition to tax lawyers and accountants, are frequent subjects of section 7206(2) prosecutions, as are taxpayers who cause a preparer to file a false or fraudulent return. *See, e.g.,* United States v. Hooks (7th Cir.1988) (liability for hiding bonds and causing estate to file false return).

E.　*Section 7207—Submitting a False Document*

It is a misdemeanor under section 7207 to willfully deliver to the IRS "any list, return, account, statement, or other document" known to be fraudulent or false as to any material matter. This provision differs from section 7206(1) in several ways.

First, the false document need not be subscribed under penalties of perjury. Second, the person who delivers the false document is liable under this section, while section 7206(1) applies only to the signer (subscriber) of the document. Thus, delivering a false document signed by another can subject a person to prosecution under section 7207.

F. Section 7212(a)—Impeding or Obstructing Administration of the Internal Revenue Code

Section 7212(a) is a felony provision that applies to two types of conduct: (1) attempts corruptly or by force or threats of force (including any threatening letter or communication) to intimidate or impede any officer or employee of the United States acting in an official capacity and (2) attempts in any other way corruptly or by force or threats of force (including any threatening letter or communication) to obstruct or impede the due administration of the tax laws. The first type of conduct generally applies to the use of force, threats or intimidation against revenue agents, while the latter applies more broadly to any act that serves to obstruct or impede the due administration of the Code. Thus, the latter provision could apply to efforts to hide income and supply false information to the IRS. It need not involve attempts to intimidate or impede, nor must it be an act that is itself illegal (i.e., forming a corporation in an attempt to hide income).

If convicted of this offense, an individual may be fined up to $3,000 or imprisoned for not more than 1 year, or both. If, however, the offense involves the use of force against an officer or employee of the United States or a member of his family, the punishment increases to $5,000 or imprisonment for up to 3 years, or both.

G. *Criminal Activities of Government Employees*

Recognizing the importance of the privacy of confidential tax return information, Congress has enacted two criminal provisions for government employees who abuse the confidentiality rules. The first, section 7213, makes it a felony for a current or former government employee to make an unauthorized disclosure of confidential tax return information. Of course, such a disclosure must be made willfully to come within the ambit of section 7213.

In 1997 Congress enacted the Taxpayer Browsing Protection Act, in which it added section 7213A to the Code. Section 7213A makes it a misdemeanor for any state, federal or other government employee willfully to inspect confidential return information without authorization to do so. These provisions apply to acts occurring after August 5, 1997. Taxpayers whose returns are subjected to unauthorized browsing may bring civil actions for damages under section 7431.

H. *Section 7216—Preparer Disclosure of Unauthorized Return Information*

Section 7216 makes it a misdemeanor for a paid preparer to knowingly and recklessly disclose confidential tax return information without the taxpayer's consent or to use such information for a purpose other than to prepare a return. A return for purposes of section 7216 includes an individual, corporate or fiduciary income tax return, an amended return or an estimated tax return. This provision is subject to a number of exceptions, however, such as where information is required under the Code, by court order, to report the commission of a crime, or pursuant to a quality or peer review.

§ 18.2 Related Federal Criminal Statutes Under Title 18

In addition to the criminal offenses under the Code, a tax offender also may be prosecuted for the same conduct under Title 18 of the U.S. Code.

A. *18 U.S.C. § 371—Conspiracy*

Probably the most frequently employed general criminal charge in tax prosecutions is conspiracy, which is a felony (punishable by up to 5 years imprisonment and a fine of up to $250,000 for individuals). The conspiracy statute provides as follows:

> If two or more persons conspire either to commit any offense against the United States, or to defraud the United States, or any agency thereof in any manner or for any purpose, and one or more of such persons do any act to effect the object of the conspiracy, each shall be fined not more than [$250,000 for crimes after January 1, 1984; 18 U.S.C. § 3623] ($500,000 in the case of a corporation) or imprisoned not more than 5 years, or both, together with the costs of prosecution.

If the underlying crime is a misdemeanor, however, the punishment for the conspiracy may not exceed the punishment for the misdemeanor. For example, a conspiracy to violate section 7207 (a misdemeanor statute) is punishable only to the same degree that a misdemeanor is punishable.

The elements of conspiracy are:

1.　An agreement by two or more persons;

2.　To commit an offense against the United States or to defraud it in any manner; and

3.　An overt act in furtherance of the object of the conspiracy committed by one or more conspirators. The overt act committed in furtherance of the conspiracy need not be illegal in and of itself.

The Government often uses the conspiracy charge to prosecute accountants and lawyers, in addition to taxpayers. Although most tax-related conspiracy prosecutions involve an alleged conspiracy to violate a specific Code provision (for example, a conspiracy to evade tax under section 7201), the conspiracy charge is a separate offense. Thus it is possible for a defendant to be acquitted of the underlying specific tax crime but convicted of conspiracy.

One of the most far-reaching applications of the conspiracy statute is in a so-called "Klein conspiracy," in which a defendant can be convicted of conspiracy to defraud the Government by impeding the lawful functions of the IRS by deceit or dishonesty. In *United States v. Klein* (2d Cir.1957), the Government prosecuted the taxpayer, lawyer, accountant, and top corporate officials of the taxpayer for evasion under section 7201 and conspiracy. The defendants, who impeded the IRS investigation by making false and misleading entries in corporate books, were acquitted of the evasion charge, but convicted of conspiracy. The Second Circuit upheld the conspiracy convictions on the basis that the defendants' conduct amounted to a conspiracy to defraud through impeding the IRS in its functions of investigating taxpayers and collecting tax. This case should provide a sobering lesson for those considering attempting to "outsmart" the IRS during an audit or subsequent criminal investigation; even if they have committed no tax crime, they may be found guilty of conspiracy to defraud the United States by impeding an IRS investigation.

The statute of limitations for a tax-related conspiracy charge is 6 years from the date the last overt act in furtherance of the object of the conspiracy is committed. I.R.C. § 6531(8). The Government may use the conspiracy statute to prosecute in situations in which the underlying tax crime is time-barred, but an overt act in furtherance of the conspiracy occurred within the 6–year period prior to the Government's discovery of the scheme.

B.   *18 U.S.C. § 1001—False Statements*

This provision makes it a felony to "knowingly and willfully" falsify, conceal or cover up any material fact by any scheme or trick, or to make or use any false writing in connection with any matter within the jurisdiction of any United States department or agency. Clearly, the filing of a false federal income tax return could be prosecuted under this section, as well as under specific criminal tax Code provisions. Taxpayers and their advisors who attempt to cover up a problem during an audit or investigation can be convicted under this section, and a tax advisor may be convicted even though the client/taxpayer is not. *See* United States v. Fern (11th Cir.1983).

C.   18 U.S.C. § 1621—Perjury

Still another federal criminal provision under which one can be prosecuted for false statements is the perjury statute, 18 U.S.C. § 1621. This statute makes it a felony to make any oral or written statement under oath that the maker knows is false or untrue as to any material matter. Thus, those who make a false statement under oath or under penalties of perjury may be prosecuted under section 1621 (the general perjury section), under section 1001 for false statements, and under one or more of the criminal tax provisions under the Internal Revenue Code, such as section 7201 (attempted evasion) or section 7206(1) (false statement made under penalty of perjury).

D.   18 U.S.C. §§ 1341, 1343, and 1961 et seq.— Mail and Wire Fraud and RICO

The federal mail fraud statute, 18 U.S.C. § 1341, applies to anyone who devises or intends to devise a scheme to defraud for the purpose of obtaining money or property by false pretense, and who uses the mail to execute the scheme. Wire fraud, 18 U.S.C. § 1343, applies to anyone who transmits across state lines by wire, radio or television any pictures, writings or sounds for the purpose of executing a fraudulent scheme. The mail and wire fraud sections, both of which are felonies carrying maximum prison sentences of 5 years, are *in pari materia*, so that decisions under one apply equally to the other.

Can the mailing of a fraudulent income tax return violate the mail fraud statute? Yes, so long as there is a scheme to defraud. Courts have upheld convictions of mail fraud in cases in which the defendant filed false income tax returns under fictitious names to obtain refunds. United States v. Anderson (8th Cir.1980); United States v. Mangan (2d Cir.1978). A defendant can be convicted of both mail fraud and tax fraud. United States v. Busher (9th Cir.1987). Because the Government need not prove "willfulness" in a mail fraud prosecution, it may elect to proceed under the mail fraud statute, rather than under a criminal tax provision.

The significance of importing the mail and wire fraud statutes into the tax fraud arena is that conviction of either will support civil and criminal penalties under RICO, the Racketeer Influenced and Corrupt Organizations Act, 18 U.S.C. §§ 1961 et seq. RICO prosecutions are statutorily authorized for violation of some federal criminal laws. Tax crimes are not included in the list of permissible predicate crimes, but mail and wire fraud are appropriate predicates. If the same conduct supports both a tax charge (under any of the tax crimes) and a mail fraud charge (because the defendant mailed his tax return as part of a scheme to defraud), then the same indictment charging those two offenses can also include a RICO charge. *See Busher, supra.*

The penalties for criminal RICO violations are stiff: maximum 20 years imprisonment, or maximum $20,000 fine, or both. In addition, RICO has a broad forfeiture provision, requiring the violator to forfeit to the Government all assets from the "criminal enterprise." It is possible that the enforced forfeiture could be grossly disproportionate to the tax offense involved. If so, the court must consider whether this violates the Eight Amendment's prohibition against disproportionality of punishment. *See* United States v. Busher (9th Cir.1989) (concluding that complete forfeiture of defendant's business interest did not violate the Eighth Amendment).

The Justice Department requires authorization of the Tax Division before charging mail fraud either independently or as a predicate for a RICO charge when the mailing charged is either the filing of a false tax return or other tax form or the mailing is to promote a tax fraud scheme such as a tax shelter. According to the amendment, "authorization [to bring a mail fraud charge in such situations] will be granted only in exceptional circumstances." The amendment explains the policy as follows: "It is the position of the Tax Division that Congress intended that tax crimes be charged as tax crimes and that the specific criminal law provisions of the Internal Revenue Code should form the focus of prosecutions when essentially tax law violation motives are involved, even though other crimes may technically have been committed." United States Attorneys' Manual, section 6–4.210.

§ 18.3 Currency Transaction Offenses

A. Money Laundering–Title 18 U.S.C. §§ 1956 and 1957

In order to avoid leaving a paper trail, many criminals engage in cash transactions. The problem this creates is that the cash may become bulky and unwieldy, making transportation difficult and causing attention to be focused on the wrongdoer. Thus, criminals engage in the process of laundering money by changing small bills into larger ones or by disguising the source or ownership of income from illegal sources to make it appear legitimate. The Money Laundering Control Act was enacted in 1986 during the Reagan Administration's war on drugs and organized crime. Section 1956 makes it a felony to engage in a financial transaction with the intent to further a criminal enterprise or to conceal the proceeds of "specified unlawful activity." Section 1957 applies to third parties and makes it a crime to knowingly engage or attempt to engage in a financial transaction of $10,000 or more with property derived from a criminal activity. The third person may be subject to prosecution under this provision for depositing, transferring or withdrawing such funds. While there is a conflict among the circuits as to whether there is a tracing requirement if tainted funds are deposited in an account with untainted funds, most courts that have considered the issue have held that no tracing is required. *See, e.g.,* United States v. Braxtonbrown–Smith (D.C. 2002). This stands to reason, because as the District of Columbia Circuit has noted, "allowing the mere commingling of legitimate funds to defeat a money laundering conviction so easily would wholly undermine Congress's intent and effectively nullify the offense." An advantage for the Government of the money laundering provisions is that the penalties are more severe than those under the tax Code and there are both civil and criminal forfeiture provisions. 18 U.S.C. §§ 981 and 982.

B. Currency Transaction Reporting—Title 26 U.S.C. § 6050I

Any person engaged in a trade or business who receives more than $10,000 in cash during the course of that trade or business, in a single transaction or two or more related transactions, must file a currency transaction report (CTR) with the IRS. This report is filed on a Form 8300 and it requires the payee to list the name and taxpayer identification number (TIN) of the payor. This raises ethical problems for attorneys who receive more than $10,000 in cash from a client who does not wish to reveal his identity to the IRS. See discussion, Chapter 3, § 3.6, *supra*.

A "related transaction" is defined as a transaction conducted within a 24–hour period or beyond if the payee knows or has reason to know that the transactions are related. Dividing a transaction into multiple transactions to avoid the reporting require- ment is called "structuring" and this also is a crime under section 6050I, as is advising a party to struc- ture a transaction to avoid the reporting require- ment. *See, e.g.,* United States v. McLamb (4th Cir. 1993) (owner of car dealership convicted of struc- turing sales to avoid the IRS reporting require- ment).

C.   Bank Secrecy Act

Section 6050I applies to those engaged in a trade or business. The Bank Secrecy Act, on the other hand, applies to financial institutions and requires the filing of CTRs for all currency transactions involving more than $10,000. The Bank Secrecy Act also requires any person who transports more than $10,000 into or out of the country to file a CTR with the U.S. Custom's Office. Any U.S. citizen or resident alien must file a CTR with the Treasury Department if that person has an interest in a foreign financial account with a value greater than $10,000.

§ 18.4   Stacking Criminal Charges; Lesser In- cluded Offenses

As should be obvious from the above discussion, there is an overlap between the "pure" tax offenses under Title 26 and the federal criminal provisions under Title 18. Prosecutors frequently seek and obtain indictments charging violations of several provisions based on the same conduct. For example, a criminal fraud case can involve charges under section 7201 (evasion), conspiracy, false statements (under the Internal Revenue Code, section 7206(1), as well as under sections 1001 and 1621 of Title 18), and possibly mail fraud and RICO, all arising from the same set of facts. When the criminal conduct supports both a felony and a misdemeanor, the defendant can be aided by application of the lesser-included-offense rule.

The lesser-included-offense rule permits a jury to convict a defendant of a lesser charge, and acquit on the greater charge, only if the greater charge requires the jury to find a fact that is not required for the lesser offense. Sansone v. United States (S.Ct. 1965). For example, if the greater offense is evasion under section 7201, which requires an affirmative act, and if the existence of the affirmative act is disputed, the lesser-included-offense rule entitles the defendant to a jury charge authorizing the jury to return a verdict of guilty either of evasion or of the lesser charge that does not require the affirmative act.

The virtue of the lesser-included-offense rule is that it permits the jury to reach a compromise verdict in cases in which it believes the defendant should not go unpunished, but it does not believe that his conduct warrants a felony conviction. However, the Supreme Court has construed the rule very narrowly in tax cases. *See, e.g., Sansone, supra* (holding lesser included offense jury instruction not required); United States v. Bishop (S.Ct.1973) (same).

§ 18.5 Punishment: Sentencing Guidelines and Increased Fines

In 1984, Congress enacted the Federal Sentencing Reform Act, which dramatically changed the federal sentencing process and thereby dramatically changed the practice of criminal defense law. This legislation created the U.S. Sentencing Commission (the "Commission"), an independent commission within the judicial branch. The Commission was charged with promulgating guidelines for use by federal judges in sentencing criminal offenders. The resulting Guidelines substantially increased the maximum fines for federal criminal violations. For federal crimes committed after November 1, 1987, the Sentencing Guidelines (codified at 18 U.S.C. §§ 1335–3742 and 28 U.S.C. §§ 991–998) provide that the maximum fines shall be the greatest of the following:

(a) the amount specified in the law describing the offense;

(b) the greater of twice the gross gain or loss, unless imposition of this fine would unduly complicate the sentencing process;

(c) for felonies, $250,000 for individuals and $500,000 for corporations; or

(d) for misdemeanors punishable by more than six months in prison, $100,000 for individuals and $200,000 for corporations.

As to sentences, the Sentencing Guidelines require sentences within ranges determined by the seriousness of the crime (there are 43 offense levels) and mitigating or aggravating circumstances. Mitigating circumstances include the defendant's cooperation in the investigation and remorse for his conduct (a/k/a "acceptance of responsibility"), while aggravating factors include obstructing the investigation. Basically, the Guidelines base the seriousness of a tax offense (the "offense level") on what is referred to as the "tax loss," the amount of tax evaded. The level of the offense can be increased if the defendant used "sophisticated means" to impede discovery of the offense or if the defendant derived a substantial portion of his income from the criminal activity.

As an example, a tax crime involving a tax loss of $80,001 to $150,000 is a level 12 offense, which has a sentencing range of 10 to 16 months imprisonment for a person with no prior convictions. If the defendant used sophisticated means to conceal the crime, this can increase the offense to a level 14, which has a sentencing range of 15 to 21 months.

The effect of the Guidelines and Justice Department policy on tax offenders has been drastic. The Sentencing Commission indicated that while prior to the implementation of the Guidelines 57% of tax offenders received probation, the effect of the Guidelines should be that only 3% of all tax offenders will avoid serving a prison sentence. In addition, the Justice Department Tax Division has stated that "the payment of the civil tax liability, plus a fine and suspended sentence, does not constitute a satisfactory disposition of a criminal case." U.S. Attorneys' Manual § 6–4.340. The result is that it is almost inevitable that a person who pleads or is found guilty of a tax crime will receive a jail sentence. Moreover, because the Government will almost inevitably seek civil penalties after the criminal phase of the case is completed, the additional fines and penalties could result in financial ruin in many cases.

Many judges and defense lawyers complained that the Guidelines operated unfairly in many cases and that contrary to the implication of the term "guidelines," there was no real discretion involved. Instead, the Guidelines mandated that sentences be imposed within a set range.

Although the Supreme Court upheld the constitutionality of the Guidelines in *Mistretta v. United States* (S.Ct.1989), more than a decade later, several justices expressed reservations about the fairness of the Guidelines in operation. In 2000, the Court held that the Sixth Amendment right to trial by jury is violated when a judge is allowed to make a finding of fact that results in the imposition of an enhanced sentence beyond the relevant statutory maximum supported by the jury's verdict or admitted to by the defendant. Apprendi v. New Jersey (S.Ct.2000). Then, in 2004, the constitutionality of the Guidelines was placed in doubt after the Court declared the Washington state sentencing system unconstitutional in *Blakely v. Washington* (S.Ct.2004). Although the decision addressed only the Washington sentencing scheme, that scheme largely mirrowed the federal Sentencing Guidelines. Indeed, after *Blakely*, several circuit courts declared the Guidelines unconstitutional as they applied to sentence enhancements after judicial determinations of facts not found by a jury. *See, e.g.,* United States v. Booker (7th Cir.2004); United States v. Fanfan (1st Cir.2004). In the wake of the uncertainty over the application of the Guidelines, the Supreme Court granted certiorari in two consolidated cases, *Booker* and *Fanfan,* and it rendered its decision in 2005. In *United States v. Booker*, the Court first reiterated its earlier holding in *Apprendi* that the Sixth Amendment right to trial by jury is violated when a judge is allowed to impose "an enhanced sentence under the United States Sentencing Guidelines based on the sentencing judge's determination of a fact (other than a prior conviction) that was not found by the jury or admitted by the defendant." The Court reasoned that because the Sentencing Guidelines are mandatory and binding on judges, they have the force and effect of law. When a judge makes a post-verdict finding of fact by a preponderance of the evidence, it violates the Sixth Amendment, which requires the jury, and not the judge, to make factual determinations relevant to sentencing.

The Court then turned to the question of what to do about the Sentencing Guidelines–should it declare the entire Guidelines unconstitutional or should it attempt to salvage a portion of the Guidelines? The Court opted for the second alternative by severing and excising the provision of the sentencing statute that makes the Guidelines mandatory. 18 U.S.C. § 3553(b) (1). Thus, the Guidelines now are advisory. A sentencing judge must consider the Guidelines but may tailor the sentence by taking other considerations into account as well, although the judge does not have the discretion to disregard a statutory minimum. In addition to the mandatory provision of the Guidelines, the Court also excised the provision that set forth standards of appellate review. 18 U.S.C. § 3742(e). Instead of applying a *de novo* standard, an appellate court now must review for "unreasonableness" a departure from the Guidelines.

CHAPTER 19

DEFENSES TO CRIMINAL CHARGES

§ 19.1 Third Party Reliance

Frequently, a criminal defendant may use the excuse that he relied on the advice of a professional and thus is not guilty of a tax offense because he did not act willfully. While this defense occasionally may shield some from criminal liability, nevertheless, the defense seldom succeeds. There are two reasons for this. First, the more complex the issue, the more successful the defense. If the issue involves an aspect of tax law that is not very complicated, such as the requirement to file a return, the defense usually will fail. Second, there are specific requirements of the defense. For instance, the defendant must have chosen a competent professional, must have made full disclosure to the professional, and must have acted on the advice of the professional. A defendant who travels down a path of criminality and merely seeks advice that will allow him to continue on that path will not be able to assert the defense. *See* United States v. Cheek (7th Cir.1993).

The defense also presents other problems for defendants. In order to use the defense, the defendant will have to waive the attorney/client or federally authorized tax practitioner privilege. (See discussion §§ 3.5., A. and 3.5.B., *supra*). In addition, it may create a conflict between the defendant and the tax advisor, because the tax advisor also may be facing criminal charges or a civil suit arising from the misconduct.

§ 19.2 Mistake of Law

The maxim that "ignorance of the law is no defense" may not hold true in a tax prosecution because the Code provisions tend to be highly complex and technical, and because it would be too easy for a taxpayer to be convicted of a crime for an error or omission in applying some Code provision about which even tax experts might be confused. Similarly, an illiterate taxpayer could be convicted of a tax crime based on a clear but innocent mistake. On the other hand, permitting every defendant to escape conviction on the mere assertion that he misunderstood the law would hardly be acceptable. The difficulty in reconciling the two extremes has plagued the courts and was most frequently cast in terms of whether the willfulness element should be construed as requiring subjective or objective intent. In other words, can a defendant's honestly held but mistaken view of the law shield him from prosecution, or is there a standard of reasonableness by which such beliefs should be tested?

Tax protestors present a difficult problem in this context. One who fails to file or who files a false return is not protected from conviction merely because he disagrees with the tax laws or believes that they are unconstitutional or bad public policy. Failure to comply with the law based on such a disagreement with it does not negate willfulness. Typical arguments raised by tax protestors are that the income tax is unconstitutional and that wages are not taxable income. Given the litany of cases in which the constitutionality of the income tax system has been upheld, and the notion that wages are not taxable income flatly rejected, some courts imposed a reasonableness test on the good faith mistake of law defense, requiring the jury to reject the defense unless the defendant's belief was reasonable.

The Supreme Court resolved a split in the Circuits on the question of subjective versus objective standards for a misunderstanding of the law in *Cheek v. United States* (S.Ct.1991). In *Cheek* the Court held that a good-faith misunderstanding of the law is a valid defense to tax evasion. Defendant John Cheek, a pilot for a major commercial airline, was a tax protestor who ceased filing federal income tax returns and filed Forms W–4 with his employer claiming he was exempt from tax. He was charged with violations of sections 7203 and 7201 (and other violations). The District court instructed the jury that it could acquit only if it found that Cheek's misunderstanding of the law was objectively reasonable. Cheek was convicted, and the Seventh Circuit affirmed the conviction.

The Supreme Court reversed the conviction, stating:

> Willfulness, as construed by our prior decisions in criminal tax cases, requires the Government to prove that the law imposed a duty on the defendant, that the defendant knew of that duty, and that he voluntarily and intentionally violated that duty. We deal first with the case where the issue is whether the defendant knew of the duty purportedly imposed by the provision of the statute or regulation he is accused of violating, a case in which there is no claim that the provision at issue is invalid. In such a case, if the Government proves actual knowledge of the pertinent legal duty, the prosecution, without more, has satisfied the knowledge component of the willfulness requirement. But carrying this burden requires negating a defendant's claim of ignorance of the law or a claim that because of a misunderstanding of the law, he had a good-faith belief that he was not violating any of the provisions of the tax laws. This is so because one cannot be aware that the law imposes a duty upon him and yet be ignorant of it, misunderstand the law, or believe that the duty does not exist. In the end, the question is whether, based on all the evidence, the Government has proved that the defendant was aware of the duty at issue, which cannot be true if the jury credits a good-faith misunderstanding and belief

submission, whether or not the claimed belief or misunderstanding is objectively reasonable.

Of course, to avoid conviction, the defendant must convince the jury that his misunderstanding of the law is genuine. As the Supreme Court stated in *Cheek*: "in deciding whether to credit Cheek's good-faith belief claim, the jury would be free to consider any admissible evidence from any source showing that Cheek was aware of his duty to file a return and treat wages as income."

§ 19.3 Lack of Notice of Illegality

A related defense to that of mistake of law is that the underlying substantive law is so unclear that a person cannot constitutionally be convicted of its violation. In 1921, the Supreme Court held that a criminal law that fails to establish an ascertainable standard of guilt, and therefore does not give full and fair notice to citizens of the type of conduct covered by the statute, is unconstitutional on two grounds. First, such a statute violates the Due Process Clause of the Fifth Amendment; second, it violates the Sixth Amendment guarantee of being informed of the nature and cause of the criminal charges. United States v. L. Cohen Grocery Co. (S.Ct.1921).

Because the tax laws are so complex, and in recent decades have been amended so frequently and thoroughly, the applicability of this defense to tax prosecutions is particularly important both to taxpayers and to Government prosecutors. To date, however, the Supreme Court has failed to provide definitive guidance, either by explaining what level of confusion in the law renders prosecution unconstitutional or by deciding whether the defendant must be aware of the uncertainty to validly invoke the defense.

The landmark Supreme Court case on the applicability of this principle in tax cases is *James v. United States* (S.Ct.1961). Unfortunately, the *James* decision left many questions unanswered. James was convicted of tax evasion for failing to report embezzled income. The Supreme Court overturned his conviction on the basis that the law was too unsettled to support a finding of willfulness. The uncertainty arose from a 1946 Supreme Court decision holding that embezzled funds do not constitute taxable income, and a subsequent Supreme Court decision holding that extorted funds do constitute taxable income. The latter case declined to overrule the previous decision, however. Thus, although it would be logical to assume that embezzled funds, like extorted funds, are taxable, the Court's failure to overrule the prior decision at the time James failed to report his embezzlement income prompted the Court to overturn his conviction. Unlike the *Cohen Grocery* case, however, the uncertainty sprang not from the statute itself but from inconsistent judicial interpretations of the statute.

Does the *James* decision stand for the proposition that uncertainty in the tax law provides an absolute defense, without regard to the defendant's knowledge of or reliance on the uncertainty? Three of the Justices so voted, but three others, also in the majority, stated that the defendant must establish that he actually relied on the authority in his favor, and that the question of reliance should be determined by the jury. The Court's failure to resolve this issue in *James* or in any subsequent case has spawned conflicting decisions in the Circuits. Some Circuits hold that convictions based on unsettled areas of the law cannot be sustained, while others inquire into the defendant's subjective knowledge of the uncertainty and reliance on precedents favorable to him.

A fascinating case illustrating the difficult issues involved in this defense is *United States v. Garber* (5th Cir.1979). The defendant in *Garber* was convicted of tax evasion for failing to report income received from the sale of her rare blood plasma. Although the medical procedures involved in extracting the plasma were "accompanied by pain and discomfort and carry the risks of hepatitis and blood clotting," the defendant had undergone the painful procedures up to six times per month during the years in question and had allegedly received more than $70,000 per year for her plasma. The company that bought her plasma also paid her a weekly salary of $200, withheld taxes on it, and furnished her a W–2 form reflecting the taxes withheld. She duly reported the salary as income each year and paid taxes on it. The payments for the plasma itself, however, were not treated as wages. Thus, the company did not withhold taxes on these payments, and Garber did not pay tax on them.

The trial court refused to let the defendant's expert testify that the law was uncertain concerning whether the sale of blood plasma or other bodily parts constituted taxable income, or possibly was a nontaxable sale of "goods" rather than a taxable sale of services. Rehearing the case *en banc*, the Fifth Circuit overturned the conviction, holding that this "uncharted area in tax law" was so uncertain as to support a defense of legal uncertainty. According to the court, criminal prosecution "is an inappropriate vehicle for pioneering interpretations of the tax law." *Id.* at 100; *accord* United States v. Harris (7th Cir.1991). The court found that the Government had simply failed to prove the element of willfulness, and that the trial judge erred in failing to instruct the jury on the unsettled nature of the law.

The court further held that "relevance of a dispute in the tax law does not depend on whether the defendant actually knew of the conflict." Thus, whether or not the defendant was aware of the legal uncertainty, or relied on expert advice or authorities supporting her position, is irrelevant. According to the court: "To hold otherwise would advocate convicting an unsophisticated taxpayer who failed to seek expert advice * * * while setting free a wise taxpayer who could find advice that taxes were not due * * *." *Id.* at 98.

Garber both illuminates the legal uncertainty defense and represents a fairly rare instance of a tax prosecution that many maintain should never have been brought. In subsequent cases, the Fifth Circuit has "limited *Garber* to its bizarre facts—where the level of uncertainty approached legal vagueness." United States v. Daly (5th Cir.1985) (affirming conviction of defendant who sold "church" chapters to investors, instructing them that their income would be tax-exempt); *see* United States v. Burton (5th Cir.1984) (issue involved not novel, so legal vagueness defense not available). Importantly, these subsequent cases involved less sympathetic defendants than the defendant in *Garber*, and the "legal uncertainty" in the subsequent cases was minimal or nonexistent. *Garber* apparently continues to obviate any need to prove reliance or knowledge of the dispute if the tax law is completely unsettled.

The Second and Sixth Circuits specifically rejected *Garber* and declined to follow it. According to these courts, "*Garber* allows juries to find that uncertainty in the law negates willfulness even when the defendant is unaware of that uncertainty. This contradicts the prior cases on willfulness, which 'consistently require factual evidence of the defendants' state of mind to negate willfulness under any theory.'" United States v. Curtis (6th Cir. 1986) (quoting United States v. Ingredient Technology Corp. (2d Cir.1983)).

The Fourth Circuit, on the other hand, has twice held that uncertainty in the law is an absolute defense. In its 1985 decision in *United States v. Mallas* (4th Cir.1985), the court explained its reasoning:

Grave penalties rest in this case on an unsubstantiated theory of tax law * * *. Whatever eventual success this proposition may enjoy as an interpretation of tax law—a destiny we do not influence here—present authority in support of the theory is far too tenuous and competing interpretations of the applicable law far too reasonable to justify these convictions.

* * * Criminal prosecution for the violation of an unclear duty itself violates the clear constitutional duty of the government to warn citizens whether particular conduct is legal or illegal. * * * Willful conduct under § 7206, which the Supreme Court described in *United States v. Pomponio* as 'voluntary, intentional violation of a known legal duty,' requires that the duty involved must be knowable.

Thus, if the law is genuinely unsettled, the Fourth Circuit will not uphold a conviction under it. Similarly, the Seventh Circuit in *United States v. Harris* (7th Cir.1991) and the Fifth Circuit in *Garber* overturned a conviction because of the completely unsettled legal question involved.

How unsettled must the law be? Currently, that is the key question. Numerous courts have observed, as did the *Mallas* court, that "due process does not require the prosecution to cite a 'litigated fact pattern directly on point.'" What it does require, especially in the context of "abusive" tax shelters designed to take advantage of both legal intricacies and gullible investors, remains uncertain.

The experience of the Ninth Circuit with this issue is instructive. In a 1983 decision in which the court cited both *Garber* and Fourth Circuit precedent, the Ninth Circuit overturned the convictions of tax shelter promoters on the basis that "the legality of the tax shelter program advocated by the appellants in this case was completely unsettled by any clearly relevant precedent on the dates alleged in the indictment." United States v. Dahlstrom (9th Cir.1983). Defendants had been convicted of conspiracy and aiding and assisting the preparation of false returns under section 7206(2) based on their promotion of tax shelter schemes involving offshore trusts. The defendants had instructed "investors" to use "blue 'copy-not' pens to sign checks so that I.R.S. agents could not read them on bank microfilm records," to alter their Social Security numbers on trust bank accounts to prevent the IRS from tracing them, and to use fictitious names. *Id.* at 1430 (Goodwin, J., dissenting). Despite this evidence, the majority overturned the convictions because the legality of the offshore trust scheme was unsettled, so that it would violate both the First and the Fifth Amendment to convict someone for promoting the scheme. According to the majority: "These appellants were prosecuted in spite of the fact that no statute, regulation or court decision gave fair warning that advocacy of the creation of lawful foreign trust corporations as a tax shelter would result in a criminal prosecution if the challenged transaction might later be held to lack economic substance * * *." *Id.* at 1429.

The dissent in *Dahlstrom* argued that the transactions advocated by the defendants were "shams" and that such schemes had long been illegal. That position has been espoused in numerous post-*Dahlstrom* decisions in which *Dahlstrom* has been distinguished and labeled as "primarily a First Amendment case involving pure advocacy." United States v. Schulman (9th Cir.1987) (*quoting* United States v. Russell (9th Cir.1986)). The test now employed by the Ninth Circuit is whether the scheme has economic substance: if it does not, then the scheme is a sham, and participating in it in any manner will support a conviction. The fact that no statute or regulation directly addresses the elements of the scheme will not prevent conviction, so long as the scheme or transaction is a sham.

The Supreme Court's refusal to grant certiorari to resolve the question of the degree of uncertainty that must exist to justify the unconstitutional vagueness defense is unfortunate. Both the willfulness requirement and the unconstitutional vagueness defense offer protection to taxpayers against imprisonment for being one of "the well-meaning, but easily confused, mass of taxpayers." United States v. Bishop (S.Ct.1973) (describing the role of the willfulness requirement). Some courts, such as the Fourth Circuit, will overturn a conviction if the tax law is objectively uncertain in that a reasonable person could not understand it, even if the defendant subjectively intended to violate the law. Most courts, on the other hand, will uphold a conviction unless the law is so extraordinarily unsettled that it is unconstitutionally vague, and prosecution is thus prohibited by the Fifth Amendment. Whether an objectively uncertain law that is not extraordinarily uncertain should preclude inquiry into the particular defendant's state of mind, and how to distinguish between mere objective uncertainty and extraordinary confusion or uncertainty, are issues the Supreme Court should address.

§ 19.4 Defendant's Education, Experience and Health

Not surprisingly, the personal and professional characteristics of a defendant influence juries' findings on the question of willfulness. For example, an experienced tax lawyer or accountant who claims a good faith misunderstanding of the tax law, particularly if the question is not novel or unsettled, stands less chance of being believed than someone who is generally unfamiliar with the complexities of the tax law. Similarly, an experienced businessman or college graduate who claims not to have known that tax returns must be filed will most likely not be believed by the jury. Simply being a lawyer or other professional does not necessarily ensure conviction, however. In a now-famous case, the Fifth Circuit took judicial notice "that most lawyers have only scant knowledge of the tax laws." Bursten v. United States (5th Cir.1968).

Physical or mental health problems are frequently asserted to negate a finding that the defendant acted willfully, particularly in prosecutions for failure to file returns. Such a defense has been successful on occasion, but it usually fails. For example, defendants who are chronic alcoholics have been convicted, and their convictions sustained on appeal. *See, e.g.*, United States v. Jalbert (1st Cir. 1974). If the defendant manages to perform adequately in his job or business, juries tend to disbelieve that emotional or physical problems prevented the defendant from acting willfully. *See also* United States v. McCaffrey (7th Cir.1999) (conviction of accountant who failed to file his own tax returns, claiming mental incompetence, upheld because he continued to file returns for others during the periods in question).

§ 19.5   Statute of Limitations

Section 6531 sets out the statutes of limitations for prosecution of tax crimes. Although the general rule is 3 years from the commission of the offense, there are numerous exceptions which render the general 3–year period almost irrelevant. For all of the crimes described above, as well as for any conspiracy to defeat or evade any tax, the statute of limitations is 6 years. The statute begins to run when the offense is committed, which is usually the date the tax return is filed. If the return is filed early, the statute begins to run on the due date of the return. If the return is filed late, the statute begins to run when the return is received by the IRS. Furthermore, if the taxpayer's post-return conduct, such as lying to IRS auditors or destroying records, is the "affirmative willful act" upon which a section 7201 evasion prosecution is premised, the statute of limitations begins to run on the date of the post-filing conduct. United States v. Beacon Brass Co. (S.Ct.1952).

GLOSSARY

Actions on Decisions (AODs) are memoranda prepared by Government lawyers explaining why the Government should or should not appeal court decisions adverse to the Government on tax issues in any federal court, including the Tax Court. See Chapter 2, § 2.3.C.

Administrative costs recoverable under I.R.C. § 7430 include the same types of costs recoverable from litigation, as well as any administrative fees or similar charges imposed by the Internal Revenue Service. See Chapter 15, § 15.3.D.

APA (Administrative Procedure Act) is a federal law codified at 5 U.S.C. §§ 551 et seq. that governs federal agency conduct and rulemaking. See Chapters 2 and 4.

Appeals Office is an administrative forum to which taxpayers may bring tax controversies for resolution after an audit. Appeals Offices, which are located throughout the United States, have exclusive and final authority to settle tax cases originating within their jurisdictions. Taxpayers are encouraged to seek resolution of their tax disputes with the Appeals Office both to avoid the delay and expense of litigation and to preserve their right to recover attorneys' fees if they prevail over the IRS. See Chapter 6.

Article I courts are "legislative" courts which are established pursuant to Article I of the United States Constitution, rather than Article III, which established many other federal courts. Examples of Article I courts include the U.S. Tax Court and the U.S. Court of Federal Claims. See Chapter 14, §§ 14.2 and 14.4.

Assessment of a tax is the recording of the tax liability, together with the taxpayer's name, address, taxpayer identification number, and the date of assessment, in the ledgers of the IRS. See Chapter 7.

Attorneys' fees are recoverable by taxpayers under I.R.C. § 7430 under certain circumstances. See § 15.3.

Audit is the examination of tax returns for irregularities. It is the method by which our system of voluntary compliance is enforced and measured. Audits range from a simple written request to substantiate certain items on a return to a detailed review of the taxpayer's books and records. See Chapter 6.

Bankruptcy petition is the first step in a bankruptcy proceeding. When a bankruptcy petition is filed, creditors (including the IRS) are automatically stayed from further collection action, a bankruptcy estate is created which includes the debtor's legal and equitable interests up to the point of the petition, and the Bankruptcy Court assumes jurisdiction over civil collection and enforcement actions. See Chapter 12.

Board of Tax Appeals was the name of the Tax Court from 1924 until 1942. See § 14.2.

CID is the Criminal Investigation Division of the IRS, which is responsible for criminal investigations of taxpayers. See § 1.2.B and Chapters 16 and 17.

Circular 230 is the shorthand description of Treasury Regulations governing practice before the Treasury. The official title of these regulations is "Regulations governing the Practice of Attorneys, Certified Public Accountants, Enrolled Agents, Enrolled Actuaries and Appraisers before the Internal Revenue Service." Attorneys and others who practice before the IRS are subject to discipline in accordance with the procedures and standards of conduct contained in Circular 230. See Chapter 3.

Claim for refund (refund claim) is a claim by a taxpayer to the IRS for refund of any overpaid taxes. The refund claim is a jurisdictional prerequisite to a refund suit, and untimely filing of the claim will preclude litigation of the controversy. See Chapter 8 and Chapter 14, § 14.3.

Closing agreement is an agreement between the taxpayer and the Government settling the taxpayer's tax liability. Because of the finality of closing agreements the IRS enters into such agreements with great caution. Closing agreements may be set aside by either the taxpayer or the Government only for fraud, misrepresentation or malfeasance. See Chapter 6, § 6.4.

Collateral estoppel is a doctrine that bars the relitigation of issues actually litigated and necessarily determined in a prior suit. See Chapter 15, § 15.2.

Commissioner is the head of the Internal Revenue Service, which is a branch of the Treasury Department. The Secretary of the Treasury has delegated much authority over the administration of the internal revenue laws to the Commissioner. The Commissioner is appointed by the President, with the advice and consent of the Senate. See Chapter 1, § 1.2.

Consent to extension of statute of limitations is possible under I.R.C. § 6501(c)(4), which permits the statute of limitations on the assessment of a tax to be extended by written agreement between the taxpayer and the Service. The agreement must be entered into before the time for assessment expires. See Chapter 7, § 7.2.F.

Court of Claims (see Claims Court).

Deficiency means the excess of tax due over the amount of tax actually paid for any taxable year. See Chapter 7, § 7.1.

Determination letter is a written statement issued by an IRS Area Director applying clearly established rules to a completed transaction. Most determination letters involve the "qualification" of employee benefit plans and the tax-exempt status of organizations. See § 2.3.C.

Equitable recoupment is an equitable doctrine employed by the courts to prevent harsh and unfair treatment that would result from application of the statutes of limitation. This doctrine is necessary because the statutes of limitation are strictly construed and cannot be waived and because it is possible that unfairness could result to the taxpayer or the Government by manipulating the time bars and taking inconsistent positions. See § 9.3.

Evasion (or tax evasion) as defined and prohibited under section 7201 of the Code is committed by "[a]ny person who willfully attempts in any manner to evade or defeat any tax imposed by this title or the payment thereof." Tax evasion under section 7201 is a felony, and section 7201 provides the harshest punishment and requires a greater quantum of proof by the Government than any other tax crime. See § 18.1.A.

Federal Circuit Court of Appeals was formed in 1982 from a merger of the former Court of Claims and the U.S. Court of Customs and Patent Appeals. The new court took over the appellate jurisdiction of the two merged courts, including jurisdiction over appeals of tax-refund suits decided by the Claims Court. Unlike the other Federal Courts of Appeals, the appellate jurisdiction of the Federal Circuit is defined by subject matter, rather than geography. See § 14.4.A.

Federal tax lien (or tax lien or general tax lien or general assessment lien) is a lien which arises automatically against all property and rights to property, whether real or personal, belonging to the taxpayer as of the date of assessment, if the taxpayer neglects or refuses to pay the assessed tax within ten days from the notice and demand for payment. See § 11.2.

Fiduciary is defined in section 7701(a)(6) of the Code as a "guardian, trustee, executor, administrator, receiver, conservator, or other person acting in any fiduciary capacity for any person." In some circumstances, a fiduciary can be liable for a taxpayer's tax liability and penalties for its nonpayment. See § 13.2.B.

Field audit is an audit in which a revenue agent examines the taxpayer's books and records, usually at the taxpayer's home or business. Field audits are used in complex cases, and the revenue agents are not restricted in the scope of the audit to specific significant items identified during the earlier screening process. See § 6.1.B.

File (or filing) is the delivering of a tax return or other document. If a return is mailed on or before the due date, the date of mailing (as evidenced by the postmark) is considered the date of filing. Returns filed early (before the due date) are treated as filed on the due date. Returns filed after the due date are not considered filed until actually received by the Service. See § 5.2.

Forum refers to the court the taxpayer chooses in which to litigate a tax dispute. The taxpayer in a civil tax controversy can select among three different courts, each with different procedures, precedents, and levels of expertise. The three available forums are the United States Tax Court, the United States District Court and the United States Claims Court (Court of Federal Claims. See Chapter 14.

Fraud is defined by the Tax Court as "the intentional commission of an act or acts for the specific purpose of evading a tax believed to be owing. Fraud implies bad faith, intentional wrongdoing and a sinister motive. It is never imputed or presumed." The essence of fraud is the taxpayer's state of mind indicating a motive or intent to evade a known tax. The IRS may recommend criminal prosecution for fraud under the tax evasion statute, section 7201, or it may seek to impose a civil penalty under section 6663 (former section 6653(b)). See §§ 10.3 and 18.1.A.

Freedom of Information Act (or FOIA) is a federal law that was enacted by Congress in 1966 as an amendment to the Administrative Procedure Act ("APA") to give individuals the right of access to much of the information possessed by the Government. Under this Act, many tax documents, such as "private" letter rulings, technical advice memoranda, and significant portions of the Internal Revenue Manual, have been disclosed to the public. See § 4.1.

Full payment rule is a rule requiring the full payment of an entire tax assessed as a jurisdictional prerequisite to filing a refund suit. See § 14.3.A.

Golsen rule is a rule adopted by the Tax Court in 1970 in Golsen v. Commissioner, which requires the Tax Court to follow the governing precedent of the Court of Appeals to which the case before it is appealable. The rule was adopted to provide certainty of how the Tax Court will rule when the Courts of Appeals are split on an issue. See § 14.2.D.

IMPACT (Improved Penalty Administration and Compliance Tax Act of 1989) was enacted in late 1989. It dramatically changed the civil penalty system of the Code. See Chapter 10.

Innocent spouse relief rules provide relief for an innocent spouse from tax liabilities, interest and penalties under certain conditions, including relief from liability for civil tax fraud when the fraud is attributable only to the culpable spouse. See § 13.1.

Installment agreements are collection devices where the IRS agrees to permit financially strapped taxpayers to pay their tax liability in a series of payments over a span of up to 3 years. See § 11.3.C.

Internal Revenue Manual (or IRM) is a lengthy volume of procedures prescribed by the IRS as procedural regulations to be followed by IRS personnel. See § 2.2 and § 6.1.A.

IRS means the Internal Revenue Service (also referred to simply as "the Service").

IRS Restructuring and Reform Act was enacted in 1998 to reorganize the structure of the IRS and to redirect its mission from collections to taxpayer service. The Act reorganized the IRS from a three-tiered geographical structure (national, regional and district offices) to four operating divisions serving taxpayers with similar needs, supported by four functional units and two shared service organizations. *See* § 1.2, B.

Last known address is the address of the taxpayer to which the notice of deficiency must be sent. The taxpayer's last known address can be the address shown on the return in question. However, if the taxpayer notifies the Service in a clear and concise manner that his address has changed, this new address must be used. If the notice is mailed to the taxpayer's last known address, the notice is valid, even if the taxpayer never receives it. See § 14.2.B.

Letter ruling (private letter ruling) is a ruling issued by the IRS at the taxpayer's request that applies the IRS view of the law to facts disclosed by the taxpayer. Letter rulings are issued in a limited number of situations and may not be relied upon by another taxpayer. See § 2.3.B.

Lien (see federal tax lien)

Litigation costs that may be recovered by a taxpayer under section 7430 include reasonable court costs, expert witness fees, attorneys' fees, and the costs of conducting any test or study necessary for the preparation of the case. See § 15.3.

Memorandum decisions are Tax Court decisions involving relatively settled legal principles. Memorandum decisions have little precedential value and are not printed in the official Tax Court Reports. These opinions are published by unofficial, commercial publishers. See § 14.2.E.

Naked assessments are assessments by the Government of a tax deficiency, usually involving purported illegal income, that trigger an exception to the general rule that the Commissioner's determination of a deficiency is entitled to a presumption of correctness. The presumption of correctness vanishes if the IRS is unable to produce admissible evidence linking the taxpayer directly with the alleged illegal income. See § 15.1.C.

90–day letter (see notice of deficiency).

Notice of deficiency (or statutory notice of deficiency) is a document informing the taxpayer that the Commissioner has determined a deficiency and that identifies the taxable year and amount of the deficiency. The notice of deficiency is also known as a "90–day letter" because the taxpayer has 90 days from the date the notice is mailed either to file a petition in Tax Court seeking a redetermination of the tax deficiency or to pay the tax. See § 7.1.A.

Offer In Compromise is a collection device in which the IRS agrees to accept less than the full amount of the tax liability in the case of taxpayer who establishes that her financial difficulties are serious enough that there is genuine doubt about her ability to pay the tax. See § 11.3.D.

Office audit is an audit performed by a tax auditor in the IRS office, as opposed to a "field audit" performed at the taxpayer's residence or place of business. See § 6.1.B.

Petition for redetermination is a petition by a taxpayer to the Tax Court for redetermination of the tax deficiency computed by the Service. The petition must be filed within 90 days from the mailing of the notice of deficiency. Without a timely filed petition, a taxpayer cannot use the Tax Court. See § 14.2.A.

Position of the United States is the position stated by the Government in the notice of deficiency sent to the taxpayer. See § 15.3.C.

Power of Attorney is a document signed by the taxpayer and filed with the IRS authorizing a third party to act on behalf of the taxpayer. Under a general power of attorney (Form 2848), the third party may negotiate with the IRS on behalf of the taxpayer, execute documents and receive tax refund checks. Under a limited power of attorney (Form 8821), the representative may receive and inspect confidential return information, but otherwise may not act on the taxpayer's behalf. See § 3.1.A.

Preparer (see return preparer).

Prevailing party is one who establishes that the position of the United States in the proceeding was not substantially justified and who substantially prevailed with respect to either the amount in controversy or the most significant issue or set of issues. See § 15.3.B.

Privacy Act is an amendment to the APA which regulates government agencies' use of information they have accumulated about individuals and prohibits the federal government from disclosing information without the prior consent of the person to whom the information pertains. The Act also ensures that individuals and organizations will have access to many types of Government records concerning them so that errors or inaccuracies in those records can be detected and corrected. See § 4.1.

Private letter ruling (see letter ruling).

Protest is a written explanation of why the taxpayer disagrees with a proposed deficiency after an audit. The protest gives the taxpayer's representative an opportunity to influence the case by thoroughly explaining and documenting in writing the taxpayer's position and why he disagrees with the proposed adjustments. In preparing a protest, it is important to emphasize that there is legal or factual uncertainty involved and that the Government would not be assured a victory in litigation. See § 6.3.B.

Protestor (or tax protestor) is the label given to those taxpayers who disagree with the federal income tax system and actively resist payment of taxes.

Redetermination is the redetermination by the Tax Court of a tax deficiency computed by the IRS. See § 14.2.A.

Regular decisions are Tax Court decisions that involve some legal interpretation, unlike many "memorandum" decisions, but the issue is often less controversial or significant than is involved in most "reviewed" decisions. Regular Tax Court decisions have less precedential value than "reviewed" decisions but more than "memorandum" decisions and are published in the official Tax Court Reports. See § 14.2.E.

Regulations are rules issued by the Treasury Secretary or the IRS Commissioner to enforce the Internal Revenue Code. There are three types of regulations governing federal tax matters: legislative, interpretive and procedural. See Chapter 2.

Reportable transactions are devices designed to curtail the use of abusive tax avoidance transactions, a/k/a tax shelters (see **Tax Shelters**, *infra*). If a taxpayer participates in a tax shelter and is required to file a return, the taxpayer must disclose his participation in the shelter on a Form 8886. In this manner, the government hopes to increase the transparency of questionable transactions so that they can be evaluated more quickly. See § 3.4.B. and § 10.2.B.

Res judicata is a doctrine that bars relitigation of a claim after a final judgment on the merits has been issued in a suit involving the same parties or their privies. See § 15.2.

Responsible person means a person who can be held liable for the 100% penalty of section 6672 for failure to collect, account for or pay over trust fund taxes withheld by an employer from its employees' wages. See § 13.3.A.

Return preparer is any person or entity that prepares for compensation any return or claim for refund or any substantial portion of a return or claim for refund. Furnishing legal advice that is directly relevant to determining the proper treatment of any item on a return can make a lawyer a "preparer," if the legal advice relates to a completed action and the item represents a substantial portion of the return. See § 3.1.B.

Revenue procedures are IRS information statements, published in the Internal Revenue Bulletin and compiled in the Cumulative Bulletin, informing the public about procedures to be followed in connection with federal tax matters. See § 2.3.C.

Revenue rulings are official agency interpretations of tax laws or treaties as applied to specific facts. Revenue rulings are binding on the Service and on taxpayers, and they are published in the Internal Revenue Bulletin and compiled in the Cumulative Bulletin. Their applicability, however, is limited by the specific fact situations to which they are addressed. See § 2.3.A.

Reviewed decisions are decisions by the Tax Court which are reviewed by all 19 judges and carry the greatest precedential value of any Tax Court decision. Reviewed decisions are always published in the United States Tax Court Reports. See § 14.2.E.

Service refers to the Internal Revenue Service (the IRS).

Small tax case procedures are available to taxpayers whose tax deficiencies are $10,000 or less for any taxable year. Small tax cases are provided to afford a less expensive and less formal alternative for taxpayers who do not have the funds or the desire to litigate their tax deficiencies in a regular Tax Court trial. See § 14.2.C.

Substantial understatement penalty is a penalty imposed on taxpayers whose tax returns reflect a "substantial understatement" of tax liability. "Substantial understatement" means that the correct tax liability exceeds the reported liability by the greater of 10% of the correct tax or $5,000 ($10,000 for corporations). This penalty is imposed routinely if a substantial understatement exists. The penalty should not be imposed if the position giving rise to the understatement either was disclosed or there was substantial authority for it. See § 10.2.B.

Summons is an investigatory mechanism by which the IRS can carry out its mission of enforcing the tax laws. The IRS may issue a summons for any statutorily authorized purpose, to compel production of books and records, take testimony under oath, and summon a taxpayer or third party to compel him to appear and produce books and records and testify under oath. The IRS may also issue a summons for the purpose of inquiring into any offense connected with the administration or enforcement of the internal revenue laws. See § 17.1.

Subpoena is the grand jury equivalent of the IRS summons. See § 17.2.B.

Tax Court (or United States Tax Court) is an Article I "legislative" court which hears only tax cases. The court is based in Washington, D.C., but its judges travel throughout the country to hear tax cases. The taxpayer is not required to pay the disputed tax as a jurisdictional prerequisite to be heard in the Tax Court, and trial by jury is not available in Tax Court. The Tax Court's 19 judges are usually experts in tax matters, and taxpayers who have the most complicated and technical issues often select the Tax Court for its supposed expertise. The Tax Court's jurisdiction is strictly limited by statute. See § 14.2.

Tax Shelters are entities, plans or arrangements, the principal purpose of which is the avoidance or evasion of federal income tax. If such a scheme is determined to be abusive, the participant, as well as the promoter, may be subject to harsh penalties. See § 10.2.B.

Tax shelter opinions are opinion letters issued by lawyers or law firms regarding the tax consequences of specific tax shelter transactions. These letters generally are intended to be used in the promotion, marketing or recommending of tax shelters to third parties. Circular 230 contains stringent requirements that must be met to protect the public if the opinions constitute "covered opinions." See § 3.3D.

Transferees are persons or entities who take or receive property from a taxpayer without consideration to the detriment of the taxpayer's creditors. The transferee may be liable to the creditor, including the Federal government, under law or equity. See § 13.2.A.

Trust fund taxes means taxes withheld by the employer from the employees' wages and subject to the statutory requirement that they be held in trust for the Government. Federal income taxes and FICA (Social Security) contributions withheld by an employer are trust fund taxes. See § 13.3.

U.S. Court of Federal Claims (formerly the Court of Claims) is a legislative court established pursuant to Article I of the U.S. Constitution that has jurisdiction over tax refund suits. The Claims Court is based in Washington, D.C., but it is authorized to hold sessions throughout the country. The taxpayer must pay the disputed tax as a jurisdictional prerequisite to be heard in the Claims Court, and a trial by jury is not available in the Claims Court. Because a significant portion of the court's docket consists of tax refund cases, Claims Court judges generally are viewed as having more tax expertise than most U.S. District Court judges, but less than Tax Court judges. The Claims Court is bound by precedent of the former Court of Claims, the U.S. Court of Appeals for the Federal Circuit, and the U.S. Supreme Court. See Chapter 14, § 14.4.

Willfulness means a voluntary, intentional violation of a known legal duty. See § 18.1.A.(1).

INDEX

References are to Pages

411